YEAR ONE

BATM

Ra's al ghul

YEAR ONE: BATMAN

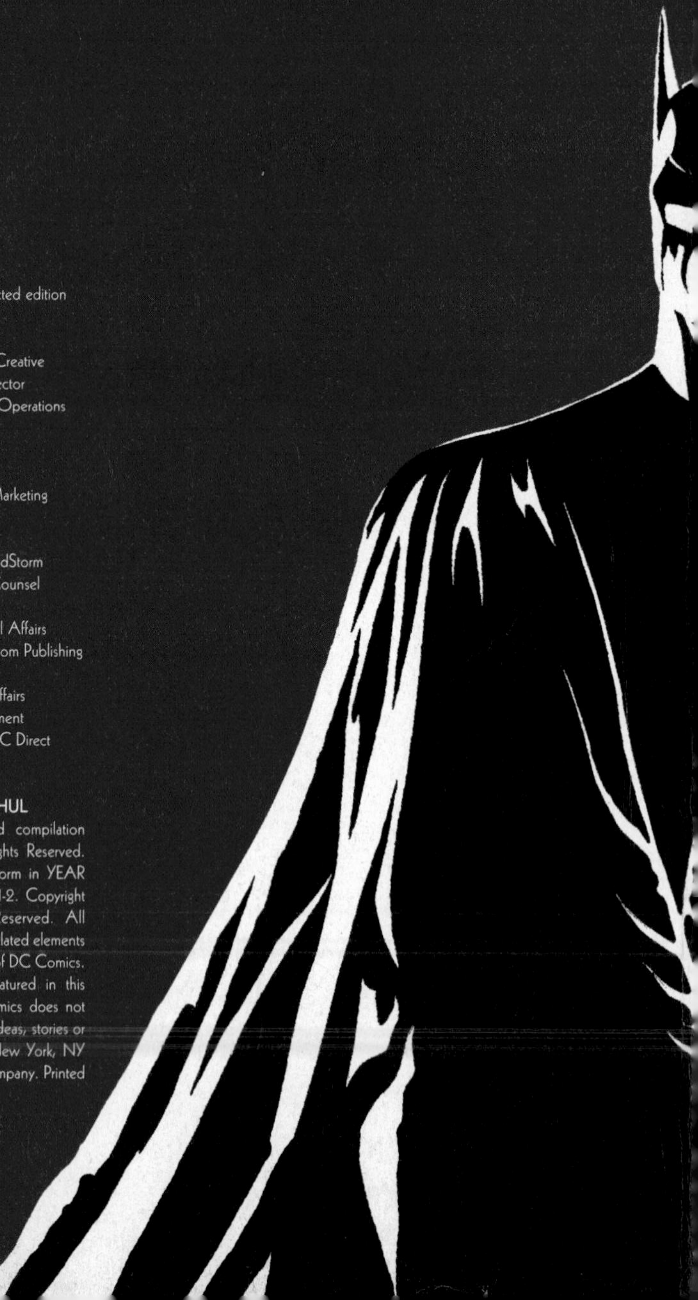

Dan DiDio Senior VP-Executive Editor
Nachie Castro Editor-original series
Robert Greenberger Senior Editor-collected edition
Robbin Brosterman Senior Art Director
Paul Levitz President & Publisher
Georg Brewer VP-Design & DC Direct Creative
Richard Bruning Senior VP-Creative Director
Patrick Caldon Executive VP-Finance & Operations
Chris Caramalis VP-Finance
John Cunningham VP-Marketing
Terri Cunningham VP-Managing Editor
Stephanie Fierman Senior VP-Sales & Marketing
Alison Gill VP-Manufacturing
Rich Johnson VP-Book Trade Sales
Hank Kanalz VP-General Manager, WildStorm
Lillian Laserson Senior VP & General Counsel
Jim Lee Editorial Director-WildStorm
Paula Lowitt Senior VP-Business & Legal Affairs
David McKillips VP-Advertising & Custom Publishing
John Nee VP-Business Development
Gregory Noveck Senior VP-Creative Affairs
Cheryl Rubin Senior VP-Brand Management
Jeff Trojan VP-Business Development, DC Direct
Bob Wayne VP-Sales

YEAR ONE: BATMAN/RA'S AL GHUL

DC Comics, 1700 Broadway, New York, NY 10019. A Warner Bros. Entertainment Company. Printed in Canada. First Printing.
ISBN: 1-4012-0904-1
ISBN-13: 978-1-4012-0904-9

Cover illustration by Paul Gulacy
Cover color by Laurie Kronenberg
Logo design by Terry Marks
Publication design by John J. Hill

WRITER **DEVIN GRAYSON**

PENCILLER **PAUL GULACY**

INKER **JIMMY PALMIOTTI**

COLORIST **LAURIE KRONENBERG**

RA'S AL GHUL

LETTERER **PHIL BALSMAN**

ORIGINAL COVERS **PAUL GULACY**
& JIMMY PALMIOTTI

BATMAN CREATED BY **BOB KANE**

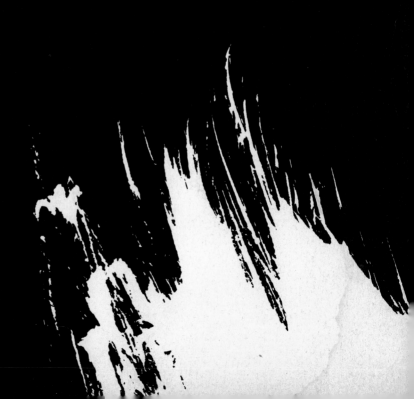

BATMAN

A family outing to the cinema ended in tragedy for eight-year-old Bruce Wayne when Dr. Thomas Wayne and his wife Martha were killed by a mugger on a street known today as Crime Alley. Bruce witnessed the act and his life changed irrevocably. Bruce swore a solemn oath to avenge his parents' deaths and he continued to live in Wayne Manor, tended to by the family valet Alfred Pennyworth. At age 14, Bruce embarked on a journey that took him to every continent, crisscrossing the globe several times over as he sought to learn every skill he would need to keep his vow. He audited courses at Cambridge and the Sorbonne. He studied criminology, forensics, and the psychology of the criminal mind. Under assumed names, Bruce apprenticed with manhunters and martial artists, learning the subtleties of detection and deduction while mastering every known fighting style. Upon his return to Gotham City, Bruce began to operate outside the law. In short order, he learned he needed a disguise to strike fear in criminal hearts. When a bat crashed through the Manor's window, he was inspired to create that disguise and so the Batman was born. In the twelve years since that night, the Batman has become not only Gotham City's protector but an inspiration for others ranging from the police force to Dick Grayson, who became the first Robin and is now Nightwing; Barbara Gordon, who became the first Batgirl and is now Oracle; and Tim Drake, the current Robin. Along the way he has encountered some of the most dangerous, grotesque and deadly foes imaginable. He and Gotham have survived much, starting with political corruption but even a plague, an earthquake and a year-long exile from the United States. And both have endured. Bruce Wayne is now a shell, a disguise to service the Batman's unending quest to give the people of Gotham City a protector against the criminal element's violence and madness.

The first recorded appearance of the man who is now known as Ra's al Ghul dates back over 600 years. Born to a tribe of Arabian desert nomads, he expressed an interest in science and left the tribe to live and pursue his research in a city. There, he met and married Sora. As a practicing physician, he discovered the alchemical combination of ingredients, harvested from the ground above electromagnetic ley lines that crisscross the planet, and built his first Lazarus Pit in order to save a dying prince. Driven insane by the body's rejuvenation, the sadistic prince strangled Sora. The prince's father charged the doctor, not the prince, with the murder and he was imprisoned with his wife's corpse. He escaped and took revenge — first killing the king and prince with his advanced scientific knowledge and then burning the city. He then took the name Ra's al Ghul, which translates to "Demon's Head." Using the Lazarus Pits to keep himself alive, Ra's spent the next several centuries traveling the world and increasing his knowledge. During this time he built many organizations, the best known being the League of Assassins. Over time, he watched, in horror, as the industrialized world began to poison the planet. Finally, he found his true calling and has set out to rid the world of most of humanity, so the ecosystem may heal itself and return Earth to a place of splendor. With the years, though, Ra's recognized that the Pits would not keep him alive forever and needed to begin building a succession plan, which brought the Batman to his attention. When Batman refused the role of heir and son-in-law, the two began a series of confrontations that grew deadlier with each meeting. Ra's never allowed himself to love again but has raised at least two daughters. The first, Nyssa, grew to hate him for his cold, unfeeling way and recently, she kidnapped her half sister, Talia, and brainwashed her, turning her into an instrument of revenge. Talia killed their father, which triggered the events in the following tale.

RA'S AL GHUL

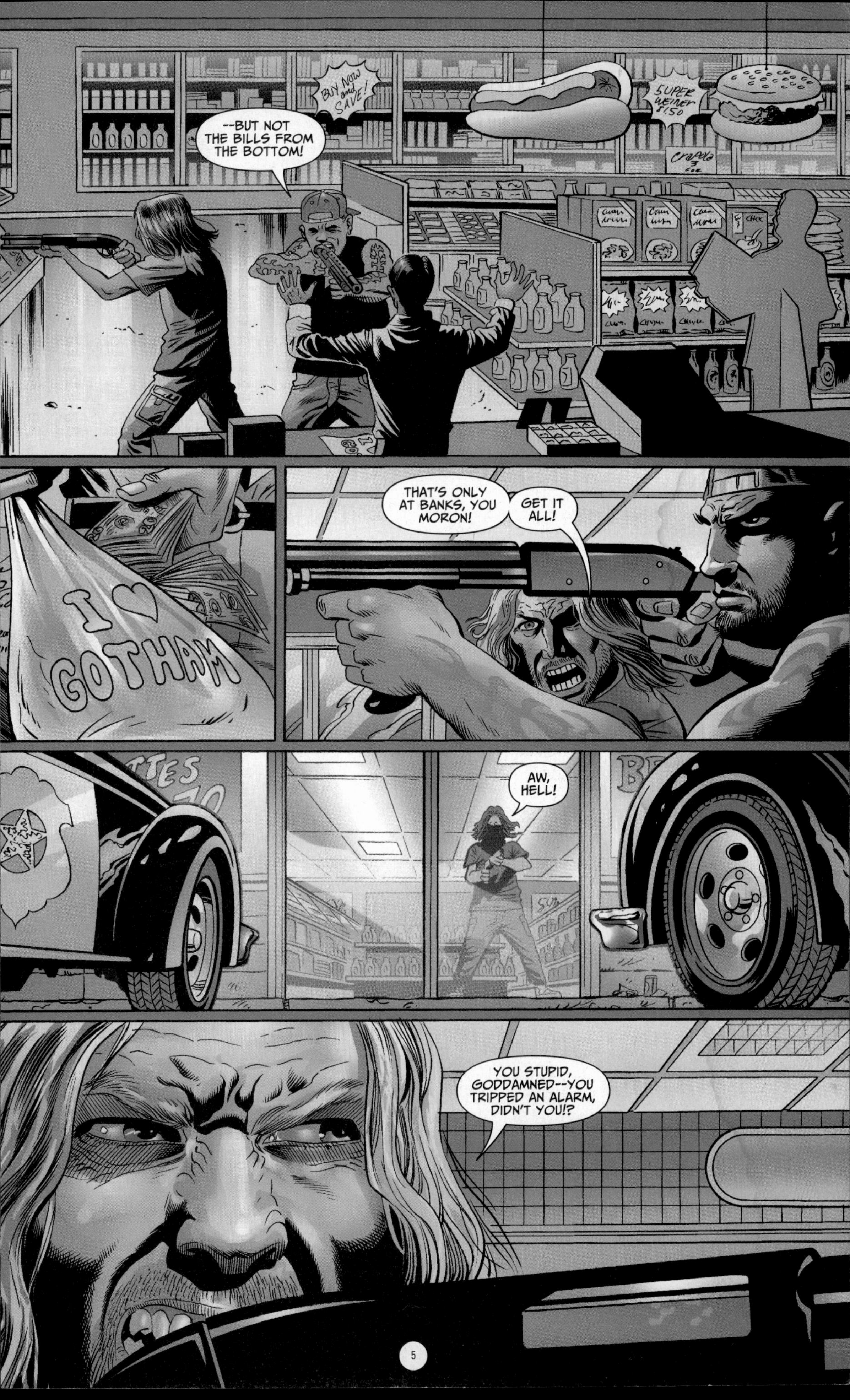
BUY NOW and SAVE!
SUPER WEINER $1.50
--BUT NOT THE BILLS FROM THE BOTTOM!
I ♥ GOTHAM
THAT'S ONLY AT BANKS, YOU MORON!
GET IT ALL!
AW, HELL!
YOU STUPID, GODDAMNED--YOU TRIPPED AN ALARM, DIDN'T YOU!?

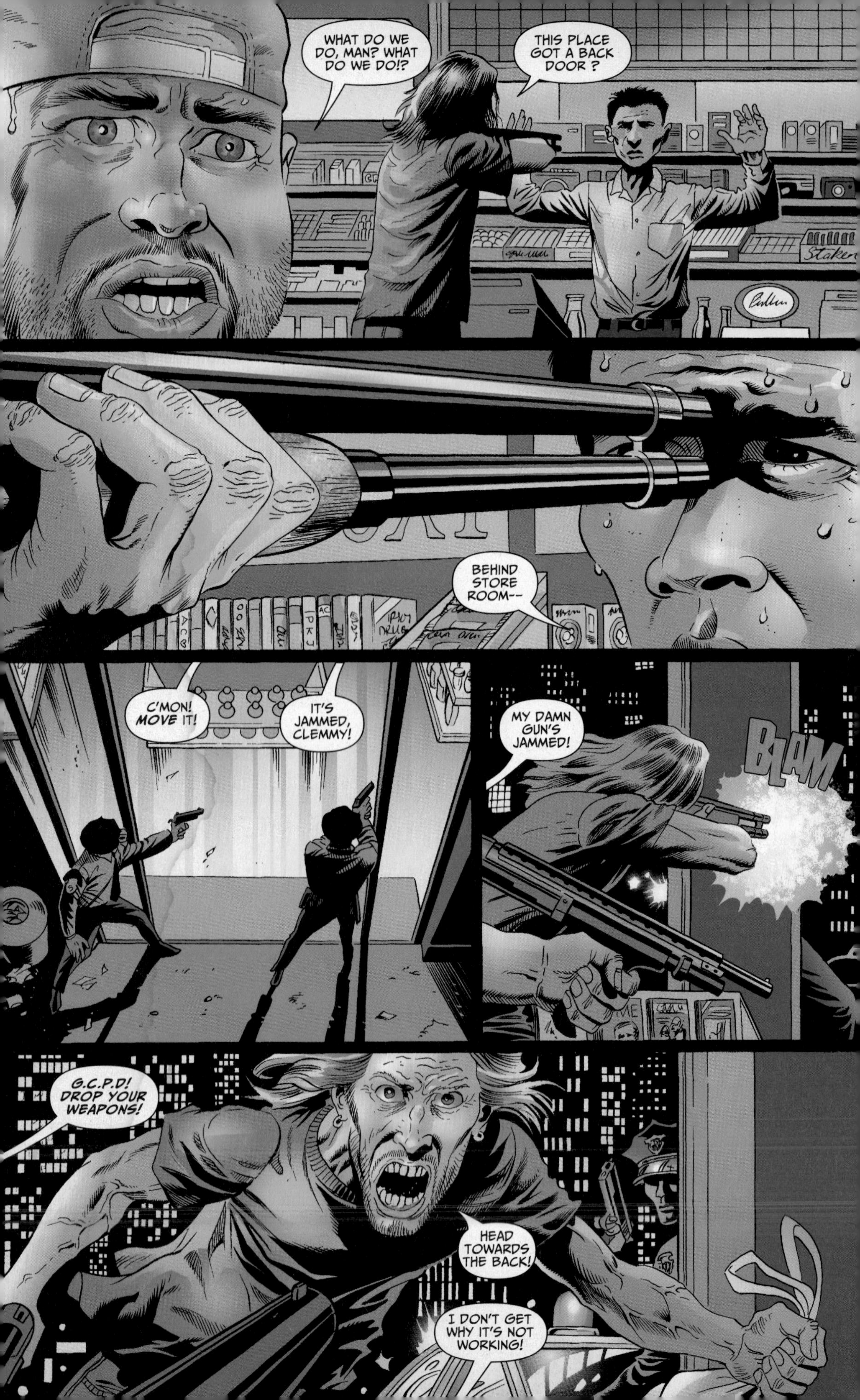
WHAT DO WE DO, MAN? WHAT DO WE DO!?
THIS PLACE GOT A BACK DOOR ?
BEHIND STORE ROOM--
C'MON! MOVE IT!
IT'S JAMMED, CLEMMY!
MY DAMN GUN'S JAMMED!
BLAM
G.C.P.D! DROP YOUR WEAPONS!
HEAD TOWARDS THE BACK!
I DON'T GET WHY IT'S NOT WORKING!

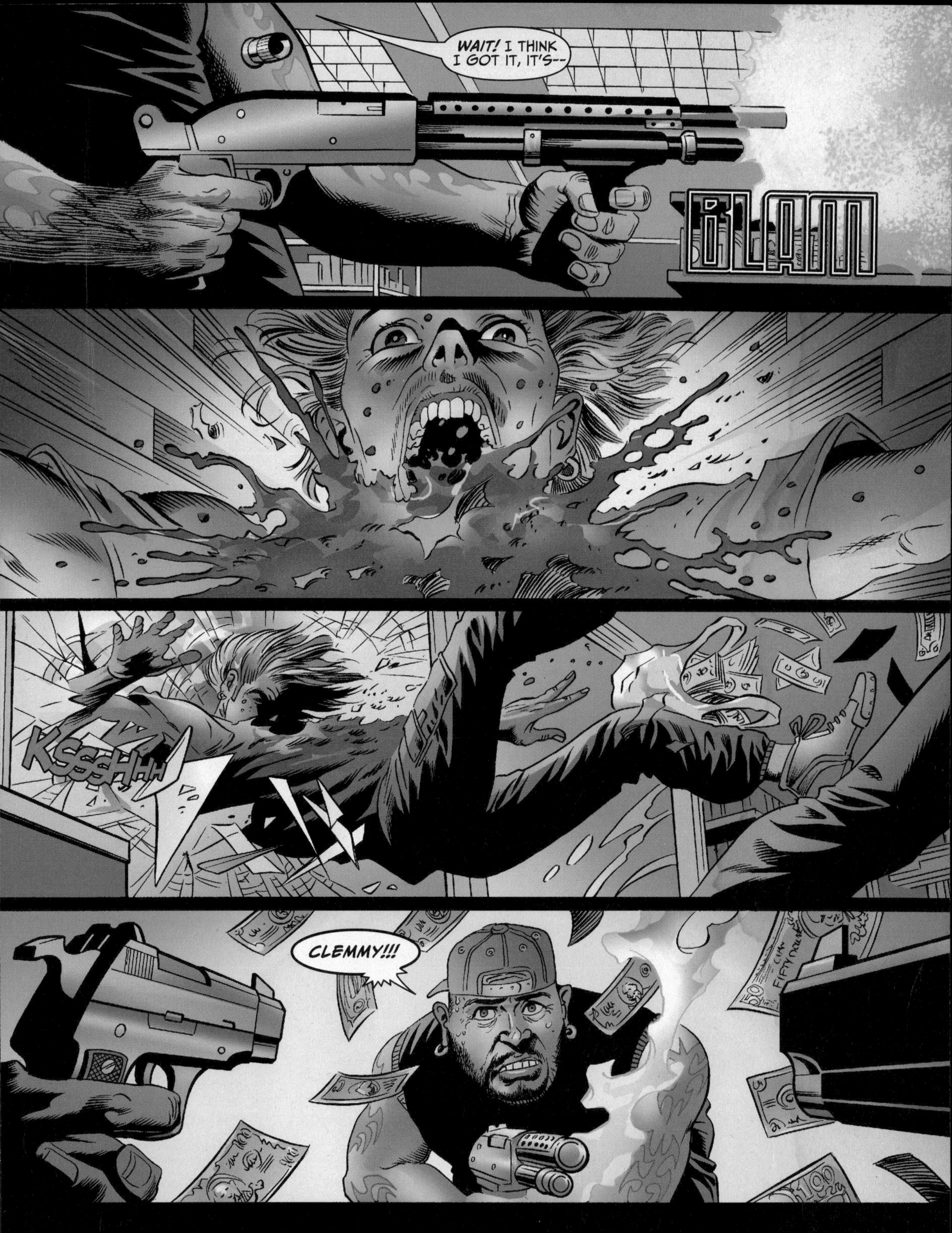
WAIT! I THINK I GOT IT, IT'S--
BLAM
KSSSHHH
CLEMMY!!!

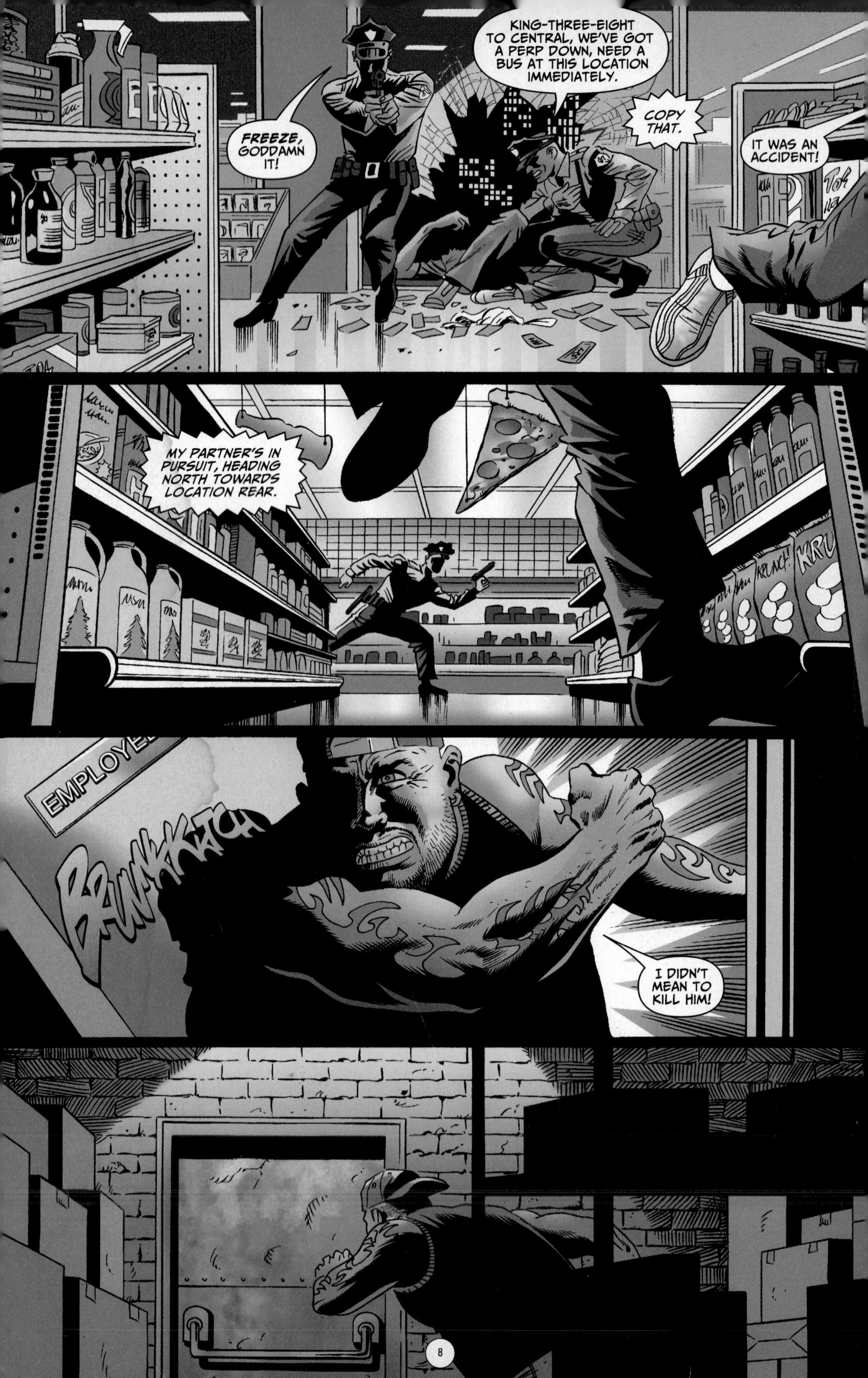
FREEZE, GODDAMN IT!
KING-THREE-EIGHT TO CENTRAL, WE'VE GOT A PERP DOWN, NEED A BUS AT THIS LOCATION IMMEDIATELY.
COPY THAT.
IT WAS AN ACCIDENT!
MY PARTNER'S IN PURSUIT, HEADING NORTH TOWARDS LOCATION REAR.
I DIDN'T MEAN TO KILL HIM!

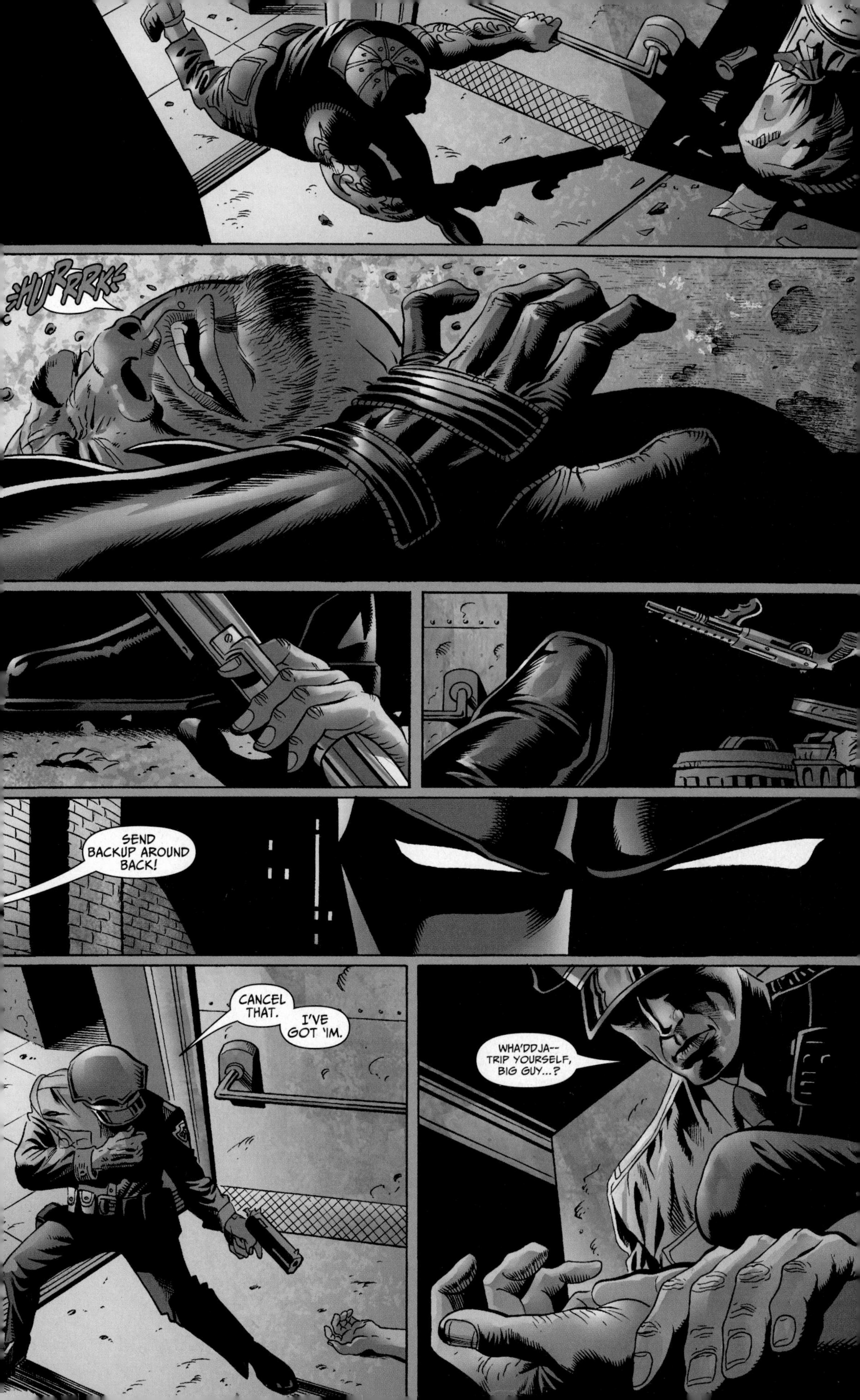
HURRRK
SEND BACKUP AROUND BACK!
CANCEL THAT.
I'VE GOT 'IM.
WHA'DDJA-- TRIP YOURSELF, BIG GUY...?

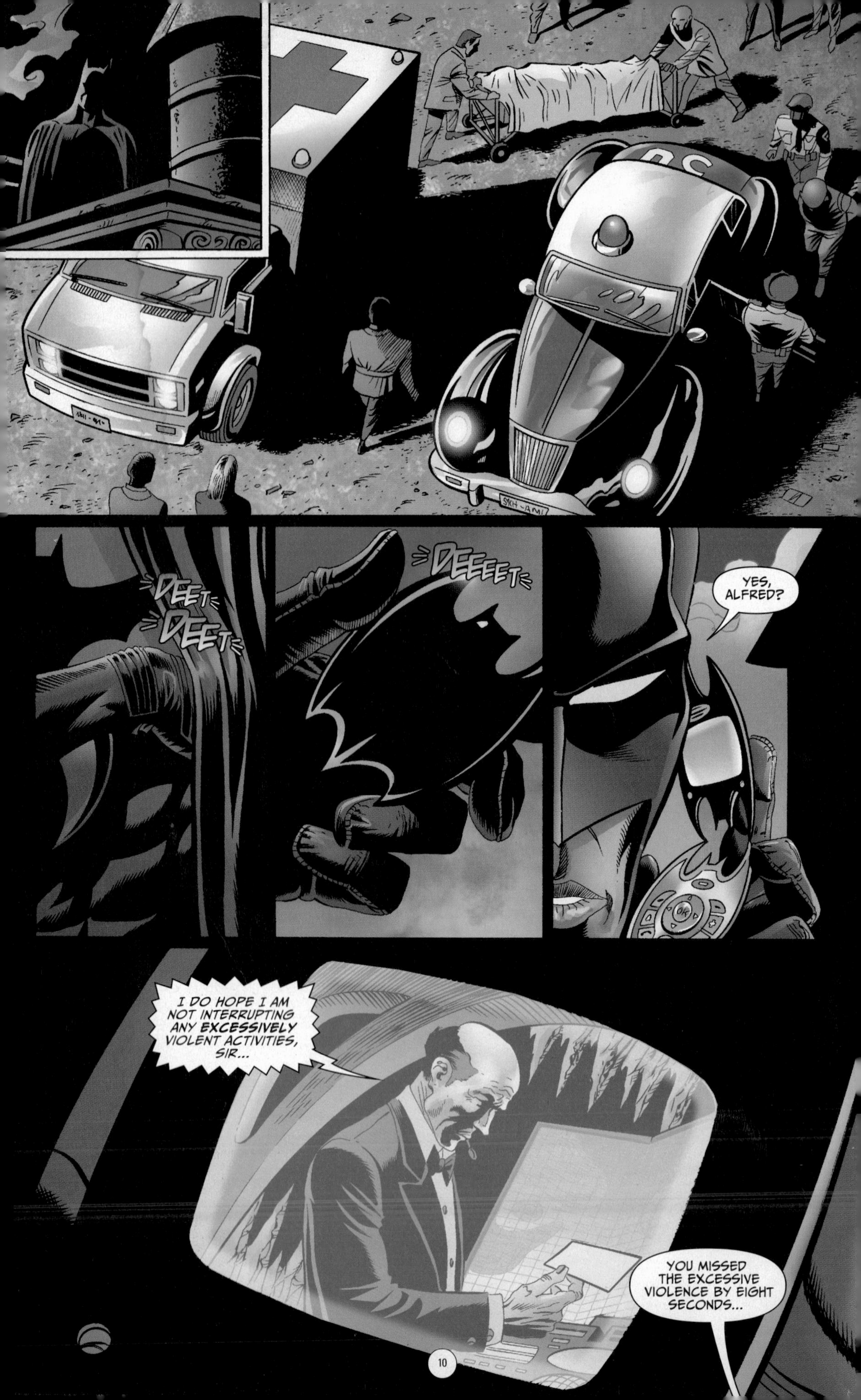
DEET
DEET
DEEEEET
YES, ALFRED?
I DO HOPE I AM NOT INTERRUPTING ANY EXCESSIVELY VIOLENT ACTIVITIES, SIR...
YOU MISSED THE EXCESSIVE VIOLENCE BY EIGHT SECONDS...

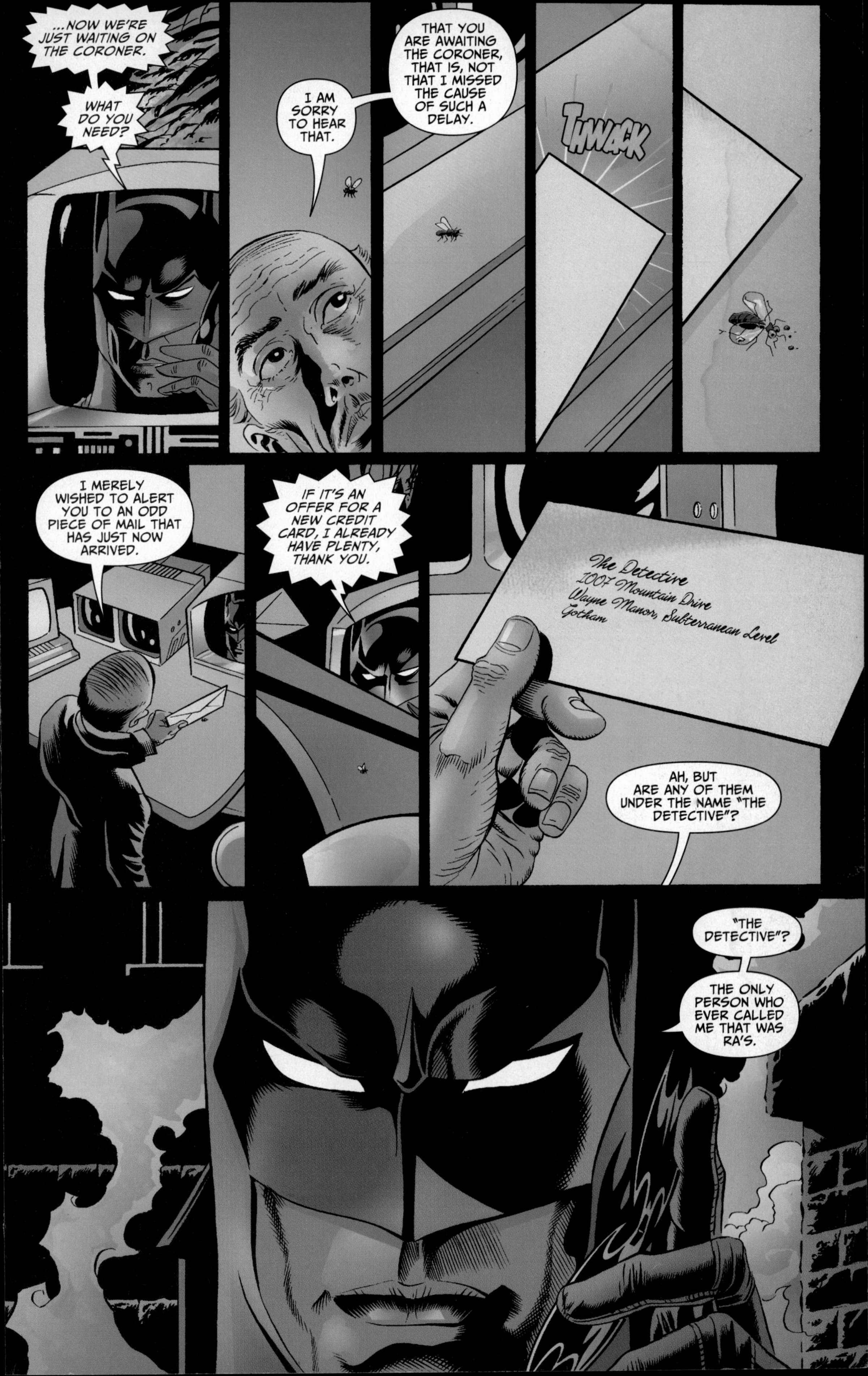
...NOW WE'RE JUST WAITING ON THE CORONER.
WHAT DO YOU NEED?
I AM SORRY TO HEAR THAT.
THAT YOU ARE AWAITING THE CORONER, THAT IS, NOT THAT I MISSED THE CAUSE OF SUCH A DELAY.
THWACK
I MERELY WISHED TO ALERT YOU TO AN ODD PIECE OF MAIL THAT HAS JUST NOW ARRIVED.
IF IT'S AN OFFER FOR A NEW CREDIT CARD, I ALREADY HAVE PLENTY, THANK YOU.
The Detective
1007 Mountain Drive
Wayne Manor, Subterranean Level
Gotham
AH, BUT ARE ANY OF THEM UNDER THE NAME "THE DETECTIVE"?
"THE DETECTIVE"?
THE ONLY PERSON WHO EVER CALLED ME THAT WAS RA'S.

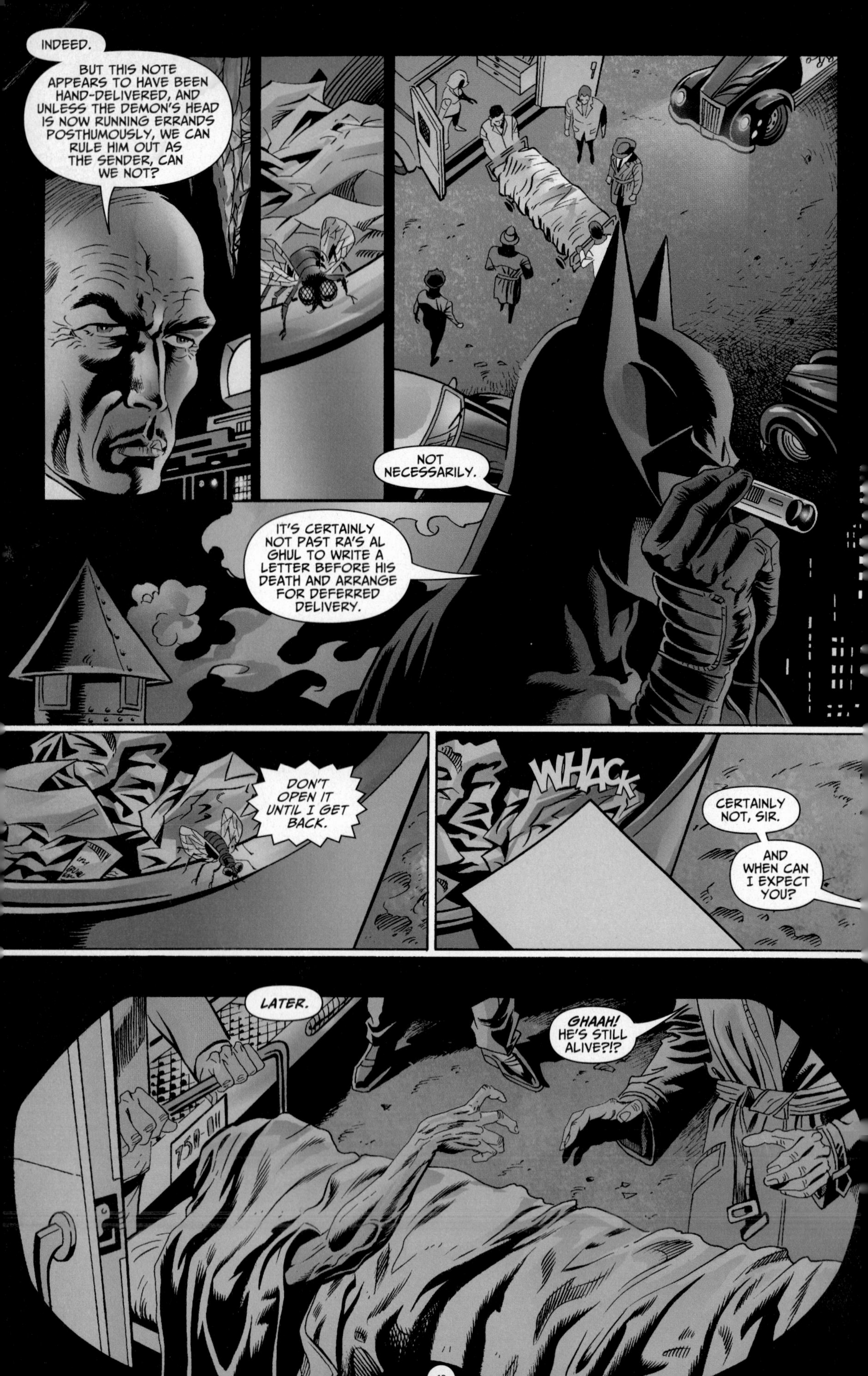
INDEED.
BUT THIS NOTE APPEARS TO HAVE BEEN HAND-DELIVERED, AND UNLESS THE DEMON'S HEAD IS NOW RUNNING ERRANDS POSTHUMOUSLY, WE CAN RULE HIM OUT AS THE SENDER, CAN WE NOT?
NOT NECESSARILY.
IT'S CERTAINLY NOT PAST RA'S AL GHUL TO WRITE A LETTER BEFORE HIS DEATH AND ARRANGE FOR DEFERRED DELIVERY.
DON'T OPEN IT UNTIL I GET BACK.
WHACK
CERTAINLY NOT, SIR.
AND WHEN CAN I EXPECT YOU?
LATER.
GHAAH! HE'S STILL ALIVE?!?
750-011

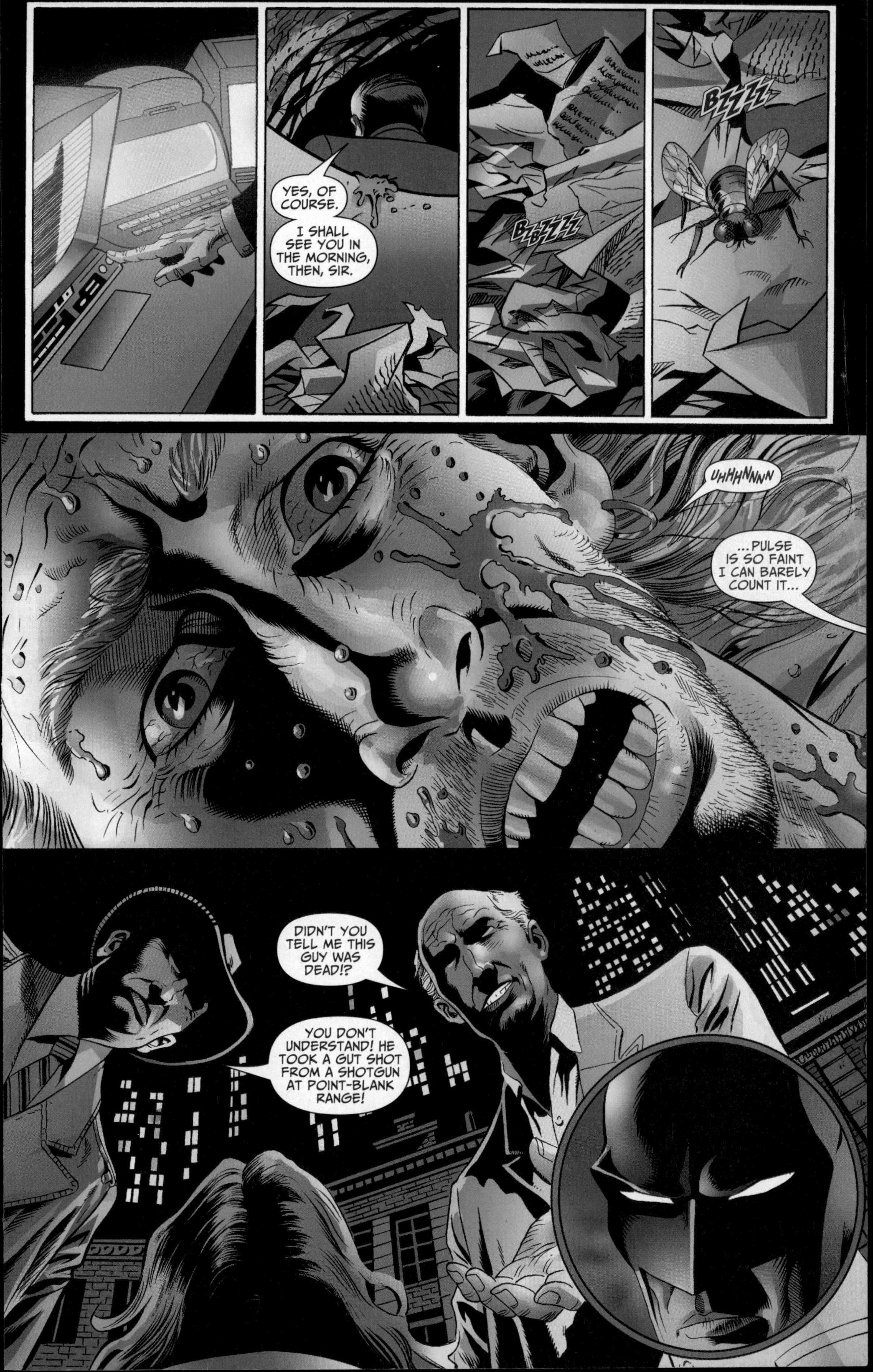
YES, OF COURSE.
I SHALL SEE YOU IN THE MORNING, THEN, SIR.
BZZZZZ
BZZZZ
UHHHNNNN
...PULSE IS SO FAINT I CAN BARELY COUNT IT...
DIDN'T YOU TELL ME THIS GUY WAS DEAD!?
YOU DON'T UNDERSTAND! HE TOOK A GUT SHOT FROM A SHOTGUN AT POINT-BLANK RANGE!

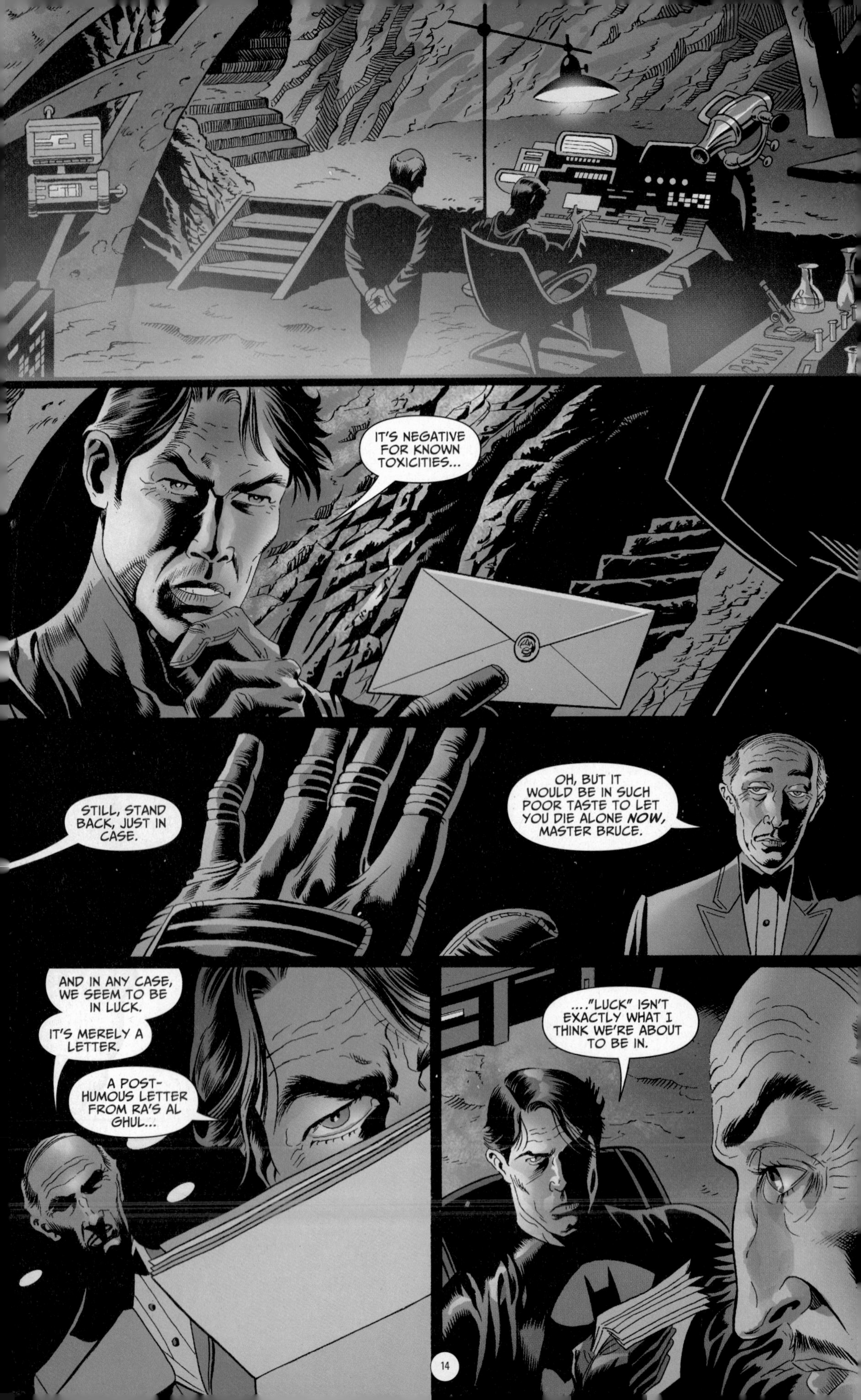
IT'S NEGATIVE FOR KNOWN TOXICITIES...
STILL, STAND BACK, JUST IN CASE.
OH, BUT IT WOULD BE IN SUCH POOR TASTE TO LET YOU DIE ALONE *NOW*, MASTER BRUCE.
AND IN ANY CASE, WE SEEM TO BE IN LUCK.
IT'S MERELY A LETTER.
A POST-HUMOUS LETTER FROM RA'S AL GHUL...
...."LUCK" ISN'T EXACTLY WHAT I THINK WE'RE ABOUT TO BE IN.

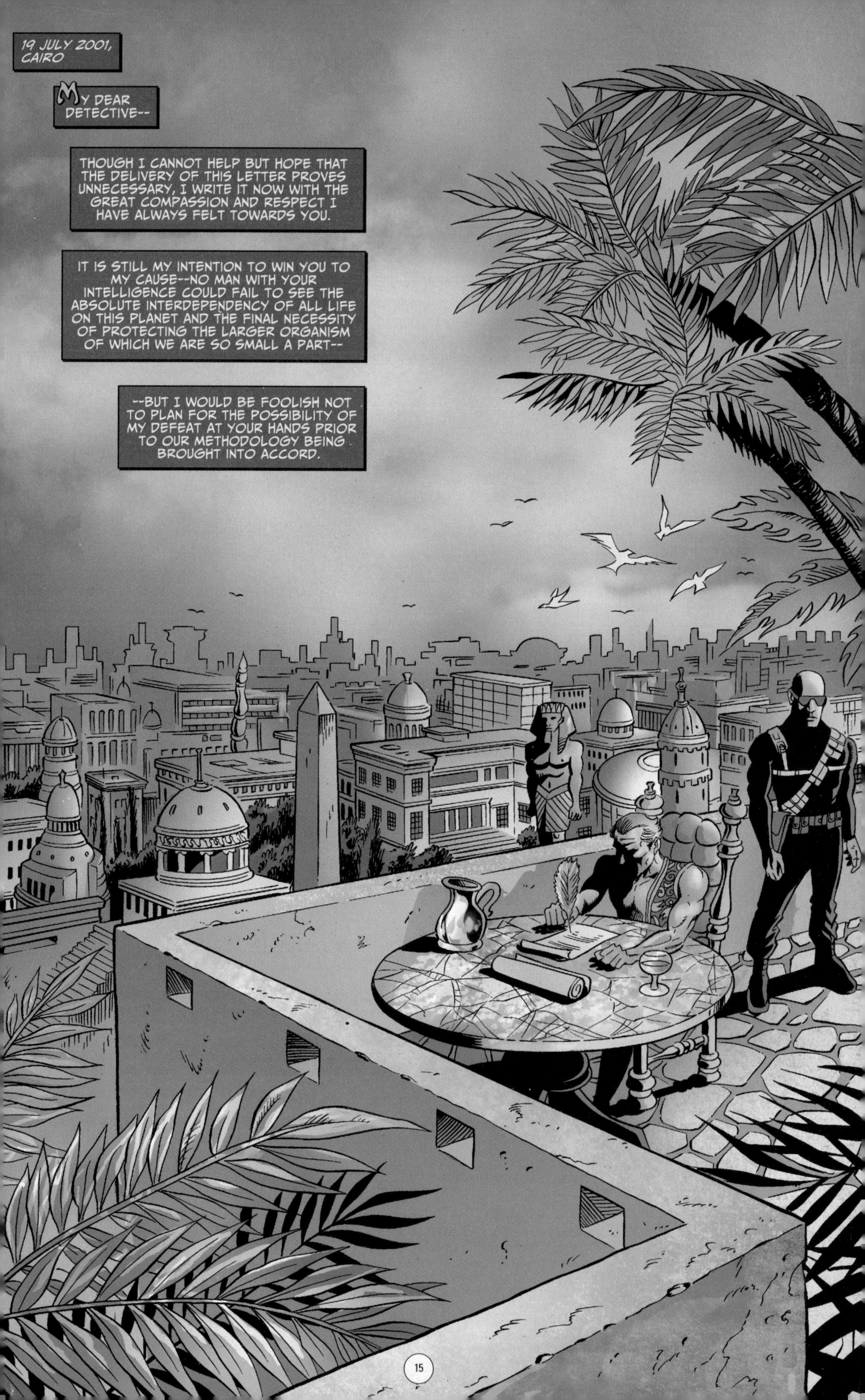
19 JULY 2001, CAIRO
MY DEAR DETECTIVE--
THOUGH I CANNOT HELP BUT HOPE THAT THE DELIVERY OF THIS LETTER PROVES UNNECESSARY, I WRITE IT NOW WITH THE GREAT COMPASSION AND RESPECT I HAVE ALWAYS FELT TOWARDS YOU.
IT IS STILL MY INTENTION TO WIN YOU TO MY CAUSE--NO MAN WITH YOUR INTELLIGENCE COULD FAIL TO SEE THE ABSOLUTE INTERDEPENDENCY OF ALL LIFE ON THIS PLANET AND THE FINAL NECESSITY OF PROTECTING THE LARGER ORGANISM OF WHICH WE ARE SO SMALL A PART--
--BUT I WOULD BE FOOLISH NOT TO PLAN FOR THE POSSIBILITY OF MY DEFEAT AT YOUR HANDS PRIOR TO OUR METHODOLOGY BEING BROUGHT INTO ACCORD.

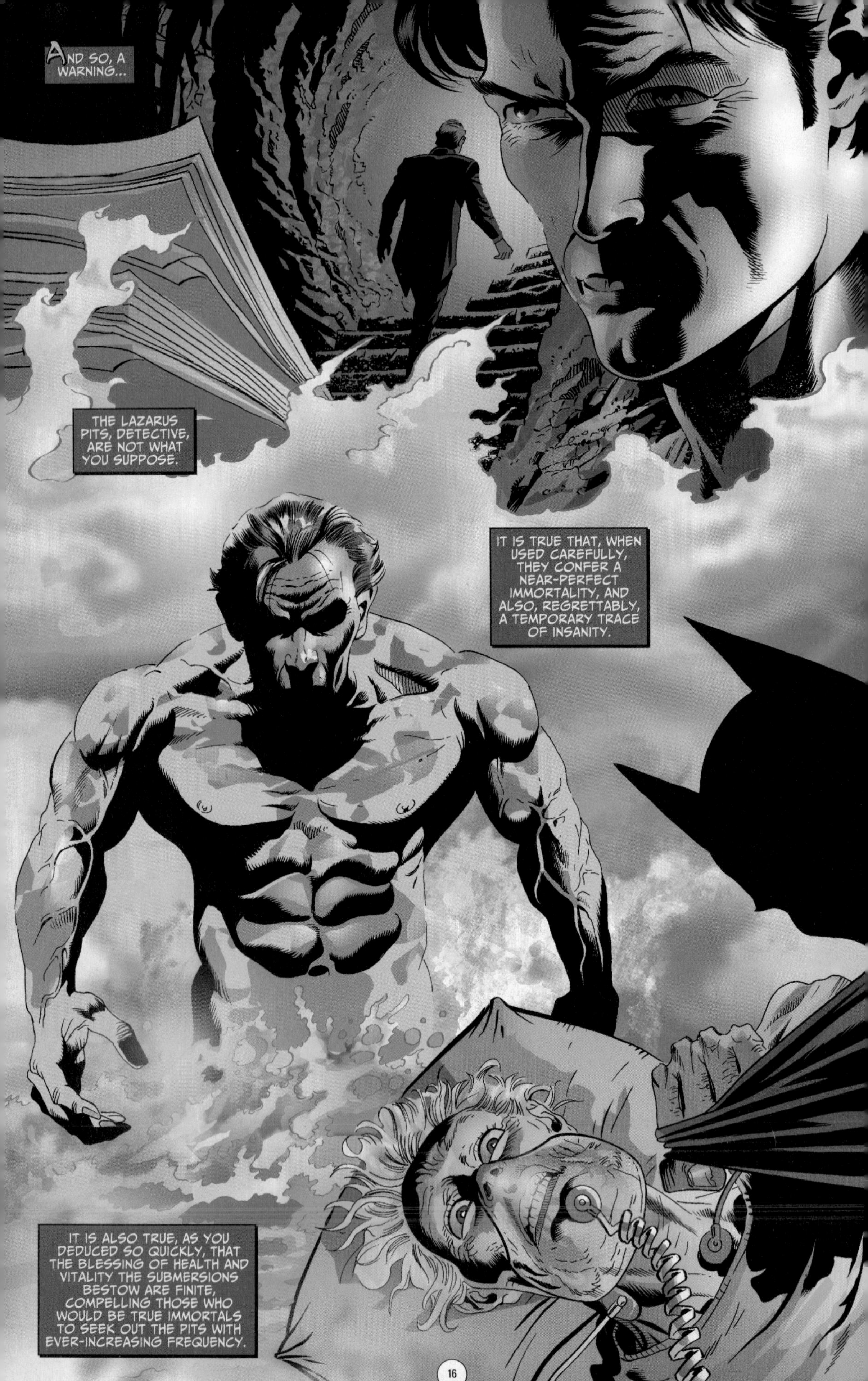
AND SO, A WARNING...
THE LAZARUS PITS, DETECTIVE, ARE NOT WHAT YOU SUPPOSE.
IT IS TRUE THAT, WHEN USED CAREFULLY, THEY CONFER A NEAR-PERFECT IMMORTALITY, AND ALSO, REGRETTABLY, A TEMPORARY TRACE OF INSANITY.
IT IS ALSO TRUE, AS YOU DEDUCED SO QUICKLY, THAT THE BLESSING OF HEALTH AND VITALITY THE SUBMERSIONS BESTOW ARE FINITE, COMPELLING THOSE WHO WOULD BE TRUE IMMORTALS TO SEEK OUT THE PITS WITH EVER-INCREASING FREQUENCY.

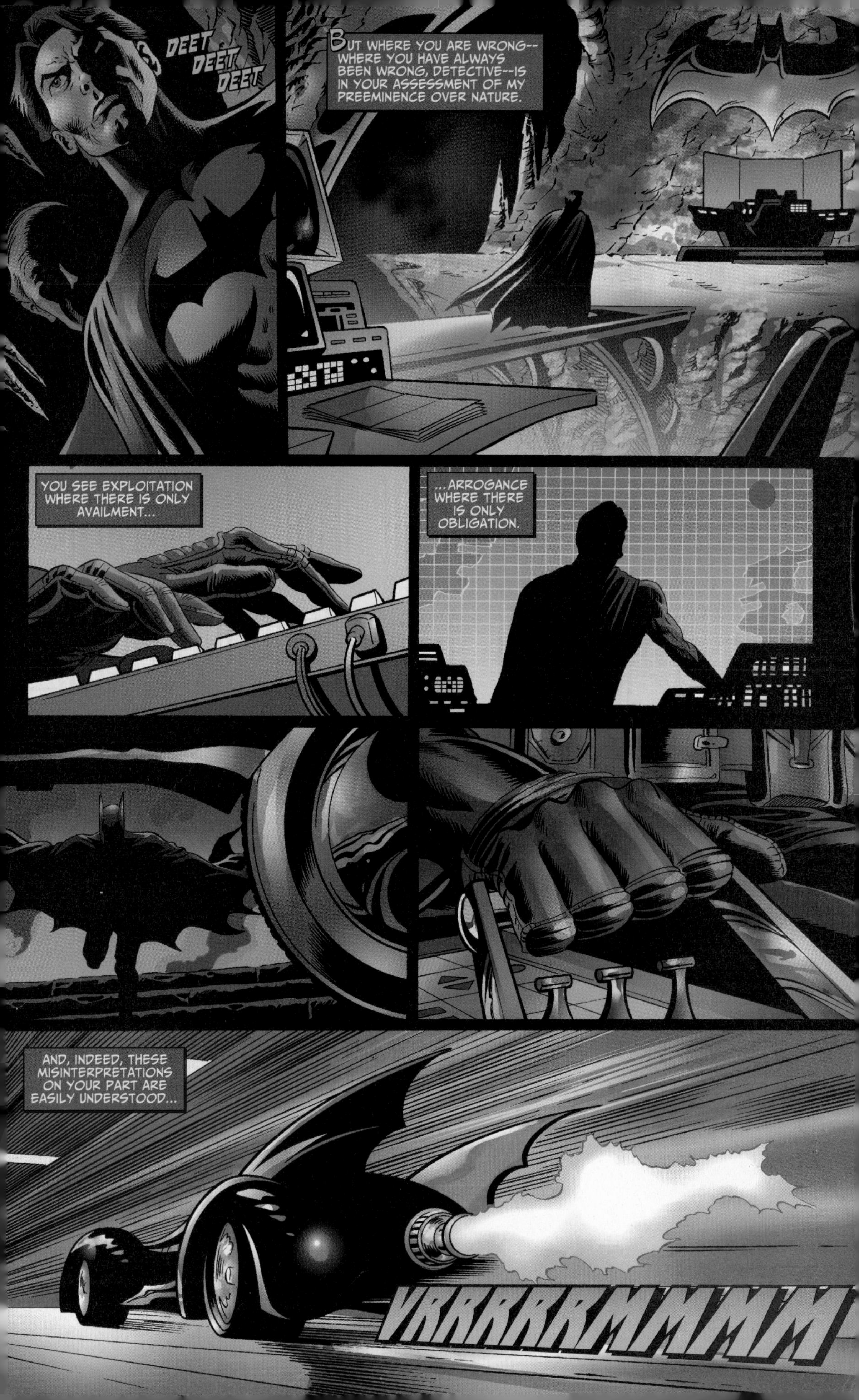
DEET DEET DEET
BUT WHERE YOU ARE WRONG--WHERE YOU HAVE ALWAYS BEEN WRONG, DETECTIVE--IS IN YOUR ASSESSMENT OF MY PREEMINENCE OVER NATURE.
YOU SEE EXPLOITATION WHERE THERE IS ONLY AVAILMENT...
...ARROGANCE WHERE THERE IS ONLY OBLIGATION.
AND, INDEED, THESE MISINTERPRETATIONS ON YOUR PART ARE EASILY UNDERSTOOD...
VRRRRRMMMM

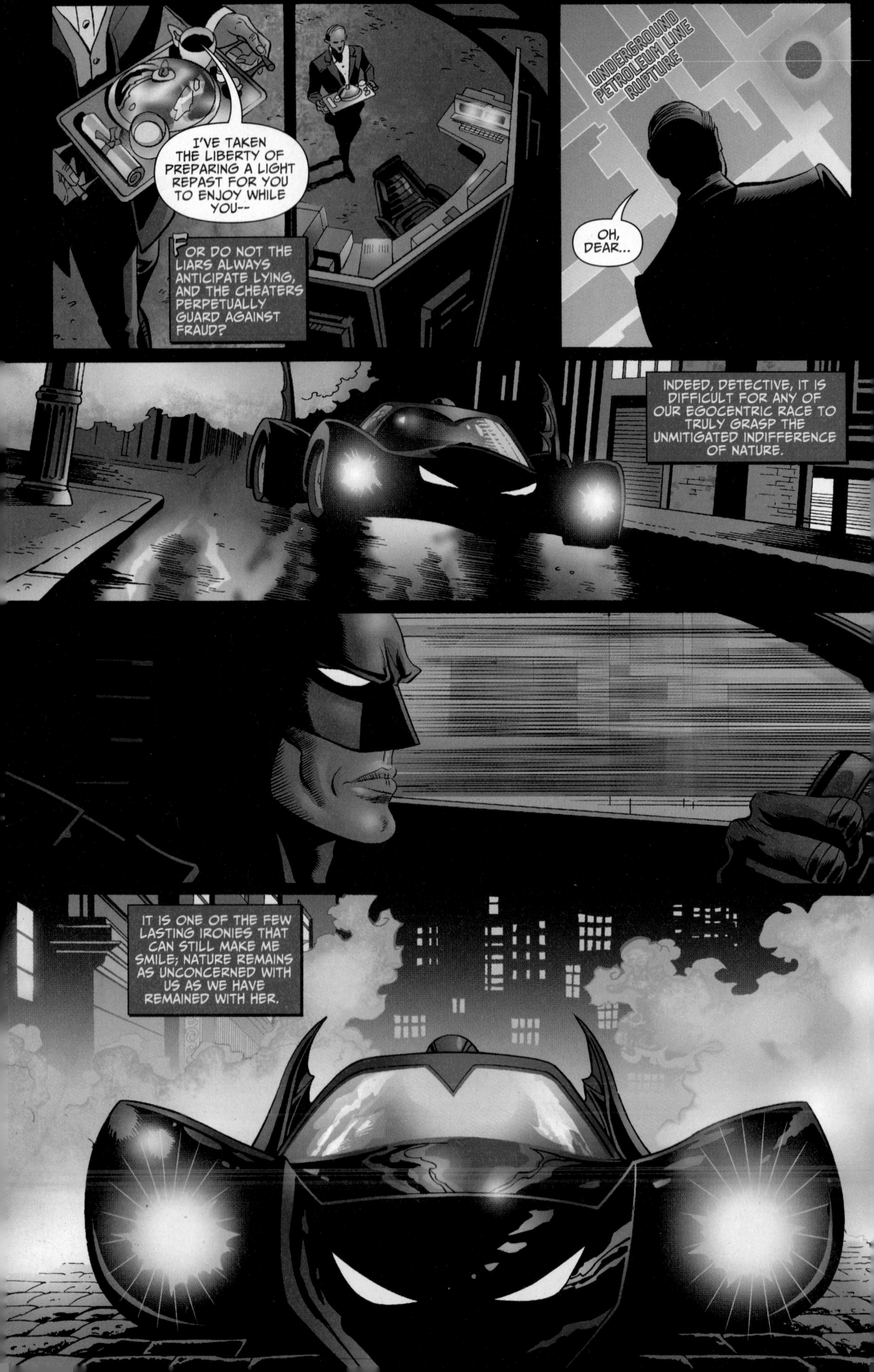
I'VE TAKEN THE LIBERTY OF PREPARING A LIGHT REPAST FOR YOU TO ENJOY WHILE YOU--
FOR DO NOT THE LIARS ALWAYS ANTICIPATE LYING, AND THE CHEATERS PERPETUALLY GUARD AGAINST FRAUD?
UNDERGROUND PETROLEUM LINE RUPTURE
OH, DEAR...
INDEED, DETECTIVE, IT IS DIFFICULT FOR ANY OF OUR EGOCENTRIC RACE TO TRULY GRASP THE UNMITIGATED INDIFFERENCE OF NATURE.
IT IS ONE OF THE FEW LASTING IRONIES THAT CAN STILL MAKE ME SMILE; NATURE REMAINS AS UNCONCERNED WITH US AS WE HAVE REMAINED WITH HER.

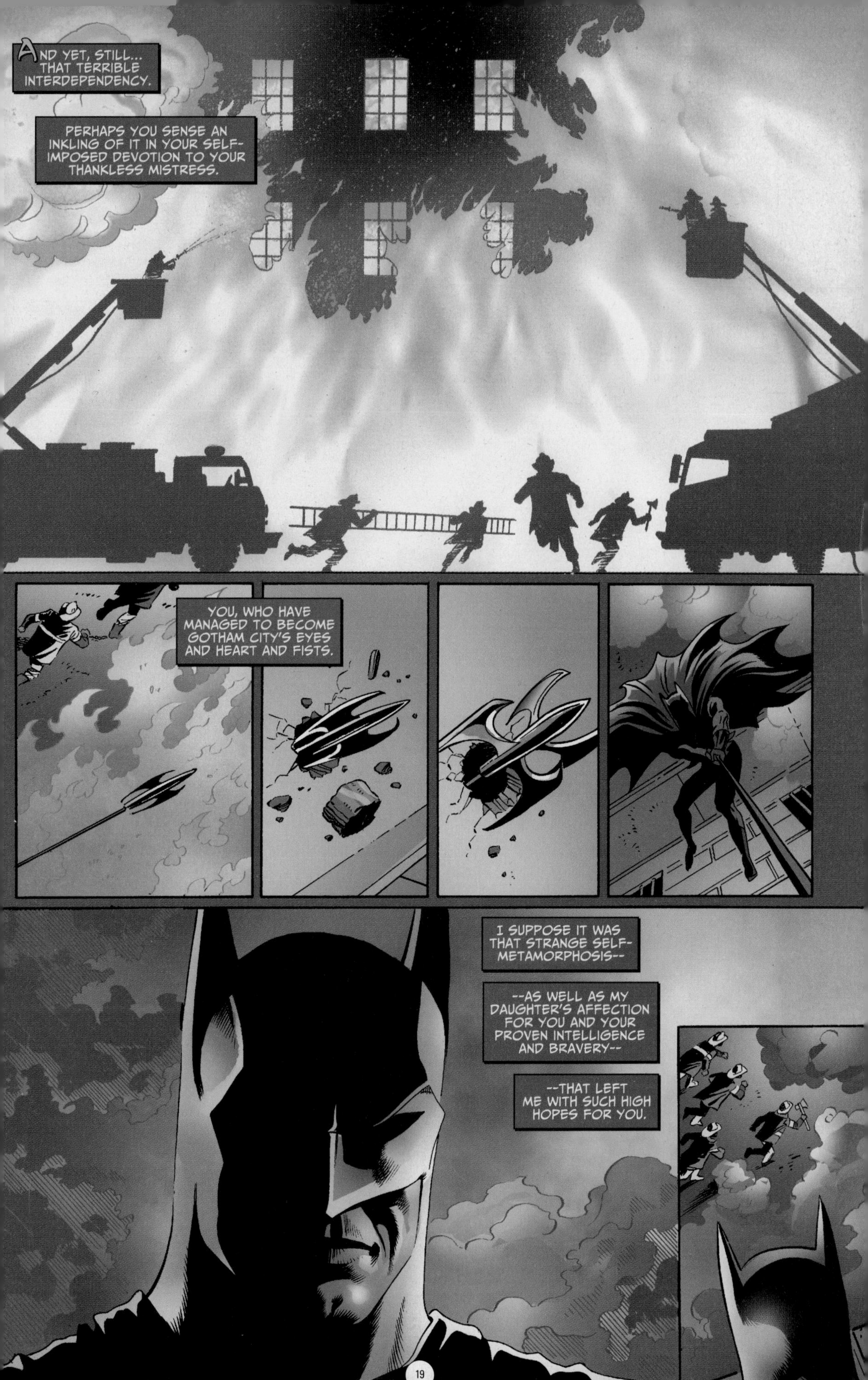
AND YET, STILL... THAT TERRIBLE INTERDEPENDENCY.
PERHAPS YOU SENSE AN INKLING OF IT IN YOUR SELF-IMPOSED DEVOTION TO YOUR THANKLESS MISTRESS.
YOU, WHO HAVE MANAGED TO BECOME GOTHAM CITY'S EYES AND HEART AND FISTS.
I SUPPOSE IT WAS THAT STRANGE SELF-METAMORPHOSIS--
--AS WELL AS MY DAUGHTER'S AFFECTION FOR YOU AND YOUR PROVEN INTELLIGENCE AND BRAVERY--
--THAT LEFT ME WITH SUCH HIGH HOPES FOR YOU.

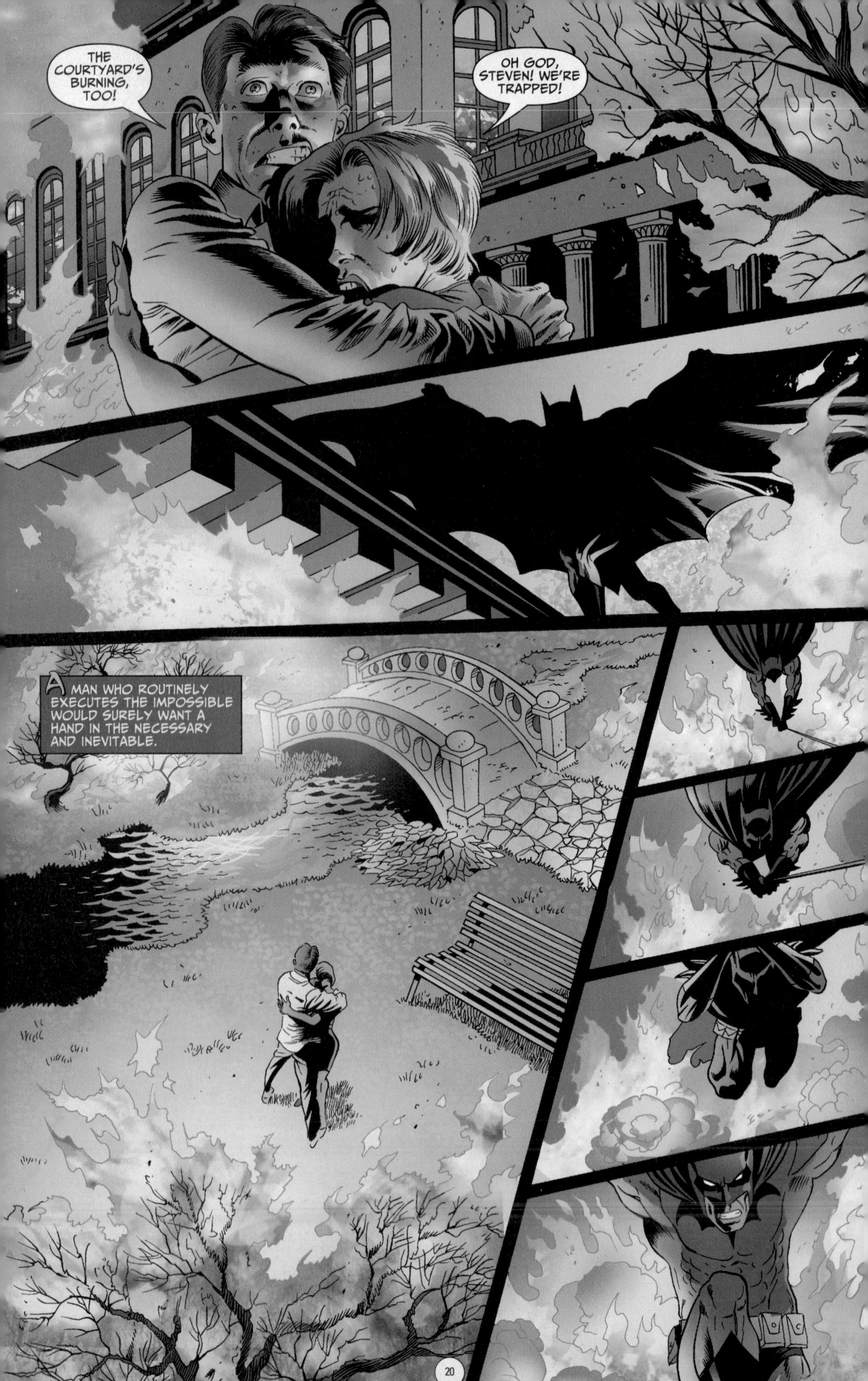
THE COURTYARD'S BURNING, TOO!
OH GOD, STEVEN! WE'RE TRAPPED!
A MAN WHO ROUTINELY EXECUTES THE IMPOSSIBLE WOULD SURELY WANT A HAND IN THE NECESSARY AND INEVITABLE.

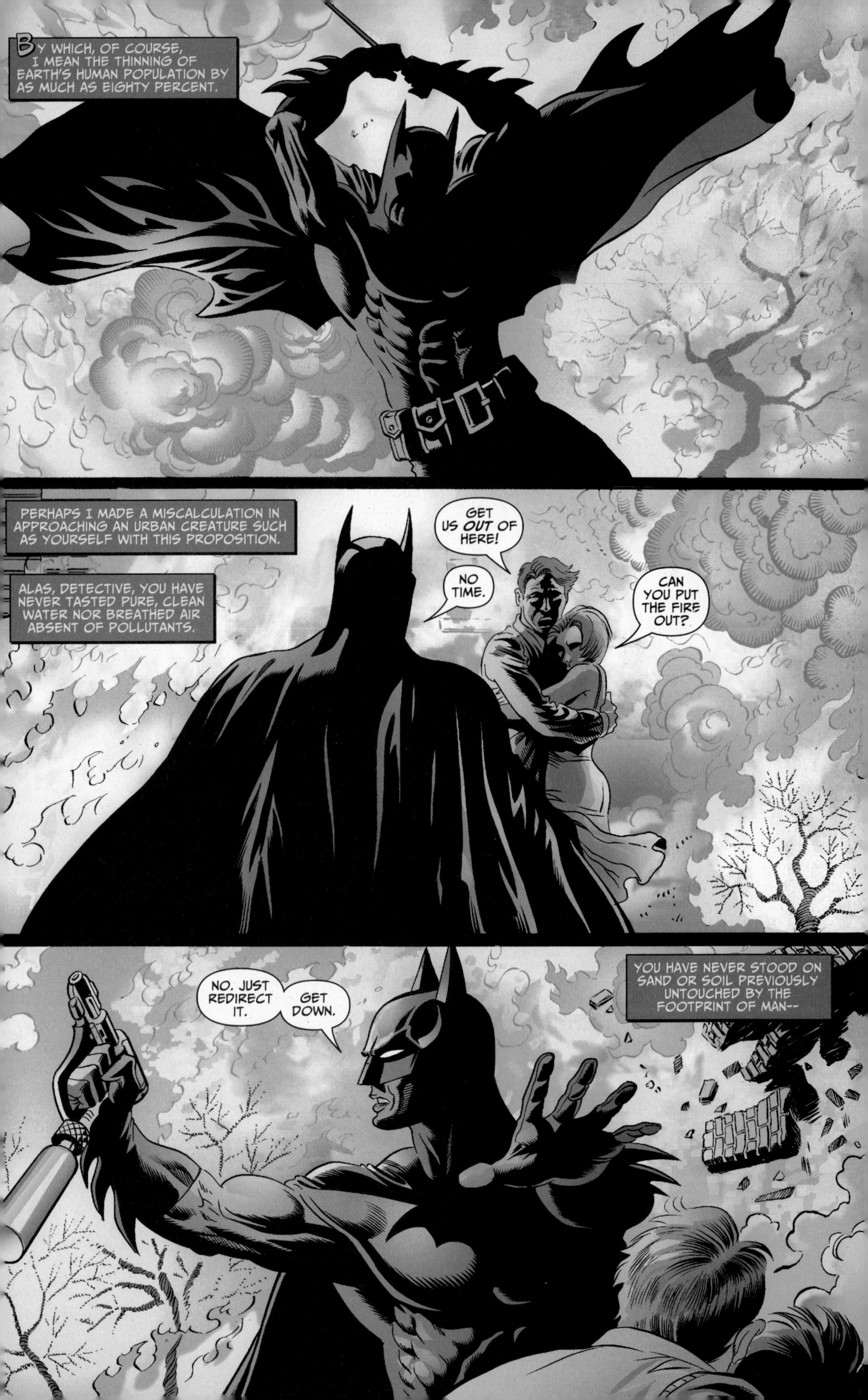
BY WHICH, OF COURSE, I MEAN THE THINNING OF EARTH'S HUMAN POPULATION BY AS MUCH AS EIGHTY PERCENT.
PERHAPS I MADE A MISCALCULATION IN APPROACHING AN URBAN CREATURE SUCH AS YOURSELF WITH THIS PROPOSITION.
GET US OUT OF HERE!
NO TIME.
ALAS, DETECTIVE, YOU HAVE NEVER TASTED PURE, CLEAN WATER NOR BREATHED AIR ABSENT OF POLLUTANTS.
CAN YOU PUT THE FIRE OUT?
NO. JUST REDIRECT IT.
GET DOWN.
YOU HAVE NEVER STOOD ON SAND OR SOIL PREVIOUSLY UNTOUCHED BY THE FOOTPRINT OF MAN--

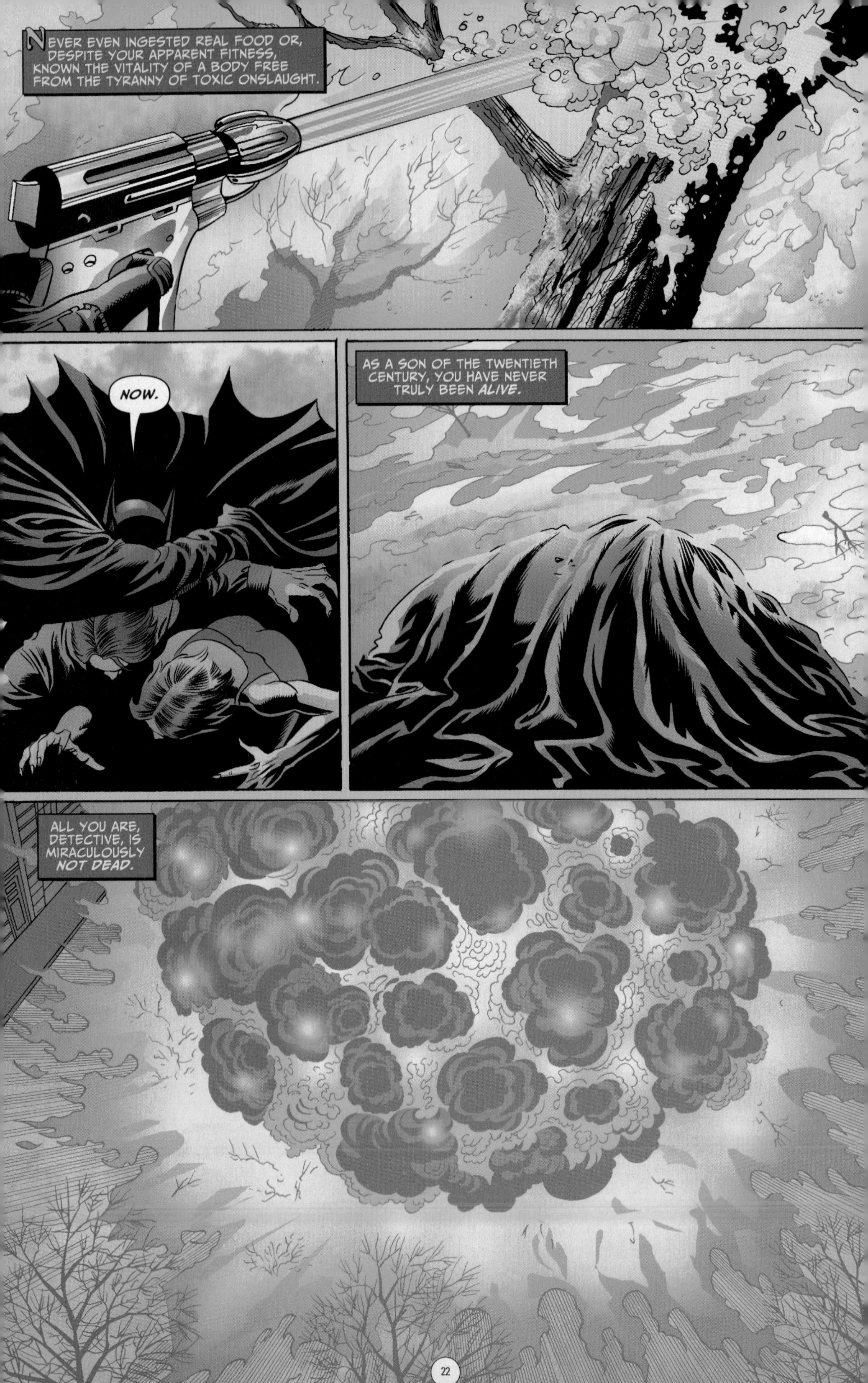
NEVER EVEN INGESTED REAL FOOD OR, DESPITE YOUR APPARENT FITNESS, KNOWN THE VITALITY OF A BODY FREE FROM THE TYRANNY OF TOXIC ONSLAUGHT.
NOW.
AS A SON OF THE TWENTIETH CENTURY, YOU HAVE NEVER TRULY BEEN *ALIVE*.
ALL YOU ARE, DETECTIVE, IS MIRACULOUSLY *NOT DEAD*.

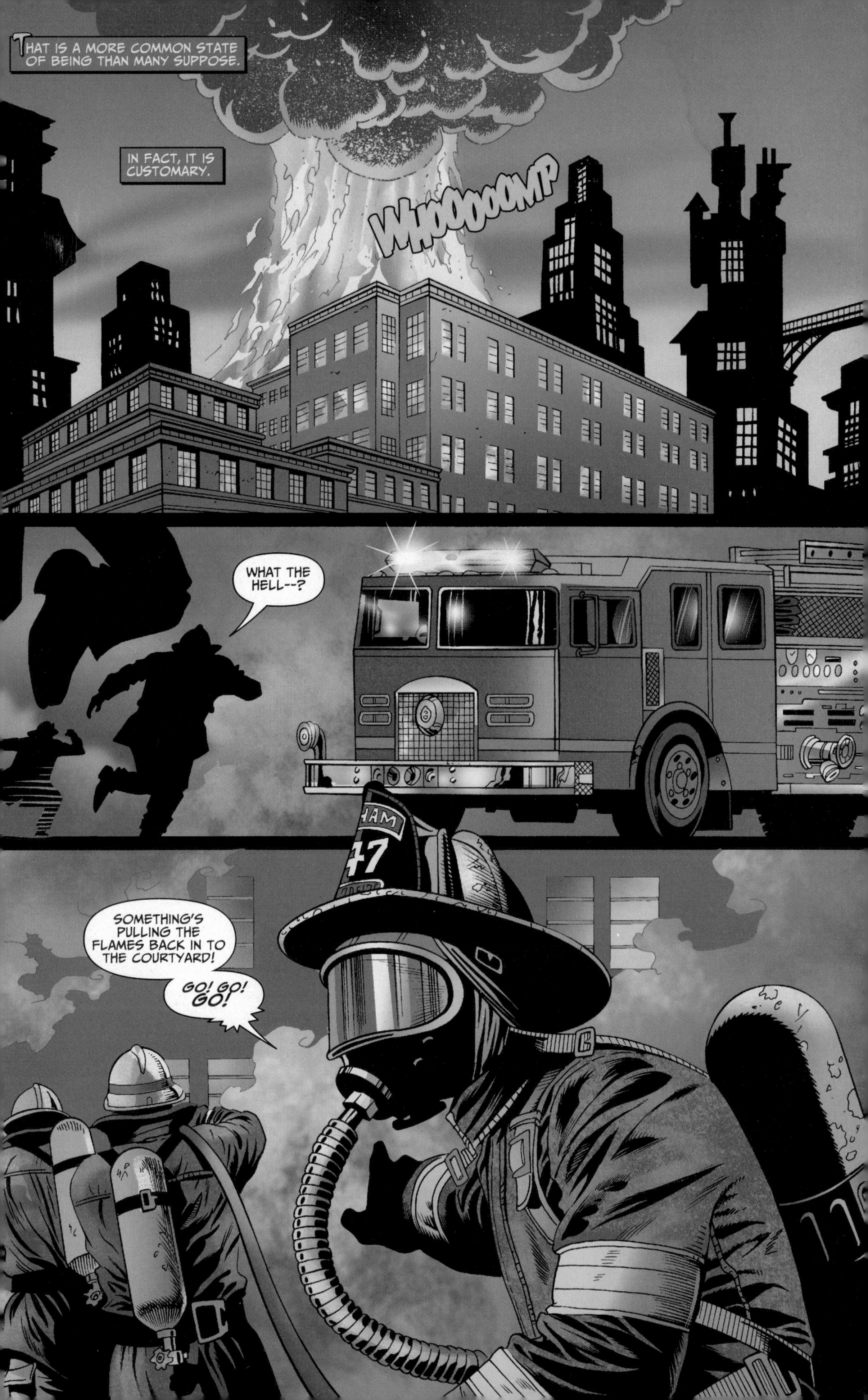
THAT IS A MORE COMMON STATE OF BEING THAN MANY SUPPOSE.
IN FACT, IT IS CUSTOMARY.
WHOOOOOOMP
WHAT THE HELL--?
SOMETHING'S PULLING THE FLAMES BACK IN TO THE COURTYARD!
GO! GO! GO!

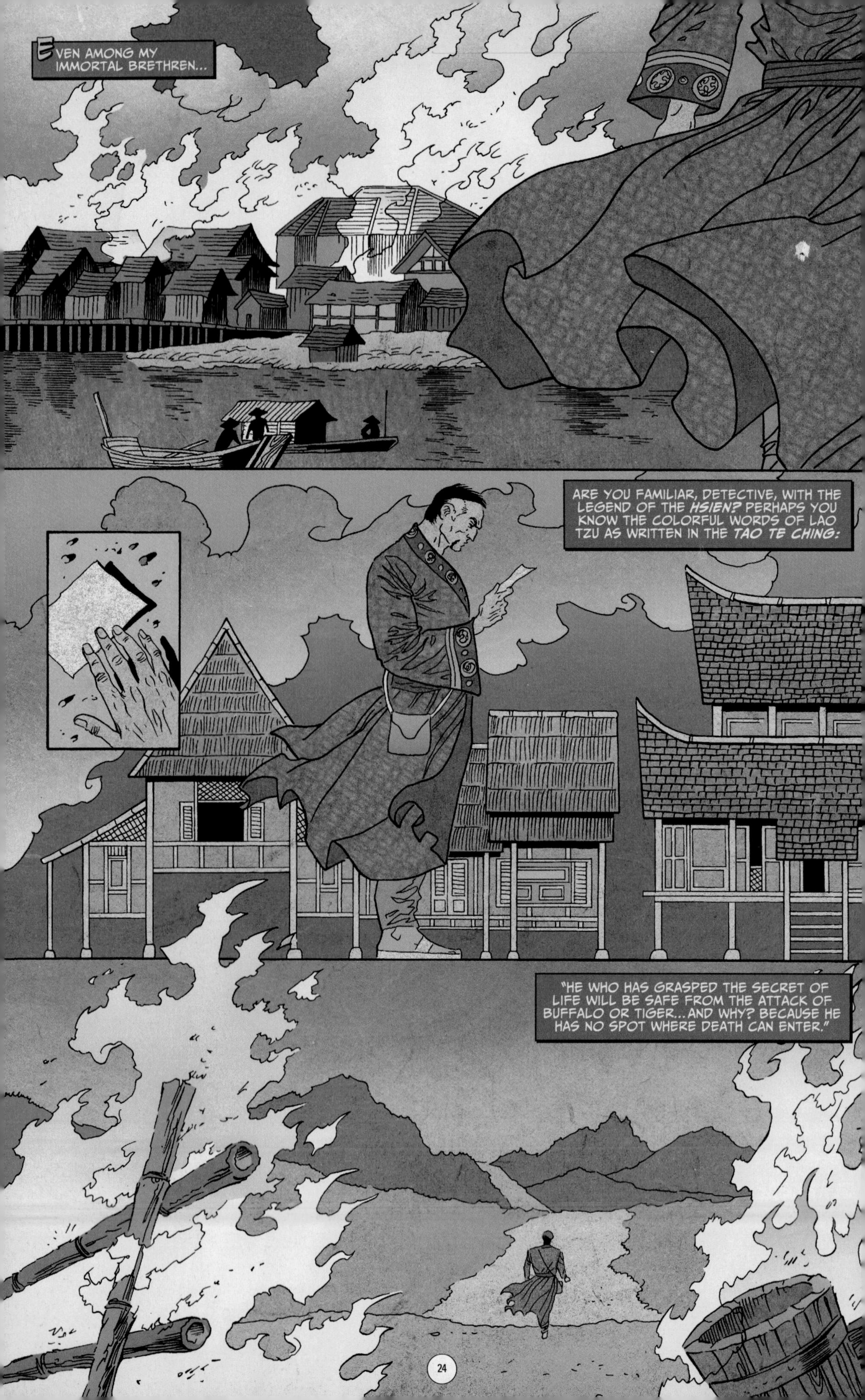
EVEN AMONG MY IMMORTAL BRETHREN...
ARE YOU FAMILIAR, DETECTIVE, WITH THE LEGEND OF THE *HSIEN?* PERHAPS YOU KNOW THE COLORFUL WORDS OF LAO TZU AS WRITTEN IN THE *TAO TE CHING:*
"HE WHO HAS GRASPED THE SECRET OF LIFE WILL BE SAFE FROM THE ATTACK OF BUFFALO OR TIGER...AND WHY? BECAUSE HE HAS NO SPOT WHERE DEATH CAN ENTER."

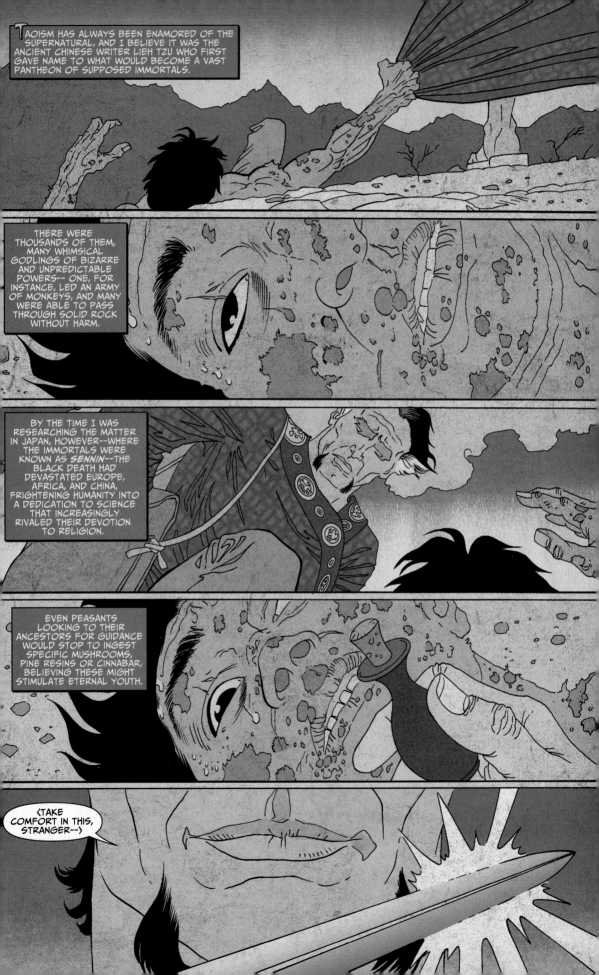

TAOISM HAS ALWAYS BEEN ENAMORED OF THE SUPERNATURAL, AND I BELIEVE IT WAS THE ANCIENT CHINESE WRITER LIEH TZU WHO FIRST GAVE NAME TO WHAT WOULD BECOME A VAST PANTHEON OF SUPPOSED IMMORTALS.

THERE WERE THOUSANDS OF THEM, MANY WHIMSICAL GODLINGS OF BIZARRE AND UNPREDICTABLE POWERS-- ONE, FOR INSTANCE, LED AN ARMY OF MONKEYS, AND MANY WERE ABLE TO PASS THROUGH SOLID ROCK WITHOUT HARM.

BY THE TIME I WAS RESEARCHING THE MATTER IN JAPAN, HOWEVER--WHERE THE IMMORTALS WERE KNOWN AS *SENNIN*--THE BLACK DEATH HAD DEVASTATED EUROPE, AFRICA, AND CHINA, FRIGHTENING HUMANITY INTO A DEDICATION TO SCIENCE THAT INCREASINGLY RIVALED THEIR DEVOTION TO RELIGION.

EVEN PEASANTS LOOKING TO THEIR ANCESTORS FOR GUIDANCE WOULD STOP TO INGEST SPECIFIC MUSHROOMS, PINE RESINS OR CINNABAR, BELIEVING THESE MIGHT STIMULATE ETERNAL YOUTH.

‹TAKE COMFORT IN THIS, STRANGER--›

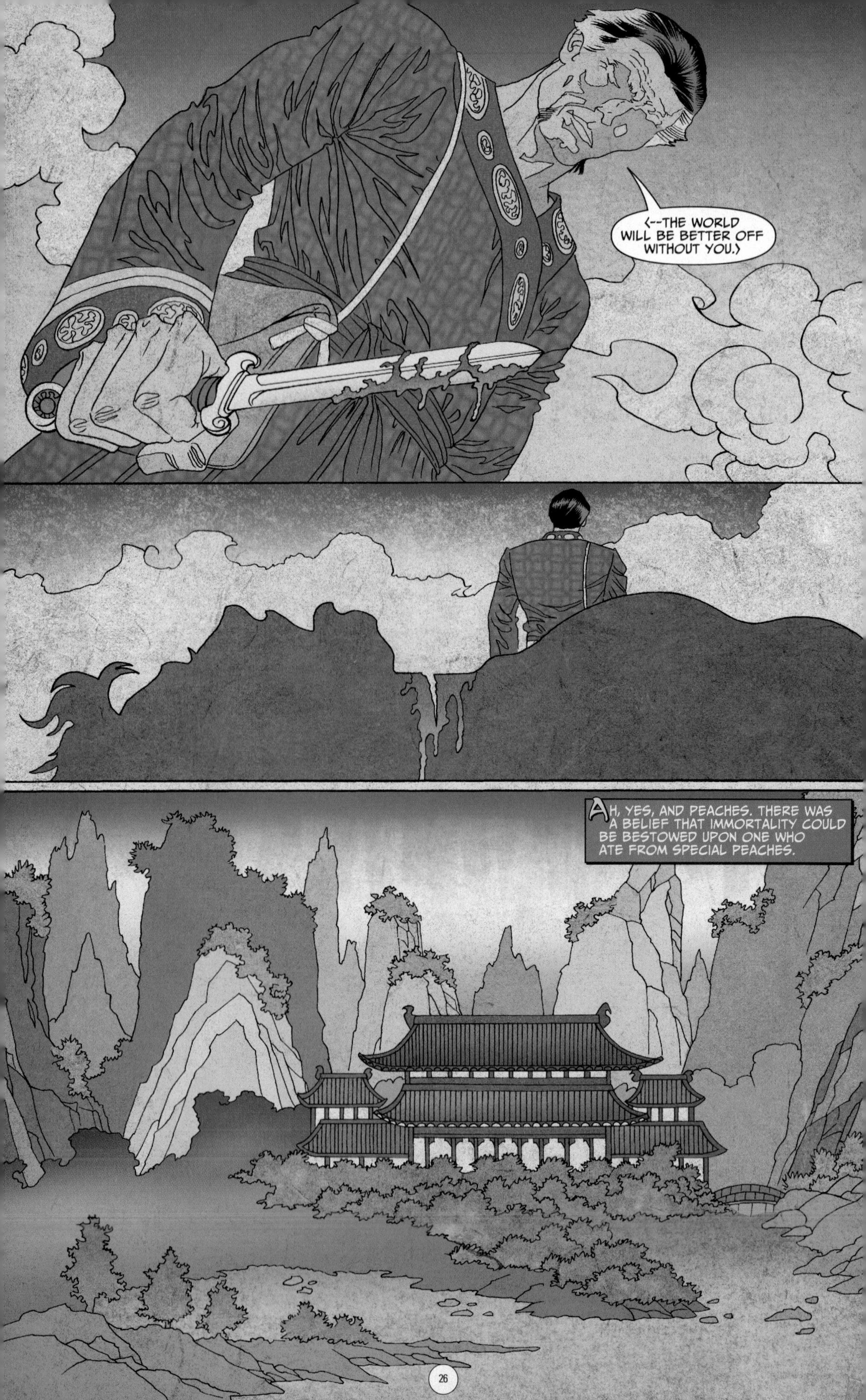

<--THE WORLD WILL BE BETTER OFF WITHOUT YOU.>
AH, YES, AND PEACHES. THERE WAS A BELIEF THAT IMMORTALITY COULD BE BESTOWED UPON ONE WHO ATE FROM SPECIAL PEACHES.

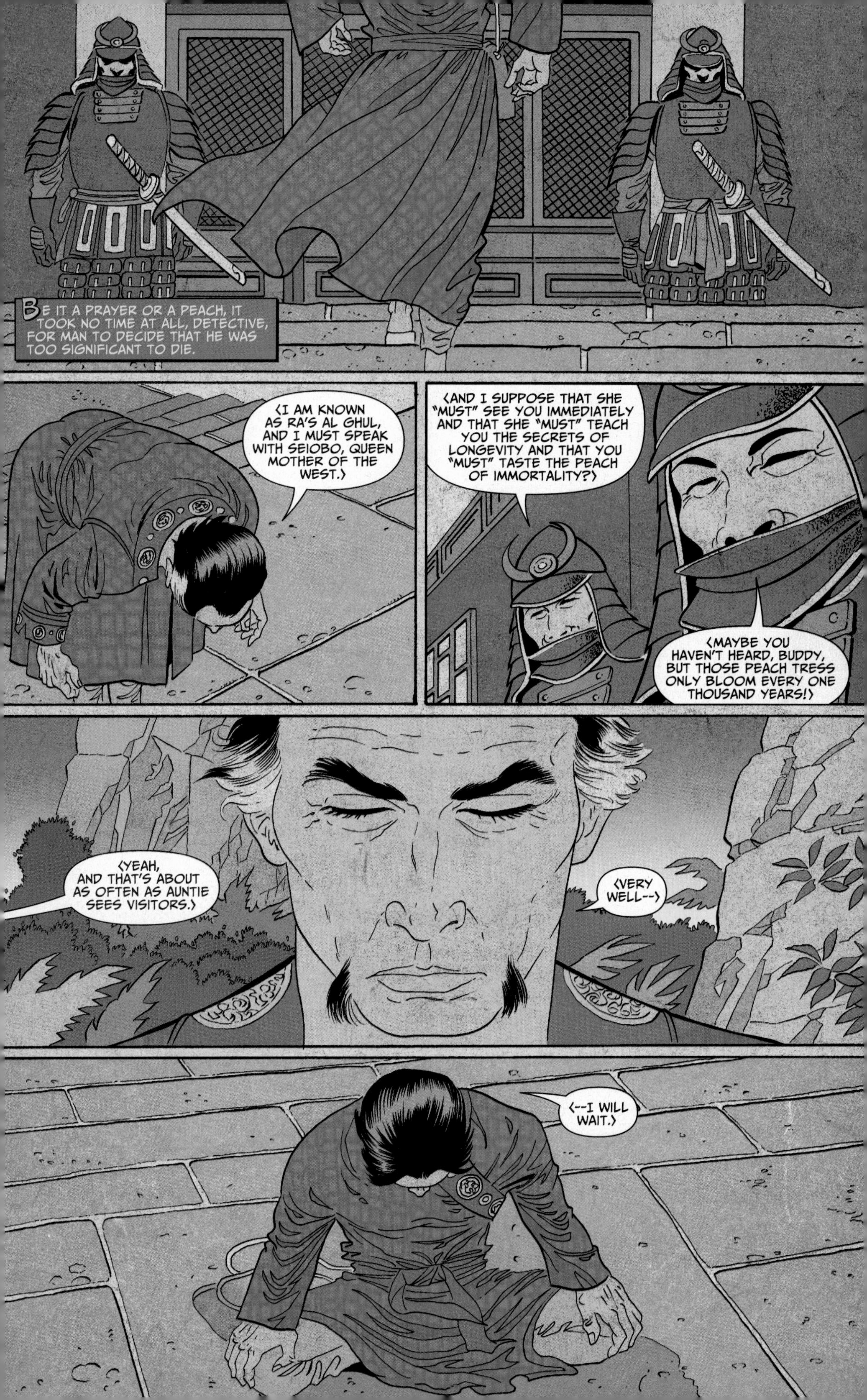
BE IT A PRAYER OR A PEACH, IT TOOK NO TIME AT ALL, DETECTIVE, FOR MAN TO DECIDE THAT HE WAS TOO SIGNIFICANT TO DIE.
‹I AM KNOWN AS RA'S AL GHUL, AND I MUST SPEAK WITH SEIOBO, QUEEN MOTHER OF THE WEST.›
‹AND I SUPPOSE THAT SHE "MUST" SEE YOU IMMEDIATELY AND THAT SHE "MUST" TEACH YOU THE SECRETS OF LONGEVITY AND THAT YOU "MUST" TASTE THE PEACH OF IMMORTALITY?›
‹MAYBE YOU HAVEN'T HEARD, BUDDY, BUT THOSE PEACH TRESS ONLY BLOOM EVERY ONE THOUSAND YEARS!›
‹YEAH, AND THAT'S ABOUT AS OFTEN AS AUNTIE SEES VISITORS.›
‹VERY WELL--›
‹--I WILL WAIT.›

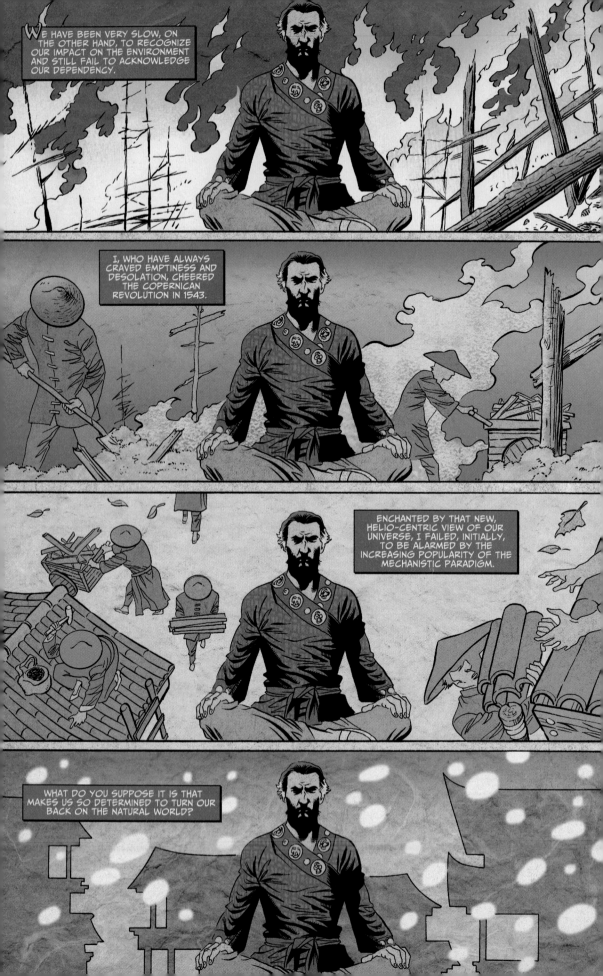

WE HAVE BEEN VERY SLOW, ON THE OTHER HAND, TO RECOGNIZE OUR IMPACT ON THE ENVIRONMENT AND STILL FAIL TO ACKNOWLEDGE OUR DEPENDENCY.

I, WHO HAVE ALWAYS CRAVED EMPTINESS AND DESOLATION, CHEERED THE COPERNICAN REVOLUTION IN 1543.

ENCHANTED BY THAT NEW, HELIO-CENTRIC VIEW OF OUR UNIVERSE, I FAILED, INITIALLY, TO BE ALARMED BY THE INCREASING POPULARITY OF THE MECHANISTIC PARADIGM.

WHAT DO YOU SUPPOSE IT IS THAT MAKES US SO DETERMINED TO TURN OUR BACK ON THE NATURAL WORLD?

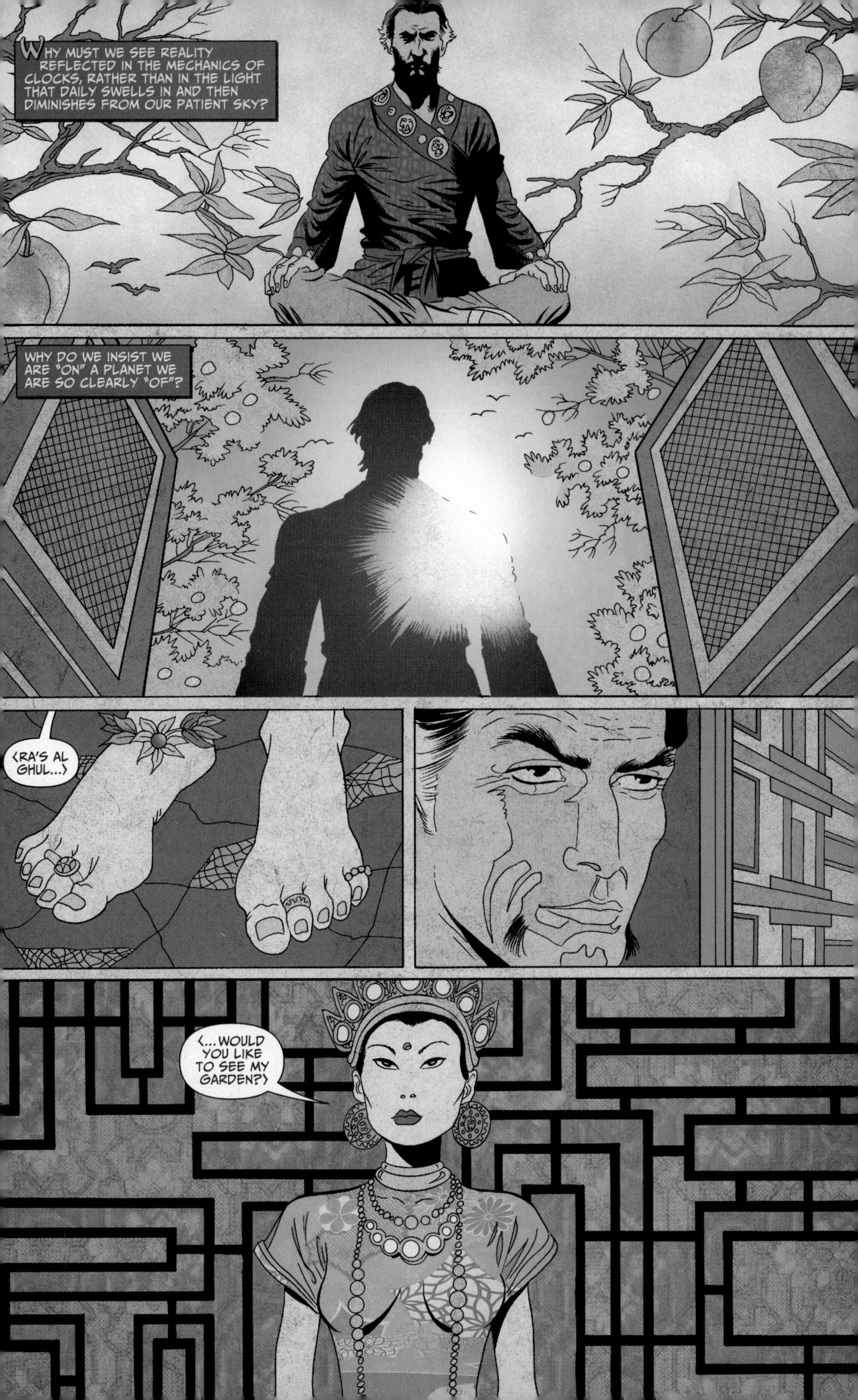
WHY MUST WE SEE REALITY REFLECTED IN THE MECHANICS OF CLOCKS, RATHER THAN IN THE LIGHT THAT DAILY SWELLS IN AND THEN DIMINISHES FROM OUR PATIENT SKY?
WHY DO WE INSIST WE ARE "ON" A PLANET WE ARE SO CLEARLY "OF"?
‹RA'S AL GHUL...›
‹...WOULD YOU LIKE TO SEE MY GARDEN?›

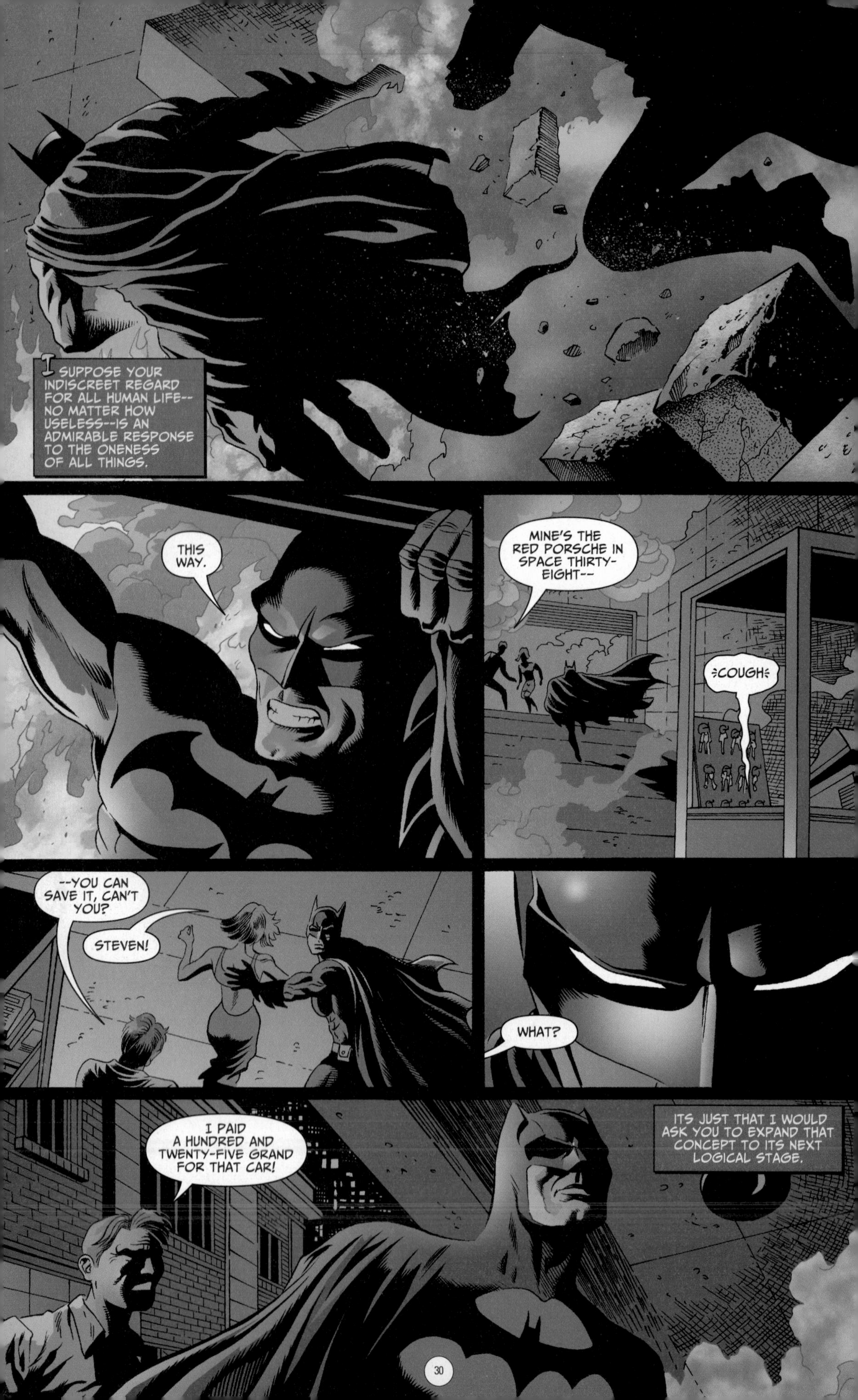
I SUPPOSE YOUR INDISCREET REGARD FOR ALL HUMAN LIFE--NO MATTER HOW USELESS--IS AN ADMIRABLE RESPONSE TO THE ONENESS OF ALL THINGS.
THIS WAY.
MINE'S THE RED PORSCHE IN SPACE THIRTY-EIGHT--
COUGH
--YOU CAN SAVE IT, CAN'T YOU?
STEVEN!
WHAT?
I PAID A HUNDRED AND TWENTY-FIVE GRAND FOR THAT CAR!
ITS JUST THAT I WOULD ASK YOU TO EXPAND THAT CONCEPT TO ITS NEXT LOGICAL STAGE.

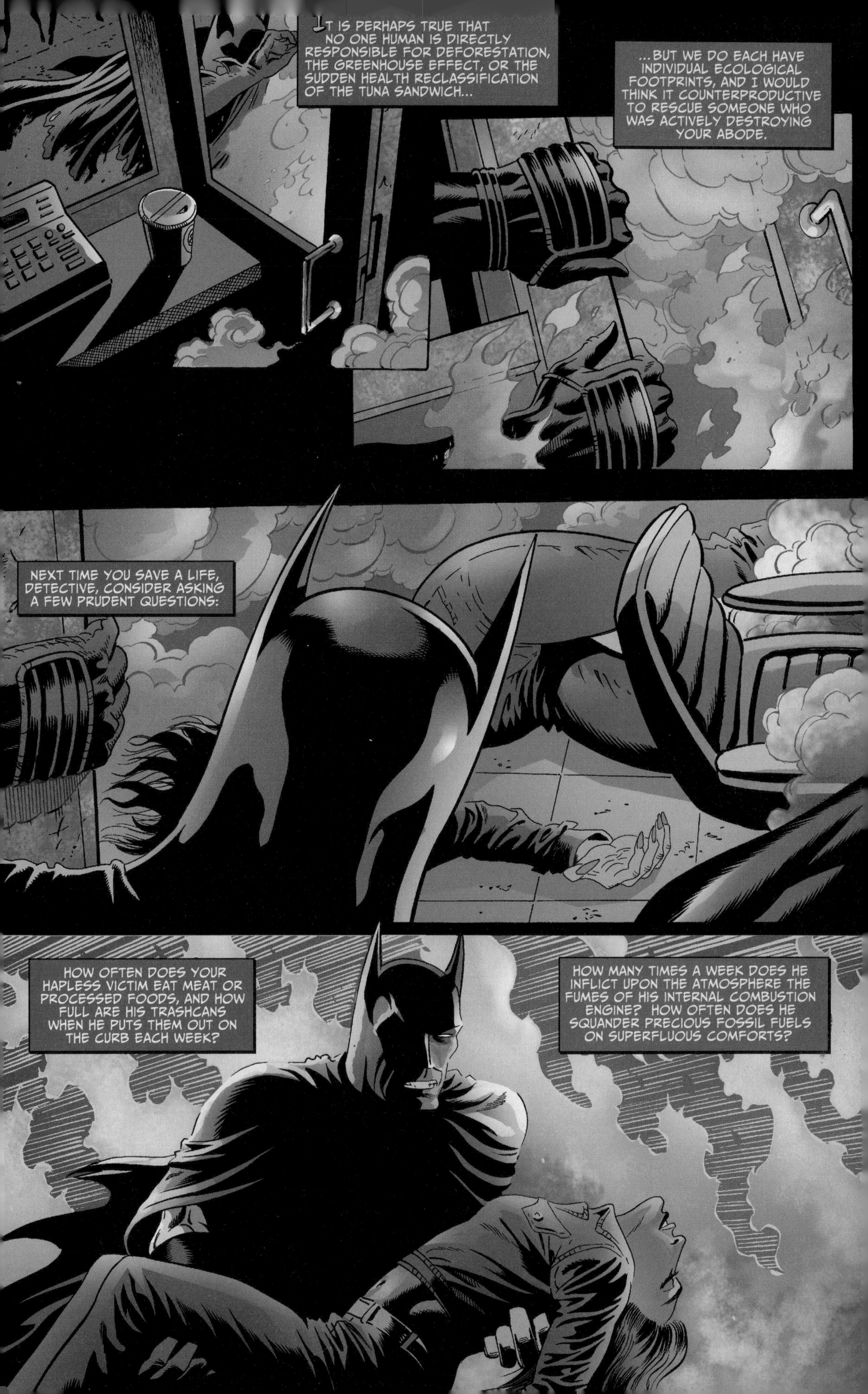
IT IS PERHAPS TRUE THAT NO ONE HUMAN IS DIRECTLY RESPONSIBLE FOR DEFORESTATION, THE GREENHOUSE EFFECT, OR THE SUDDEN HEALTH RECLASSIFICATION OF THE TUNA SANDWICH...
...BUT WE DO EACH HAVE INDIVIDUAL ECOLOGICAL FOOTPRINTS, AND I WOULD THINK IT COUNTERPRODUCTIVE TO RESCUE SOMEONE WHO WAS ACTIVELY DESTROYING YOUR ABODE.
NEXT TIME YOU SAVE A LIFE, DETECTIVE, CONSIDER ASKING A FEW PRUDENT QUESTIONS:
HOW OFTEN DOES YOUR HAPLESS VICTIM EAT MEAT OR PROCESSED FOODS, AND HOW FULL ARE HIS TRASHCANS WHEN HE PUTS THEM OUT ON THE CURB EACH WEEK?
HOW MANY TIMES A WEEK DOES HE INFLICT UPON THE ATMOSPHERE THE FUMES OF HIS INTERNAL COMBUSTION ENGINE? HOW OFTEN DOES HE SQUANDER PRECIOUS FOSSIL FUELS ON SUPERFLUOUS COMFORTS?

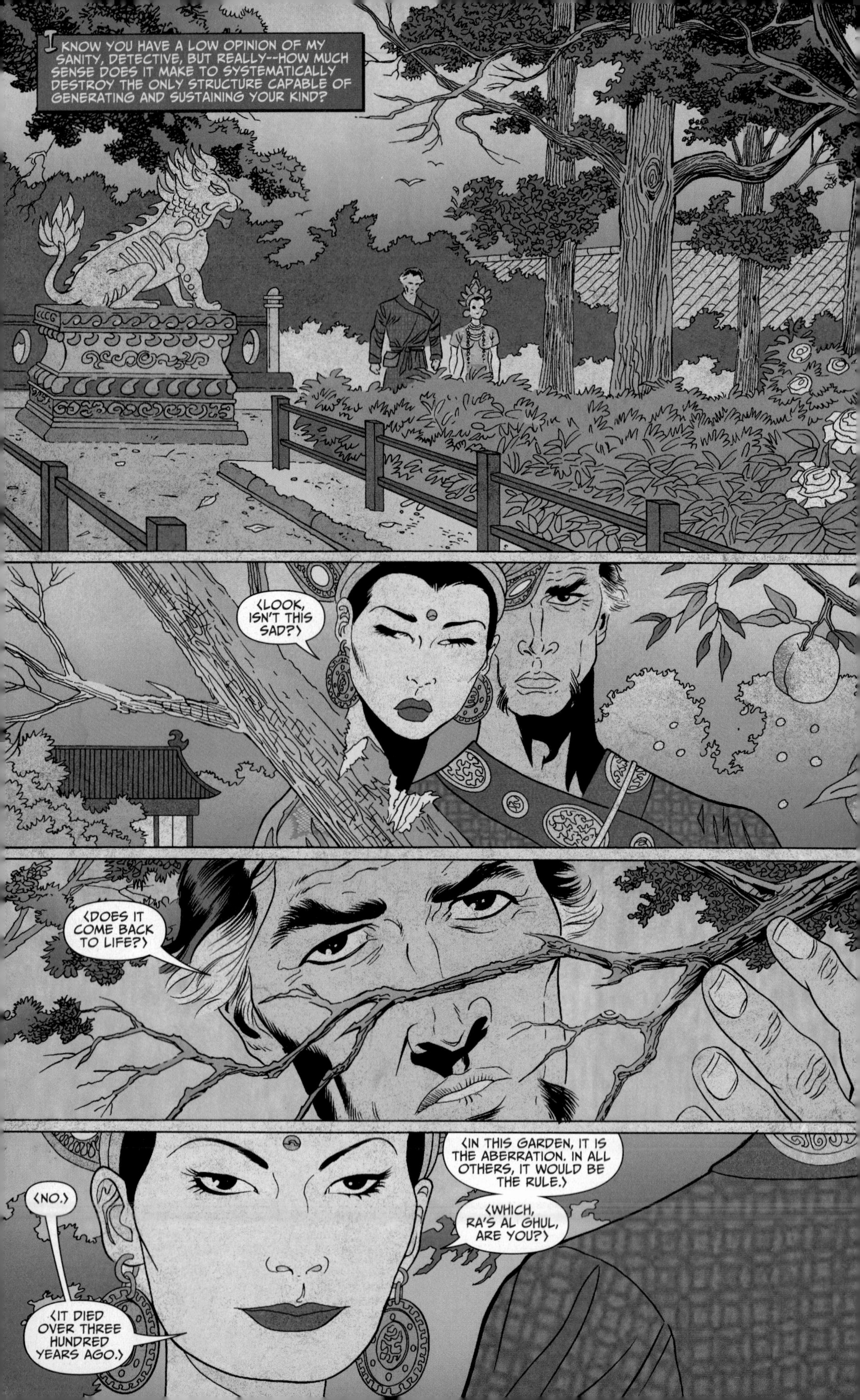
I KNOW YOU HAVE A LOW OPINION OF MY SANITY, DETECTIVE, BUT REALLY--HOW MUCH SENSE DOES IT MAKE TO SYSTEMATICALLY DESTROY THE ONLY STRUCTURE CAPABLE OF GENERATING AND SUSTAINING YOUR KIND?
<LOOK, ISN'T THIS SAD?>
<DOES IT COME BACK TO LIFE?>
<NO.>
<IT DIED OVER THREE HUNDRED YEARS AGO.>
<IN THIS GARDEN, IT IS THE ABERRATION. IN ALL OTHERS, IT WOULD BE THE RULE.>
<WHICH, RA'S AL GHUL, ARE YOU?>

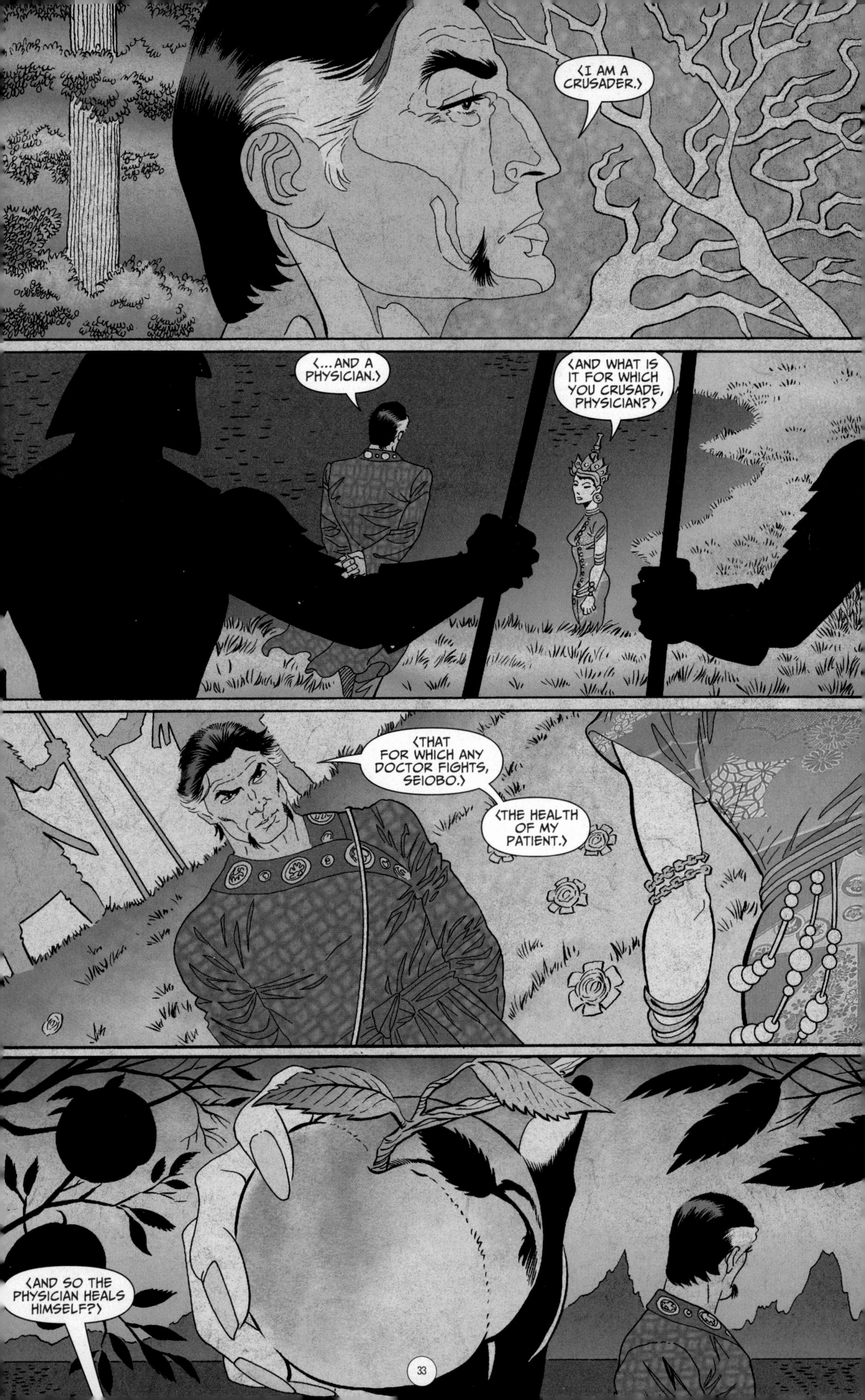

⟨I AM A CRUSADER.⟩
⟨...AND A PHYSICIAN.⟩
⟨AND WHAT IS IT FOR WHICH YOU CRUSADE, PHYSICIAN?⟩
⟨THAT FOR WHICH ANY DOCTOR FIGHTS, SEIOBO.⟩
⟨THE HEALTH OF MY PATIENT.⟩
⟨AND SO THE PHYSICIAN HEALS HIMSELF?⟩

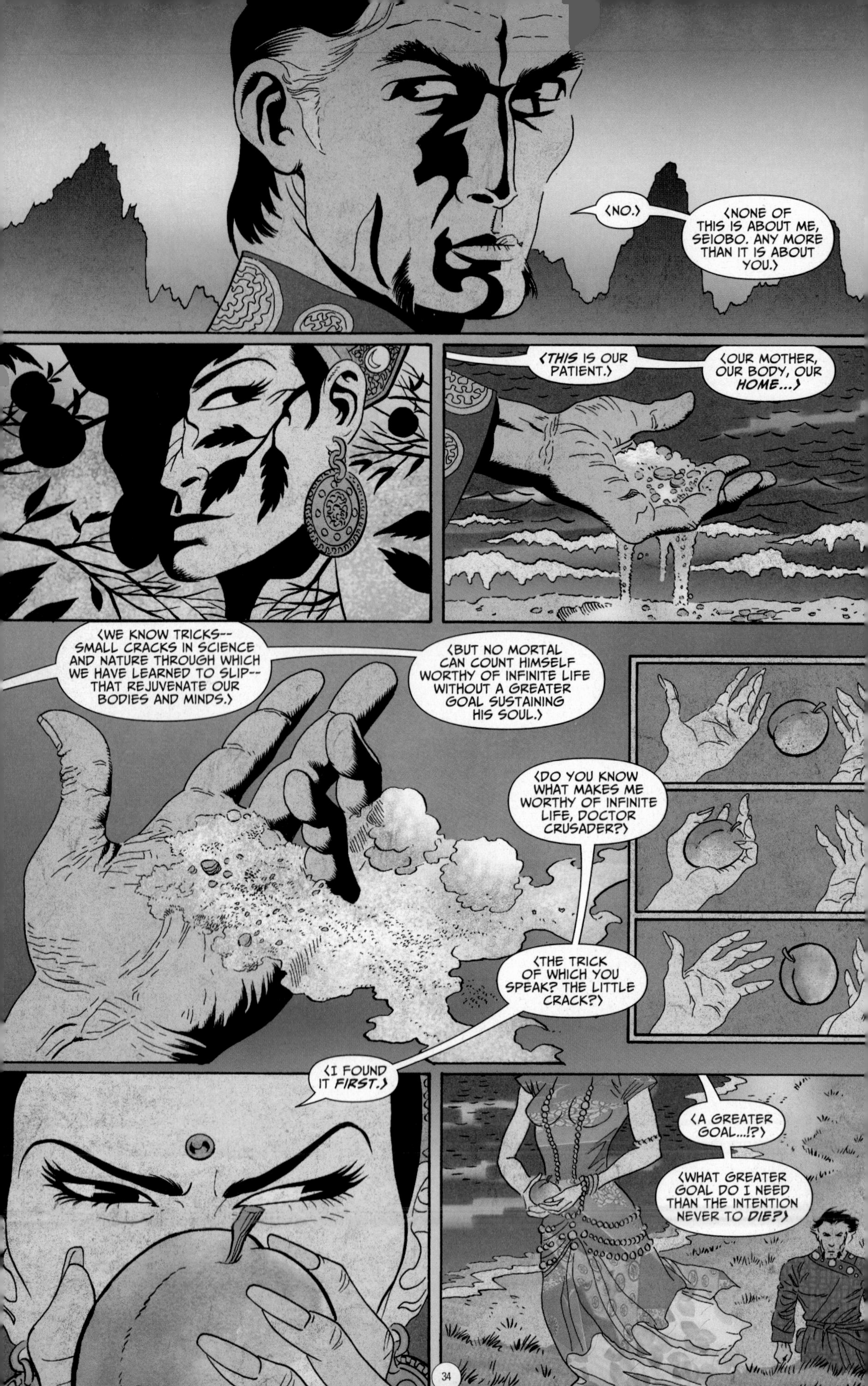

‹NO.›
‹NONE OF THIS IS ABOUT ME, SEIOBO. ANY MORE THAN IT IS ABOUT YOU.›
‹THIS IS OUR PATIENT.›
‹OUR MOTHER, OUR BODY, OUR HOME...›
‹WE KNOW TRICKS-- SMALL CRACKS IN SCIENCE AND NATURE THROUGH WHICH WE HAVE LEARNED TO SLIP-- THAT REJUVENATE OUR BODIES AND MINDS.›
‹BUT NO MORTAL CAN COUNT HIMSELF WORTHY OF INFINITE LIFE WITHOUT A GREATER GOAL SUSTAINING HIS SOUL.›
‹DO YOU KNOW WHAT MAKES ME WORTHY OF INFINITE LIFE, DOCTOR CRUSADER?›
‹THE TRICK OF WHICH YOU SPEAK? THE LITTLE CRACK?›
‹I FOUND IT FIRST.›
‹A GREATER GOAL...!?›
‹WHAT GREATER GOAL DO I NEED THAN THE INTENTION NEVER TO DIE?›

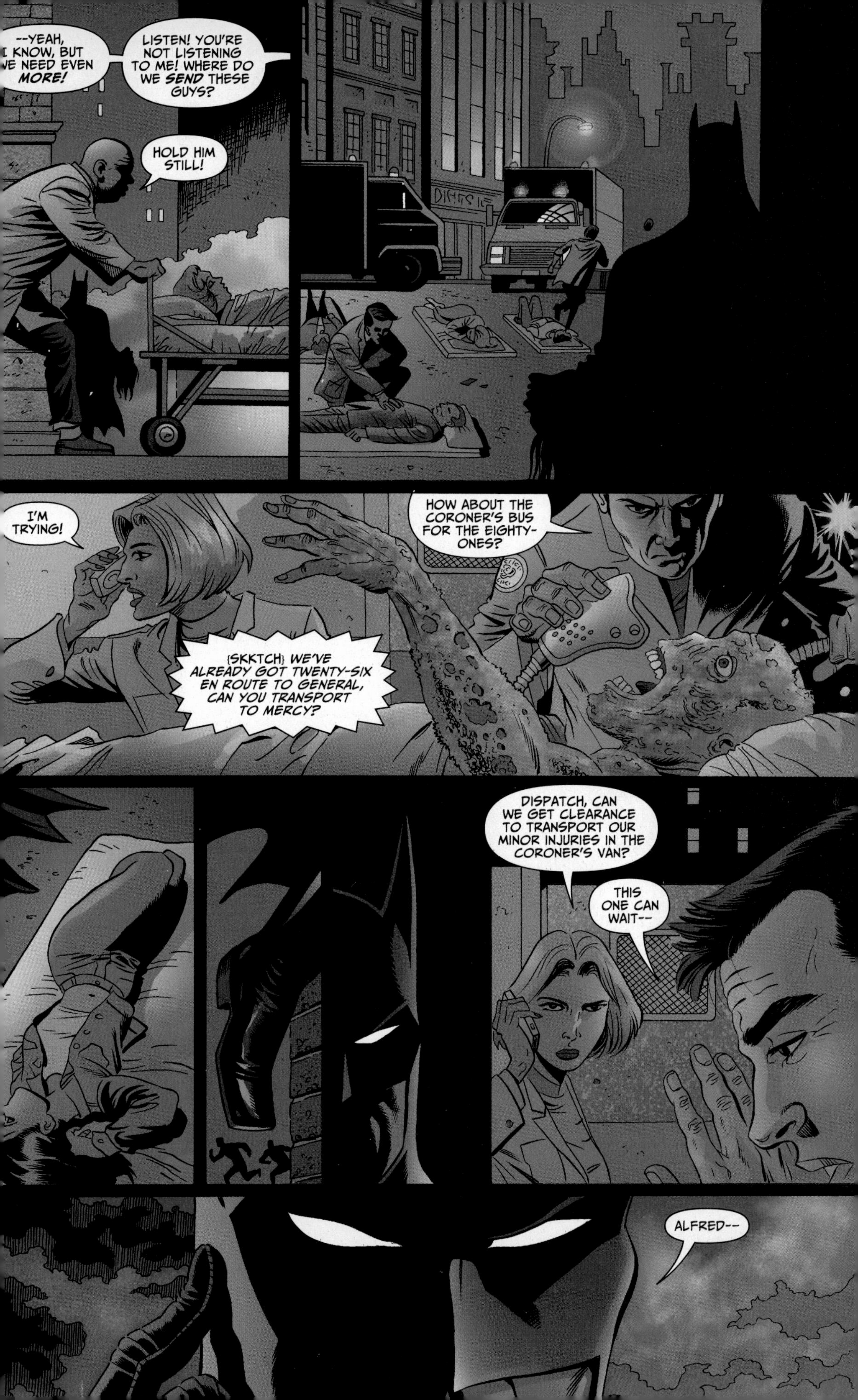
--YEAH, I KNOW, BUT WE NEED EVEN MORE!
LISTEN! YOU'RE NOT LISTENING TO ME! WHERE DO WE SEND THESE GUYS?
HOLD HIM STILL!
I'M TRYING!
HOW ABOUT THE CORONER'S BUS FOR THE EIGHTY-ONES?
{SKKTCH} WE'VE ALREADY GOT TWENTY-SIX EN ROUTE TO GENERAL, CAN YOU TRANSPORT TO MERCY?
DISPATCH, CAN WE GET CLEARANCE TO TRANSPORT OUR MINOR INJURIES IN THE CORONER'S VAN?
THIS ONE CAN WAIT--
ALFRED--

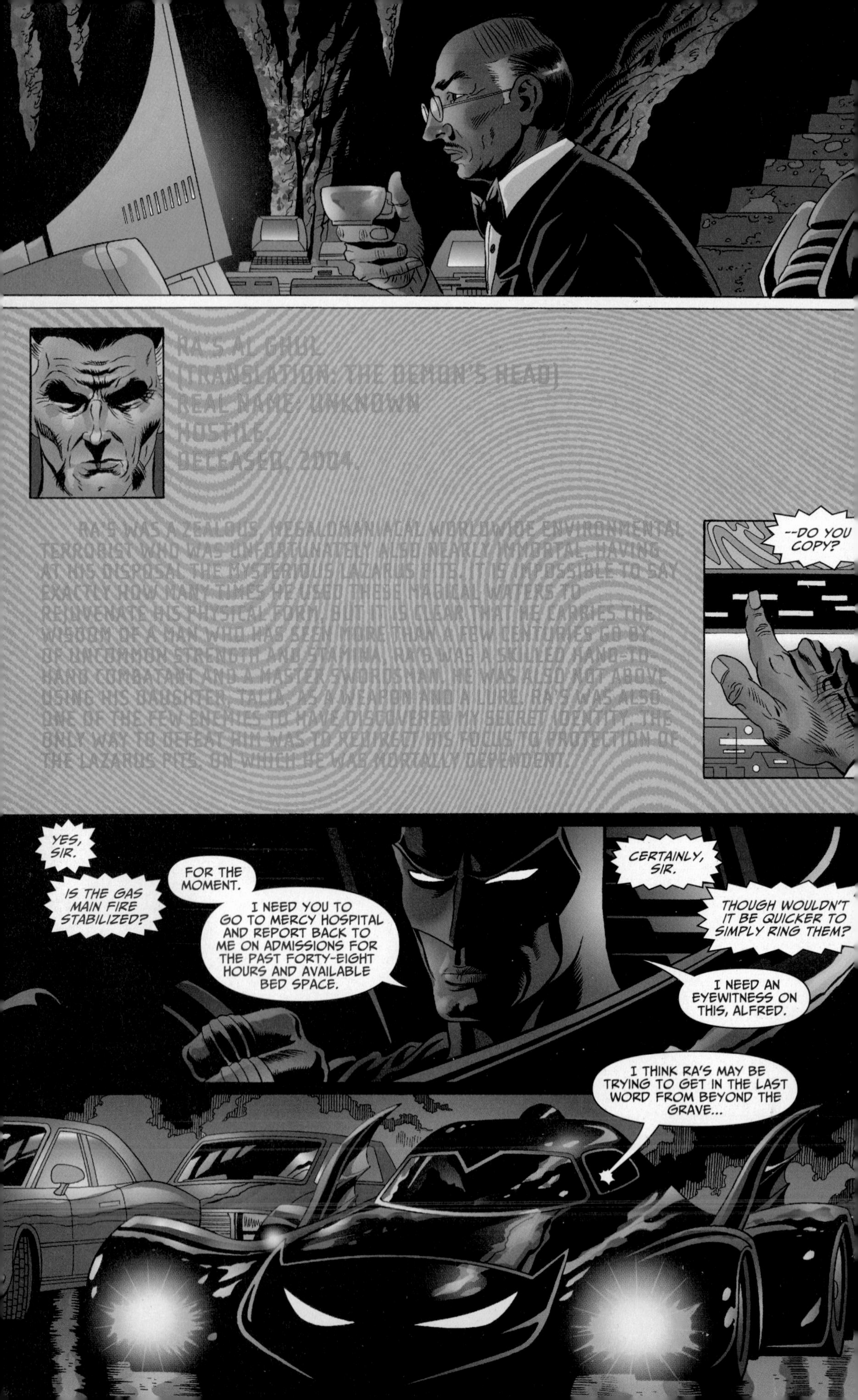

RA'S AL GHUL
(TRANSLATION: THE DEMON'S HEAD)
REAL NAME: UNKNOWN
HOSTILE.
DECEASED, 2004.
RA'S WAS A ZEALOUS, MEGALOMANIACAL WORLDWIDE ENVIRONMENTAL TERRORIST WHO WAS UNFORTUNATELY ALSO NEARLY IMMORTAL, HAVING AT HIS DISPOSAL THE MYSTERIOUS LAZARUS PITS. IT IS IMPOSSIBLE TO SAY EXACTLY HOW MANY TIMES HE USED THESE MAGICAL WATERS TO REJUVENATE HIS PHYSICAL FORM, BUT IT IS CLEAR THAT HE CARRIES THE WISDOM OF A MAN WHO HAS SEEN MORE THAN A FEW CENTURIES GO BY. OF UNCOMMON STRENGTH AND STAMINA, RA'S WAS A SKILLED HAND-TO-HAND COMBATANT AND A MASTER SWORDSMAN. HE WAS ALSO NOT ABOVE USING HIS DAUGHTER, TALIA, AS A WEAPON AND A LURE. RA'S WAS ALSO ONE OF THE FEW ENEMIES TO HAVE DISCOVERED MY SECRET IDENTITY. THE ONLY WAY TO DEFEAT HIM WAS TO REDIRECT HIS FOCUS TO PROTECTION OF THE LAZARUS PITS, ON WHICH HE WAS MORTALLY DEPENDENT.
--DO YOU COPY?
YES, SIR.
IS THE GAS MAIN FIRE STABILIZED?
FOR THE MOMENT.
I NEED YOU TO GO TO MERCY HOSPITAL AND REPORT BACK TO ME ON ADMISSIONS FOR THE PAST FORTY-EIGHT HOURS AND AVAILABLE BED SPACE.
CERTAINLY, SIR.
THOUGH WOULDN'T IT BE QUICKER TO SIMPLY RING THEM?
I NEED AN EYEWITNESS ON THIS, ALFRED.
I THINK RA'S MAY BE TRYING TO GET IN THE LAST WORD FROM BEYOND THE GRAVE...

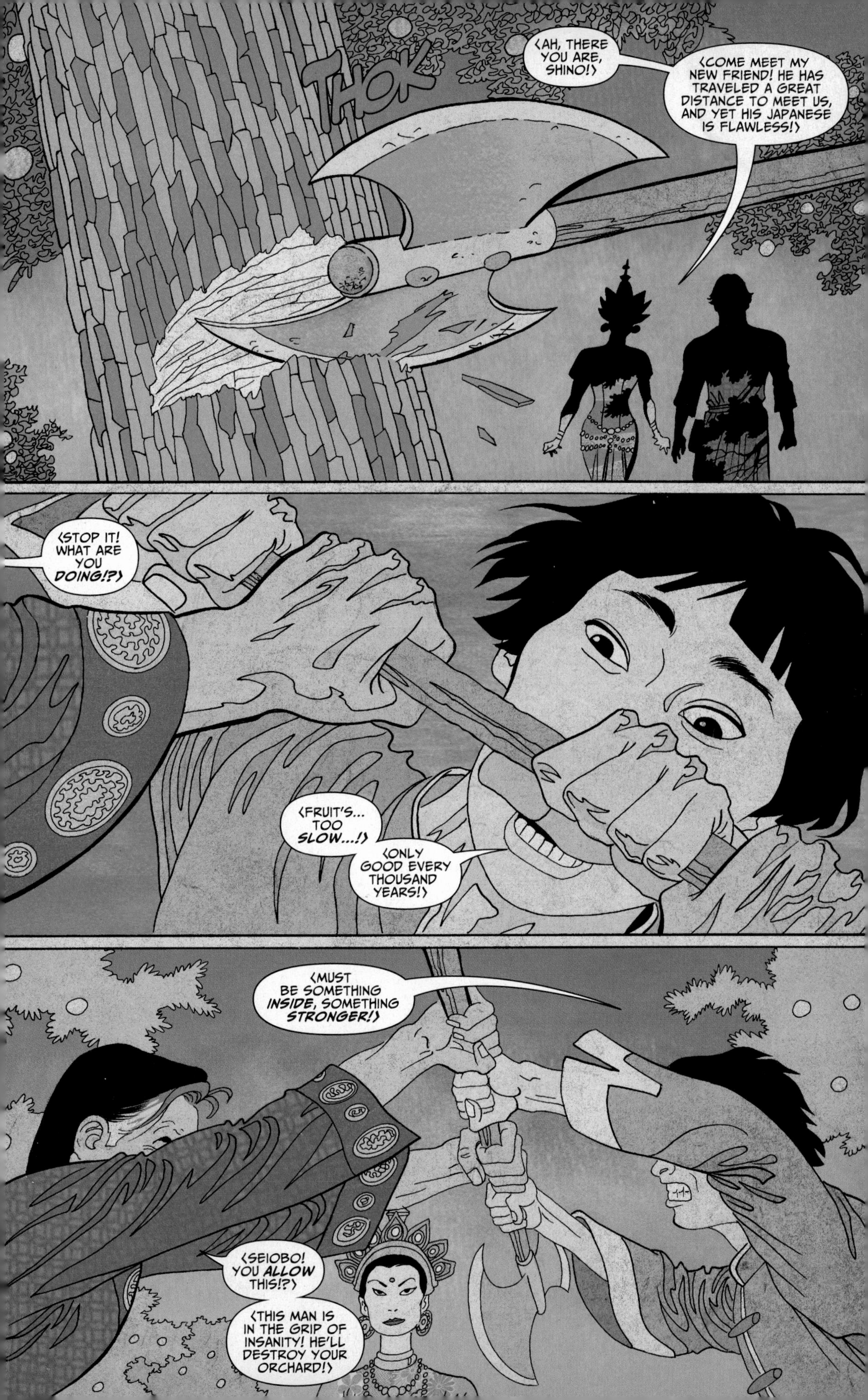
THOK
<AH, THERE YOU ARE, SHINO!>
<COME MEET MY NEW FRIEND! HE HAS TRAVELED A GREAT DISTANCE TO MEET US, AND YET HIS JAPANESE IS FLAWLESS!>
<STOP IT! WHAT ARE YOU DOING!?>
<FRUIT'S... TOO SLOW...!>
<ONLY GOOD EVERY THOUSAND YEARS!>
<MUST BE SOMETHING INSIDE, SOMETHING STRONGER!>
<SEIOBO! YOU ALLOW THIS!?>
<THIS MAN IS IN THE GRIP OF INSANITY! HE'LL DESTROY YOUR ORCHARD!>

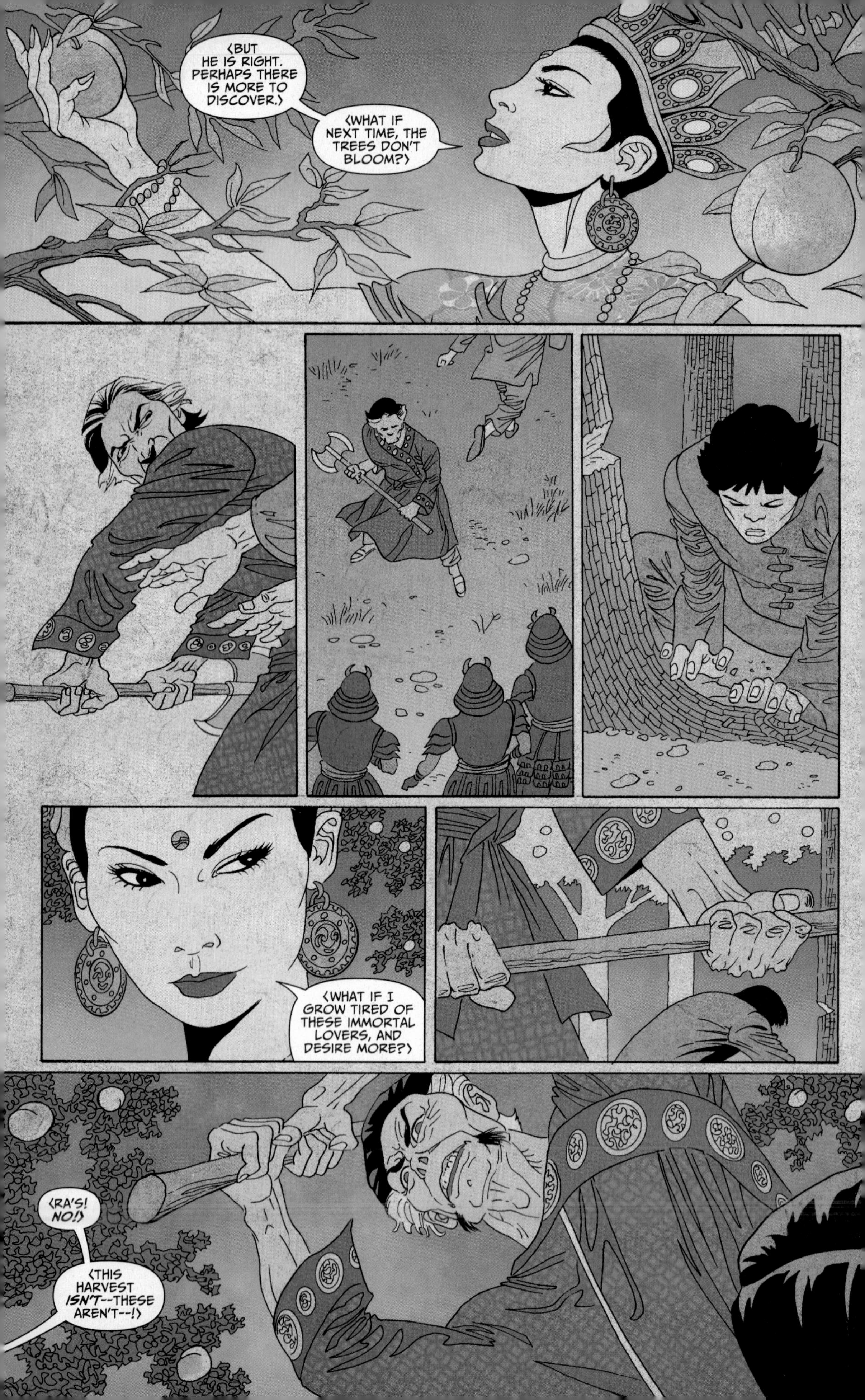
‹BUT HE IS RIGHT. PERHAPS THERE IS MORE TO DISCOVER.›
‹WHAT IF NEXT TIME, THE TREES DON'T BLOOM?›
‹WHAT IF I GROW TIRED OF THESE IMMORTAL LOVERS, AND DESIRE MORE?›
‹RA'S! *NO!*›
‹THIS HARVEST *ISN'T*--THESE AREN'T--!›

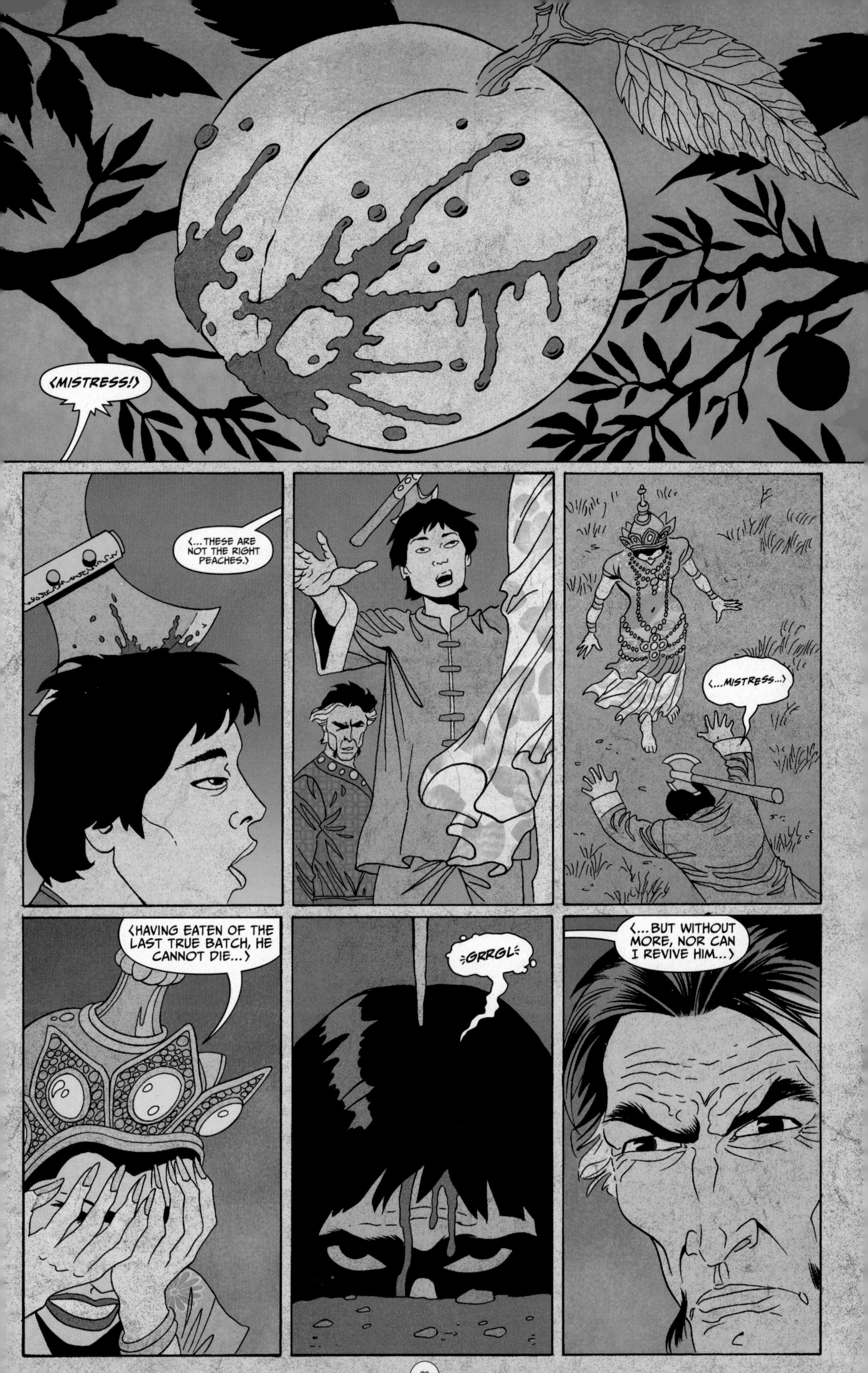
⟨MISTRESS!⟩
⟨...THESE ARE NOT THE RIGHT PEACHES.⟩
⟨...MISTRESS...⟩
⟨HAVING EATEN OF THE LAST TRUE BATCH, HE CANNOT DIE...⟩
GRRGL
⟨...BUT WITHOUT MORE, NOR CAN I REVIVE HIM...⟩

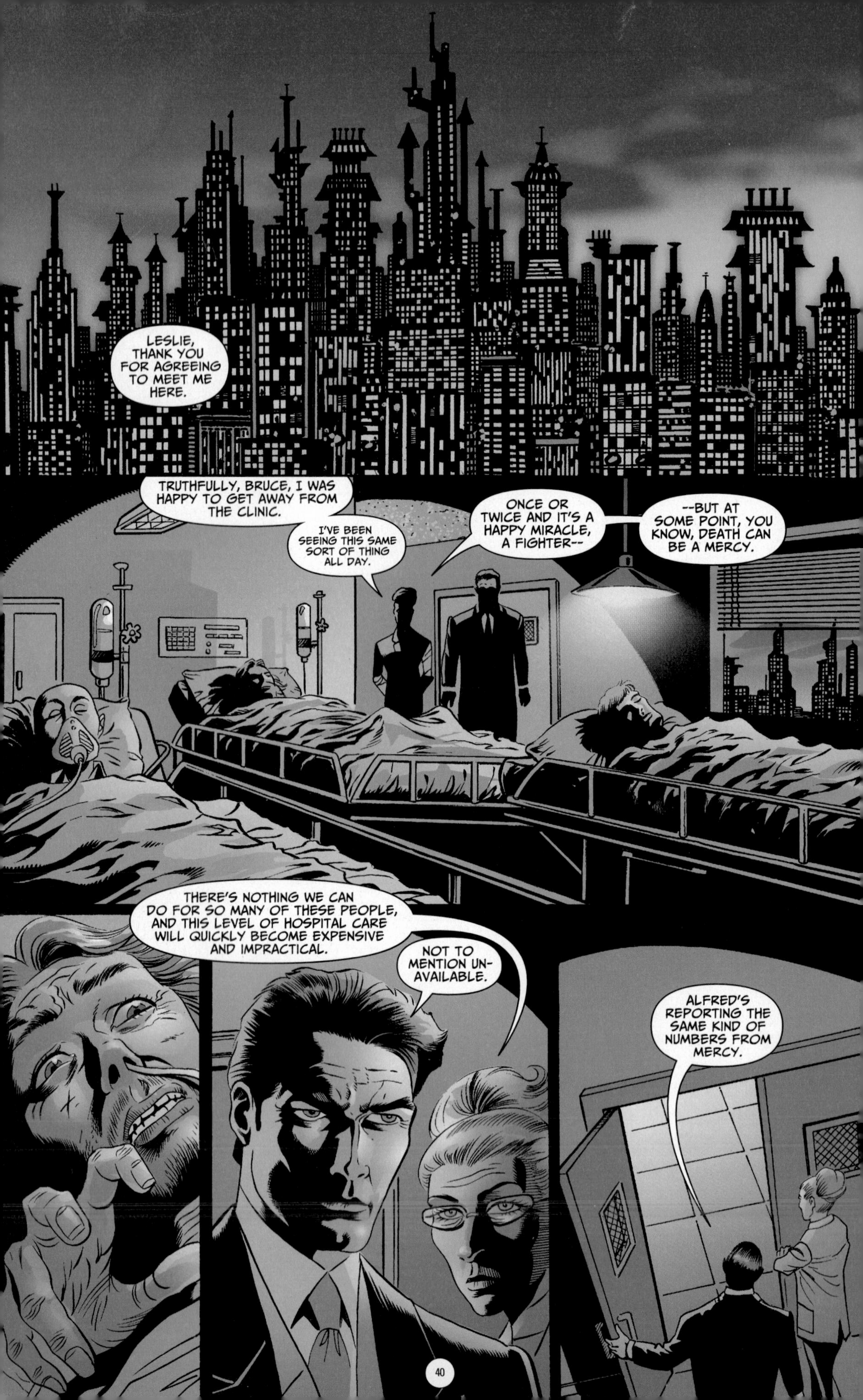
LESLIE, THANK YOU FOR AGREEING TO MEET ME HERE.
TRUTHFULLY, BRUCE, I WAS HAPPY TO GET AWAY FROM THE CLINIC.
I'VE BEEN SEEING THIS SAME SORT OF THING ALL DAY.
ONCE OR TWICE AND IT'S A HAPPY MIRACLE, A FIGHTER--
--BUT AT SOME POINT, YOU KNOW, DEATH CAN BE A MERCY.
THERE'S NOTHING WE CAN DO FOR SO MANY OF THESE PEOPLE, AND THIS LEVEL OF HOSPITAL CARE WILL QUICKLY BECOME EXPENSIVE AND IMPRACTICAL.
NOT TO MENTION UN-AVAILABLE.
ALFRED'S REPORTING THE SAME KIND OF NUMBERS FROM MERCY.

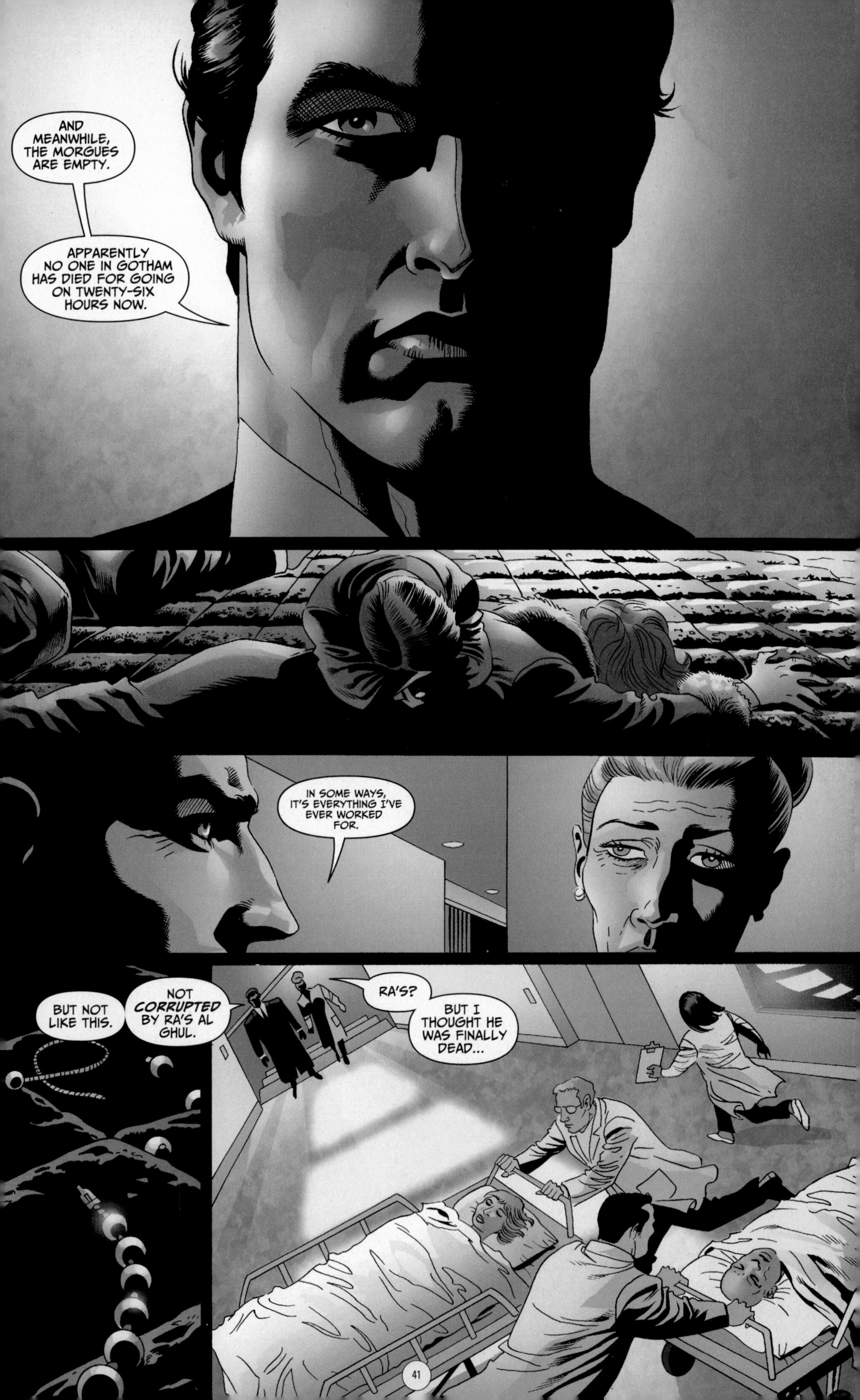
AND MEANWHILE, THE MORGUES ARE EMPTY.
APPARENTLY NO ONE IN GOTHAM HAS DIED FOR GOING ON TWENTY-SIX HOURS NOW.
IN SOME WAYS, IT'S EVERYTHING I'VE EVER WORKED FOR.
BUT NOT LIKE THIS.
NOT CORRUPTED BY RA'S AL GHUL.
RA'S?
BUT I THOUGHT HE WAS FINALLY DEAD...

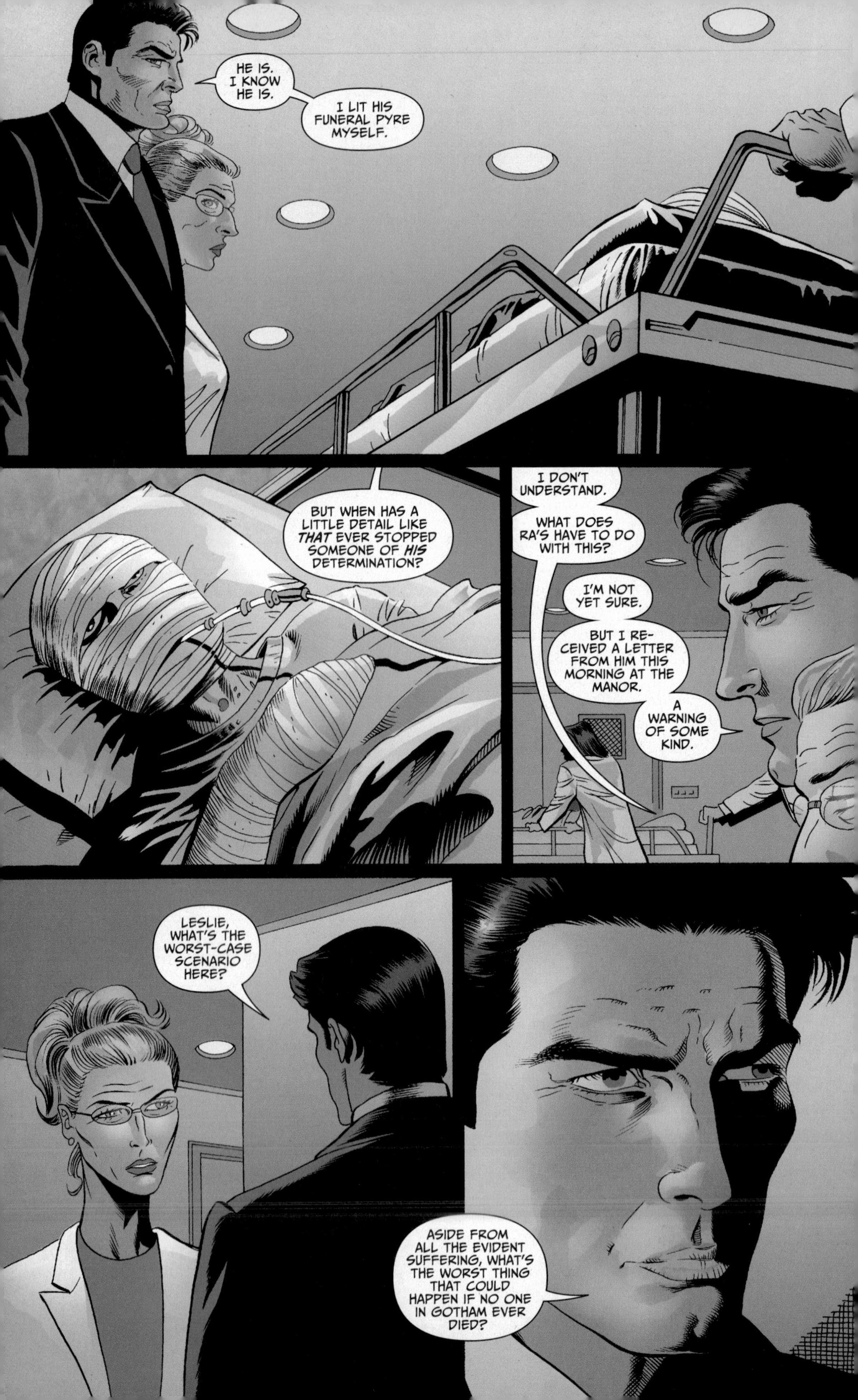
HE IS. I KNOW HE IS.
I LIT HIS FUNERAL PYRE MYSELF.
BUT WHEN HAS A LITTLE DETAIL LIKE *THAT* EVER STOPPED SOMEONE OF *HIS* DETERMINATION?
I DON'T UNDERSTAND.
WHAT DOES RA'S HAVE TO DO WITH THIS?
I'M NOT YET SURE.
BUT I RECEIVED A LETTER FROM HIM THIS MORNING AT THE MANOR.
A WARNING OF SOME KIND.
LESLIE, WHAT'S THE WORST-CASE SCENARIO HERE?
ASIDE FROM ALL THE EVIDENT SUFFERING, WHAT'S THE WORST THING THAT COULD HAPPEN IF NO ONE IN GOTHAM EVER DIED?

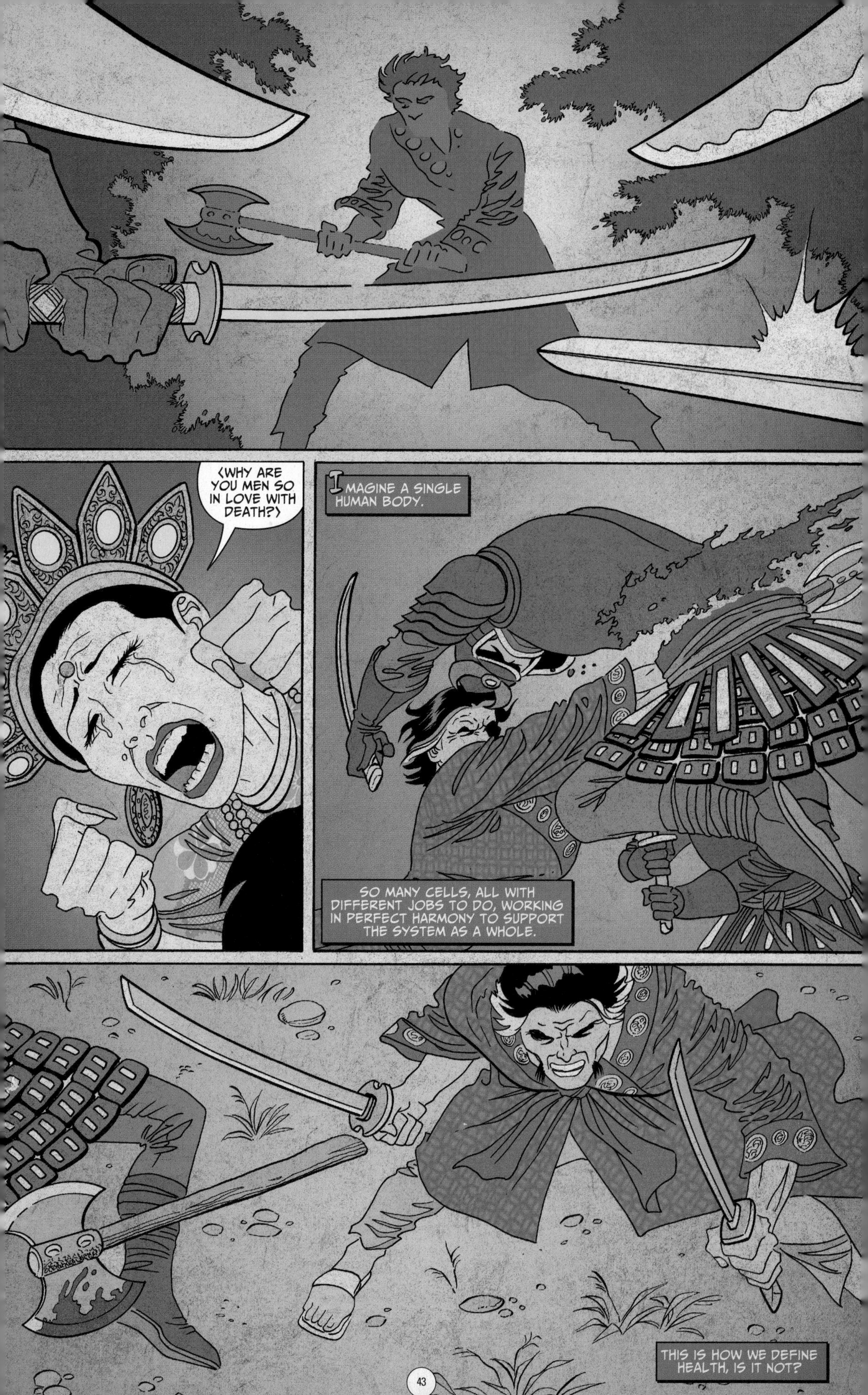
⟨WHY ARE YOU MEN SO IN LOVE WITH DEATH?⟩
IMAGINE A SINGLE HUMAN BODY.
SO MANY CELLS, ALL WITH DIFFERENT JOBS TO DO, WORKING IN PERFECT HARMONY TO SUPPORT THE SYSTEM AS A WHOLE.
THIS IS HOW WE DEFINE HEALTH, IS IT NOT?

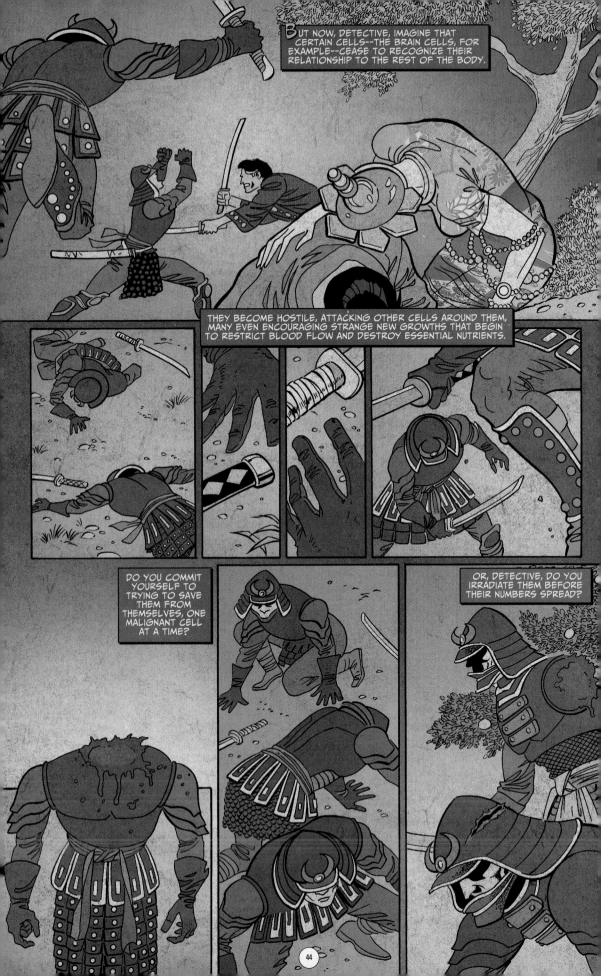

BUT NOW, DETECTIVE, IMAGINE THAT CERTAIN CELLS--THE BRAIN CELLS, FOR EXAMPLE--CEASE TO RECOGNIZE THEIR RELATIONSHIP TO THE REST OF THE BODY.

THEY BECOME HOSTILE, ATTACKING OTHER CELLS AROUND THEM, MANY EVEN ENCOURAGING STRANGE NEW GROWTHS THAT BEGIN TO RESTRICT BLOOD FLOW AND DESTROY ESSENTIAL NUTRIENTS.

DO YOU COMMIT YOURSELF TO TRYING TO SAVE THEM FROM THEMSELVES, ONE MALIGNANT CELL AT A TIME?

OR, DETECTIVE, DO YOU IRRADIATE THEM BEFORE THEIR NUMBERS SPREAD?

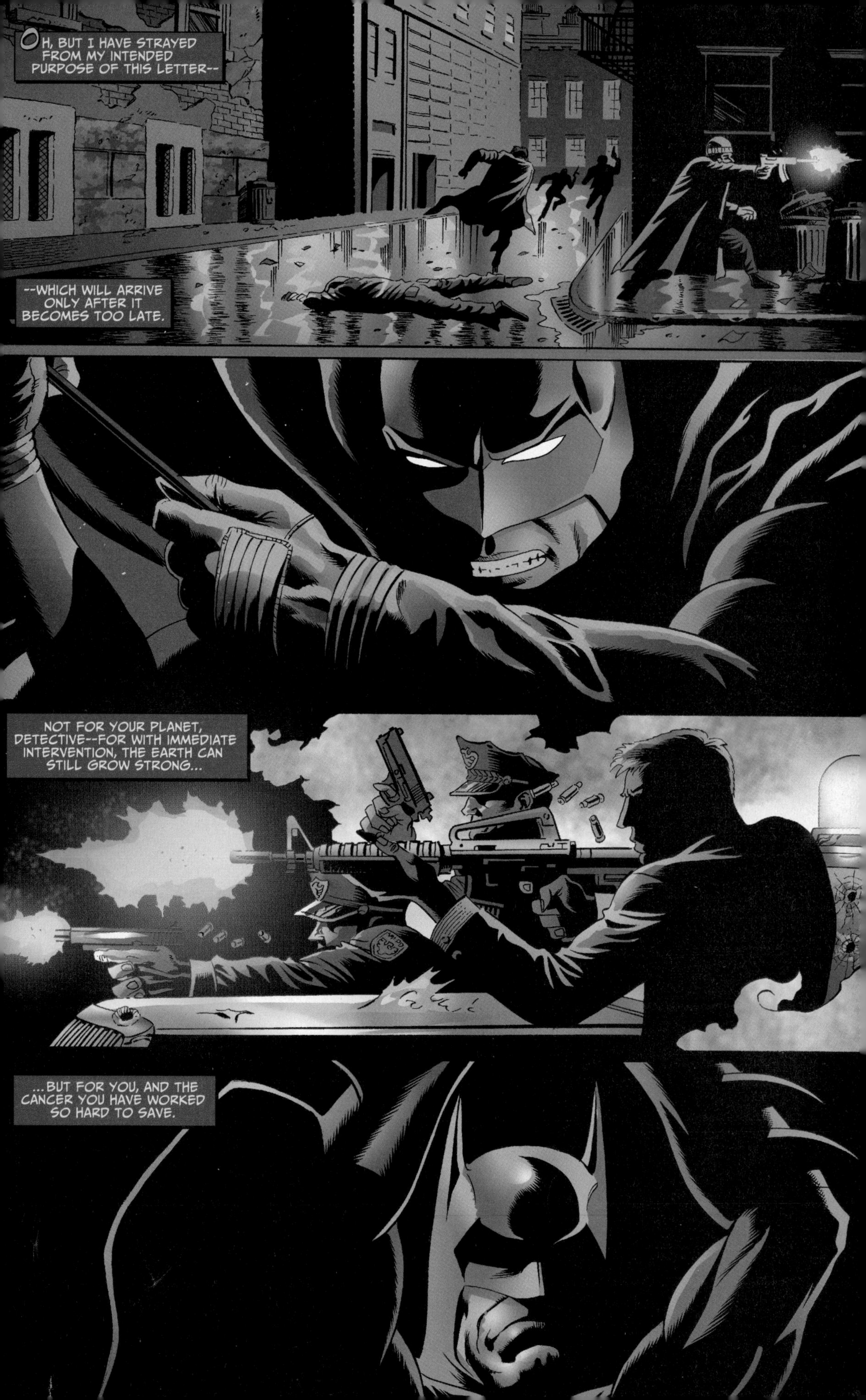
OH, BUT I HAVE STRAYED FROM MY INTENDED PURPOSE OF THIS LETTER--
--WHICH WILL ARRIVE ONLY AFTER IT BECOMES TOO LATE.
NOT FOR YOUR PLANET, DETECTIVE--FOR WITH IMMEDIATE INTERVENTION, THE EARTH CAN STILL GROW STRONG...
...BUT FOR YOU, AND THE CANCER YOU HAVE WORKED SO HARD TO SAVE.

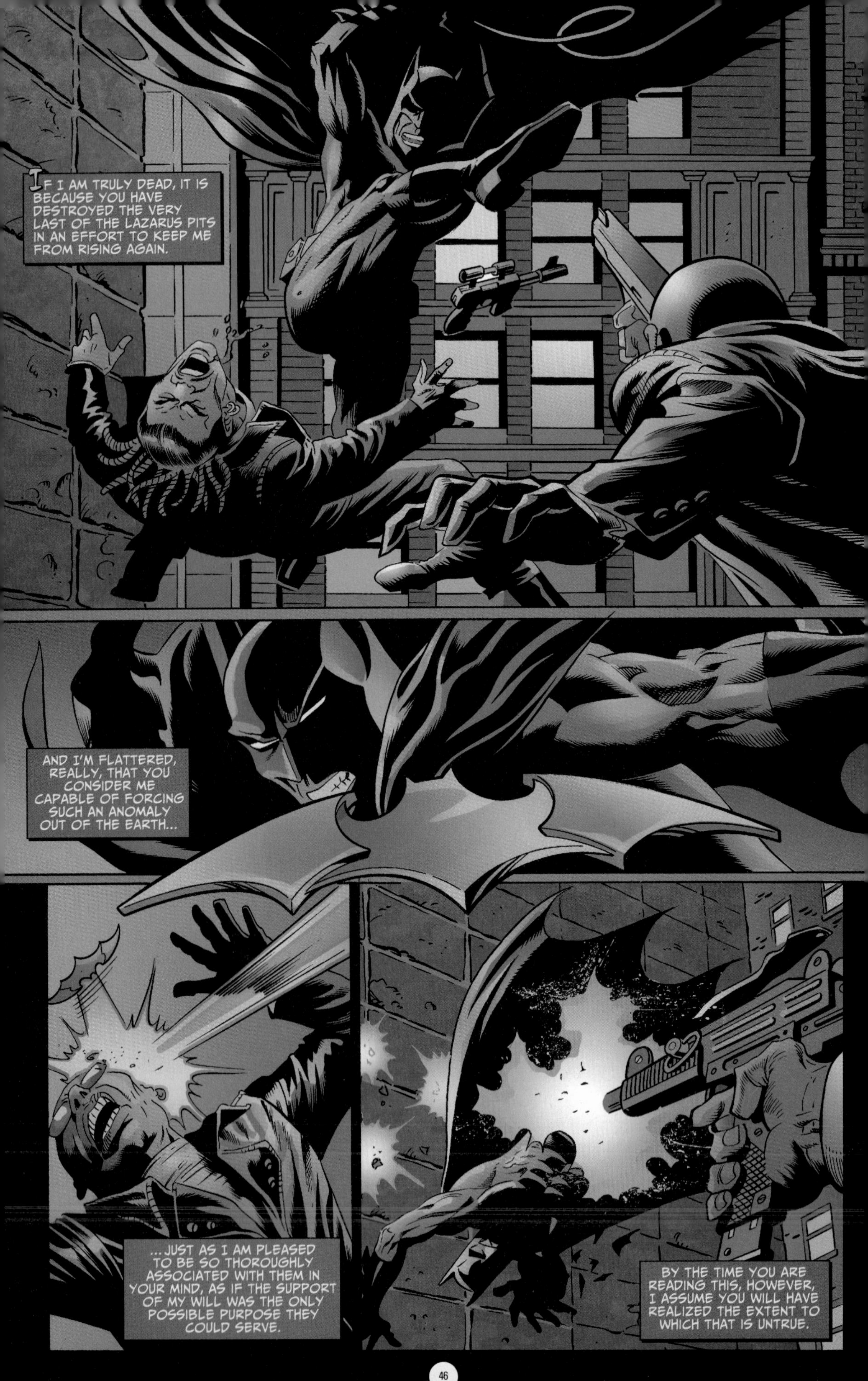
IF I AM TRULY DEAD, IT IS BECAUSE YOU HAVE DESTROYED THE VERY LAST OF THE LAZARUS PITS IN AN EFFORT TO KEEP ME FROM RISING AGAIN.
AND I'M FLATTERED, REALLY, THAT YOU CONSIDER ME CAPABLE OF FORCING SUCH AN ANOMALY OUT OF THE EARTH...
...JUST AS I AM PLEASED TO BE SO THOROUGHLY ASSOCIATED WITH THEM IN YOUR MIND, AS IF THE SUPPORT OF MY WILL WAS THE ONLY POSSIBLE PURPOSE THEY COULD SERVE.
BY THE TIME YOU ARE READING THIS, HOWEVER, I ASSUME YOU WILL HAVE REALIZED THE EXTENT TO WHICH THAT IS UNTRUE.

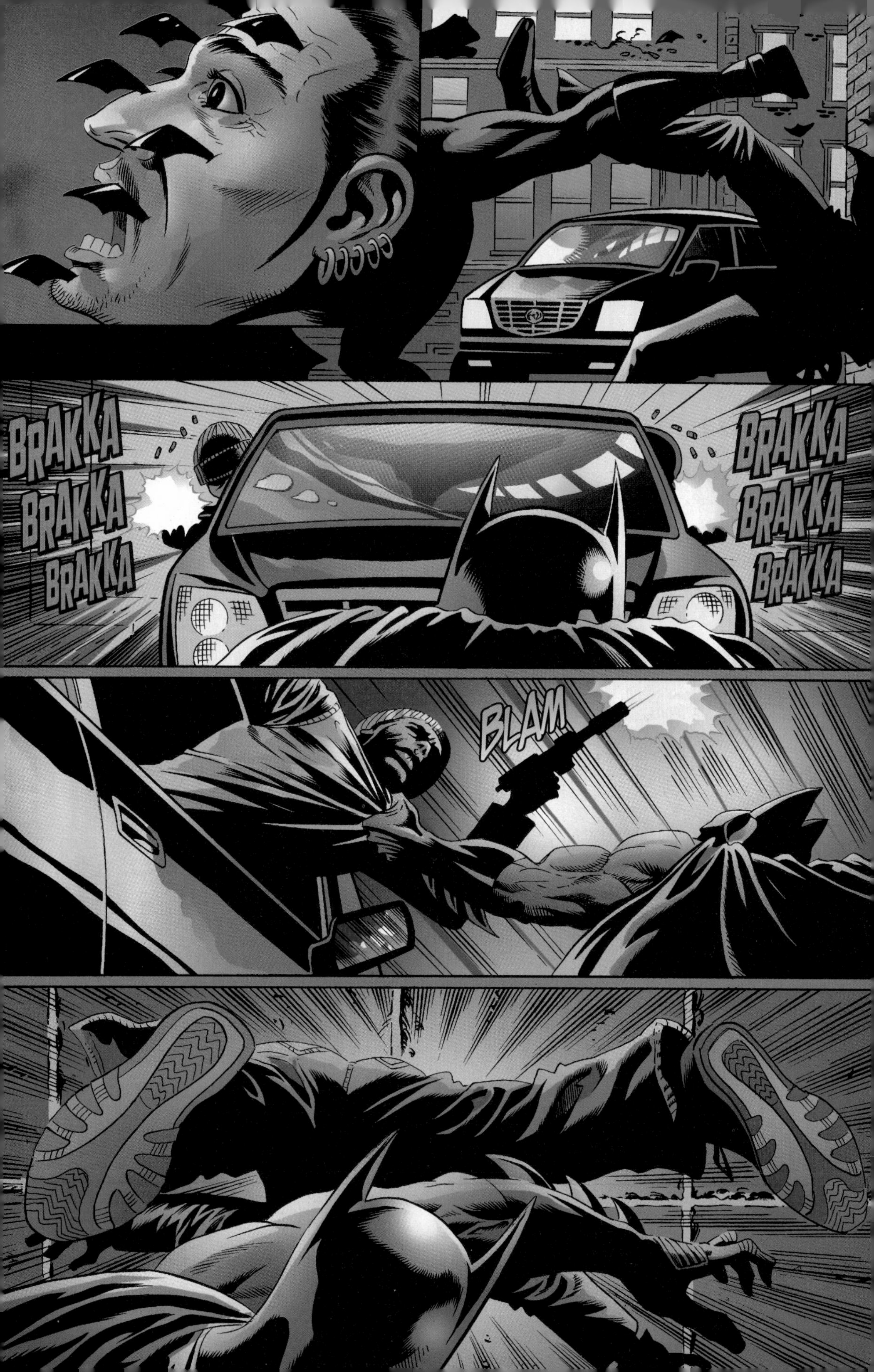
BRAKKA
BRAKKA
BRAKKA
BRAKKA
BRAKKA
BRAKKA
BLAM

BLAM BLAM BLAM

ZKRAAK

BLAM BLAM

KRAAK

KRAAK KRAAK

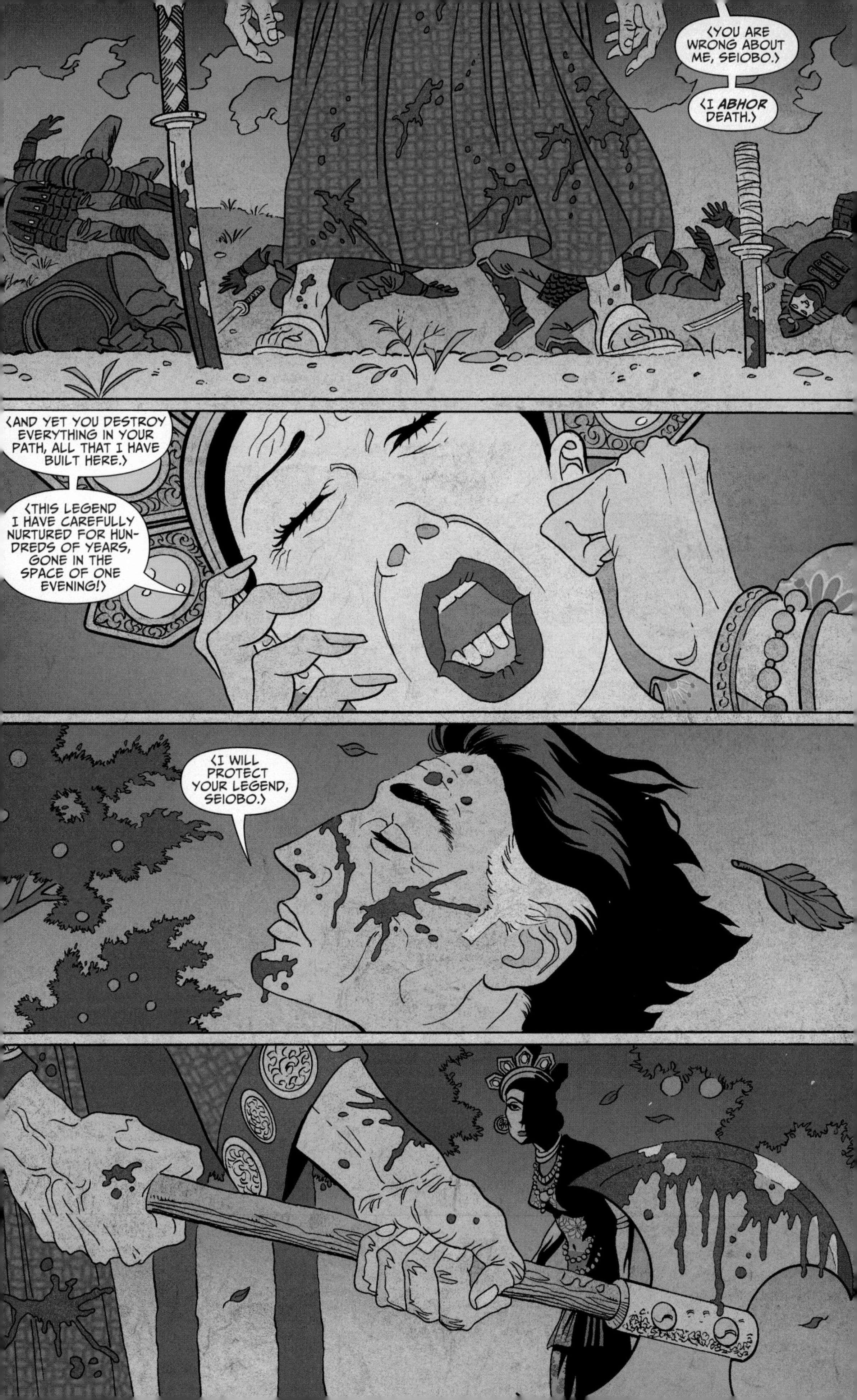
‹YOU ARE WRONG ABOUT ME, SEIOBO.›
‹I ABHOR DEATH.›
‹AND YET YOU DESTROY EVERYTHING IN YOUR PATH, ALL THAT I HAVE BUILT HERE.›
‹THIS LEGEND I HAVE CAREFULLY NURTURED FOR HUNDREDS OF YEARS, GONE IN THE SPACE OF ONE EVENING!›
‹I WILL PROTECT YOUR LEGEND, SEIOBO.›

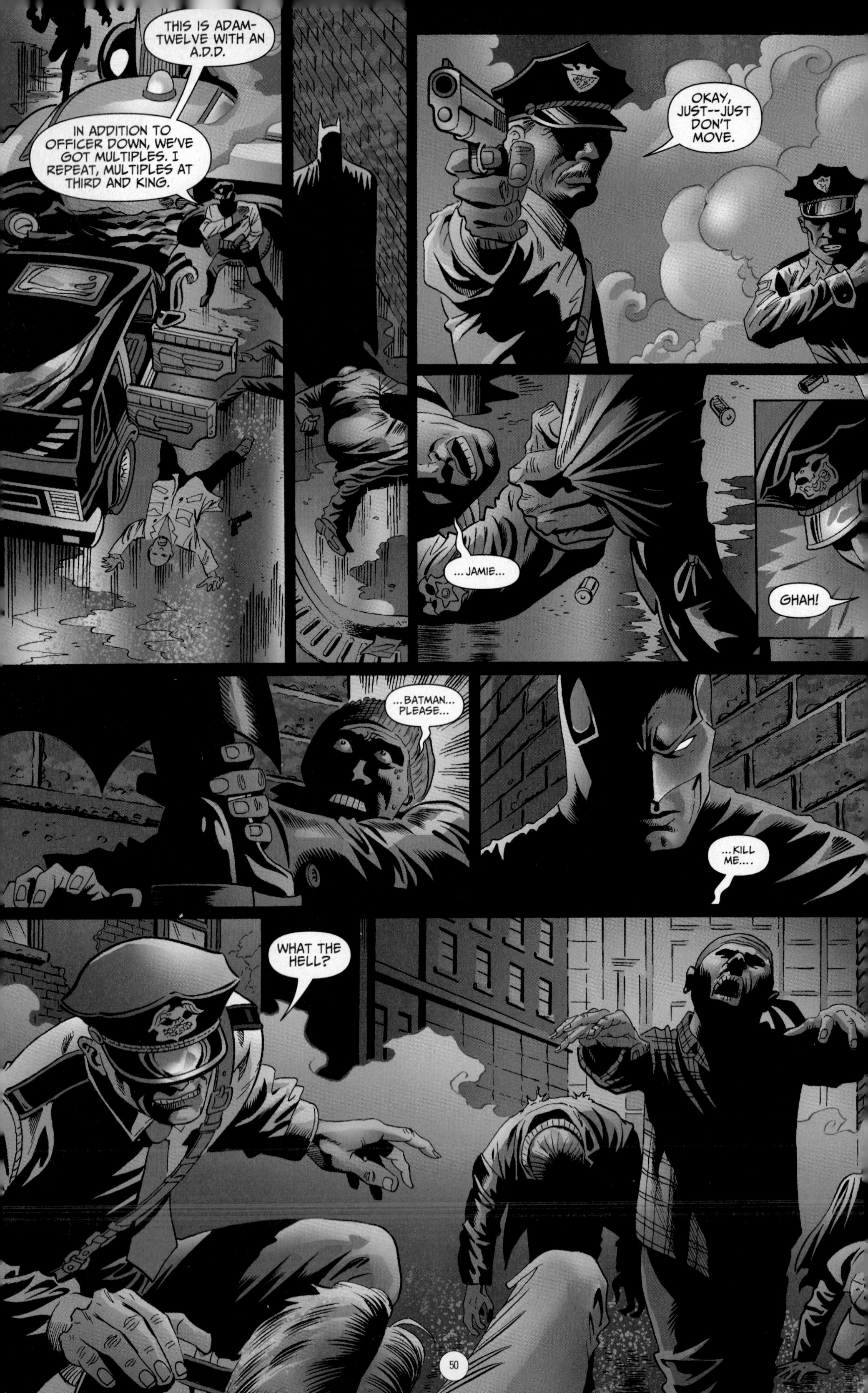
THIS IS ADAM-TWELVE WITH AN A.D.D.
IN ADDITION TO OFFICER DOWN, WE'VE GOT MULTIPLES. I REPEAT, MULTIPLES AT THIRD AND KING.
OKAY, JUST--JUST DON'T MOVE.
...JAMIE...
GHAH!
...BATMAN... PLEASE...
...KILL ME....
WHAT THE HELL?

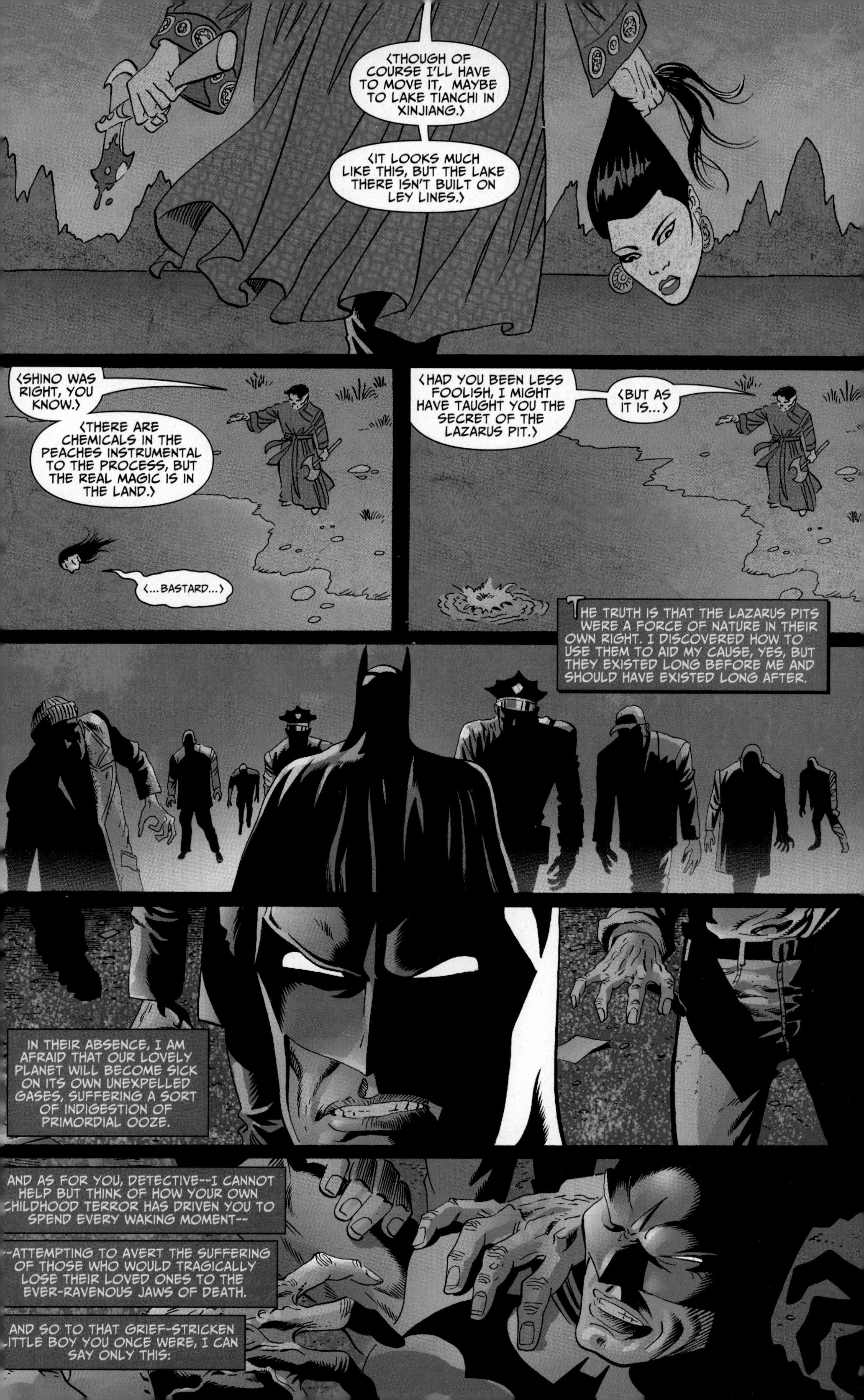

‹THOUGH OF COURSE I'LL HAVE TO MOVE IT, MAYBE TO LAKE TIANCHI IN XINJIANG.›
‹IT LOOKS MUCH LIKE THIS, BUT THE LAKE THERE ISN'T BUILT ON LEY LINES.›
‹SHINO WAS RIGHT, YOU KNOW.›
‹THERE ARE CHEMICALS IN THE PEACHES INSTRUMENTAL TO THE PROCESS, BUT THE REAL MAGIC IS IN THE LAND.›
‹...BASTARD...›
‹HAD YOU BEEN LESS FOOLISH, I MIGHT HAVE TAUGHT YOU THE SECRET OF THE LAZARUS PIT.›
‹BUT AS IT IS...›
THE TRUTH IS THAT THE LAZARUS PITS WERE A FORCE OF NATURE IN THEIR OWN RIGHT. I DISCOVERED HOW TO USE THEM TO AID MY CAUSE, YES, BUT THEY EXISTED LONG BEFORE ME AND SHOULD HAVE EXISTED LONG AFTER.
IN THEIR ABSENCE, I AM AFRAID THAT OUR LOVELY PLANET WILL BECOME SICK ON ITS OWN UNEXPELLED GASES, SUFFERING A SORT OF INDIGESTION OF PRIMORDIAL OOZE.
AND AS FOR YOU, DETECTIVE--I CANNOT HELP BUT THINK OF HOW YOUR OWN CHILDHOOD TERROR HAS DRIVEN YOU TO SPEND EVERY WAKING MOMENT--
--ATTEMPTING TO AVERT THE SUFFERING OF THOSE WHO WOULD TRAGICALLY LOSE THEIR LOVED ONES TO THE EVER-RAVENOUS JAWS OF DEATH.
AND SO TO THAT GRIEF-STRICKEN LITTLE BOY YOU ONCE WERE, I CAN SAY ONLY THIS:

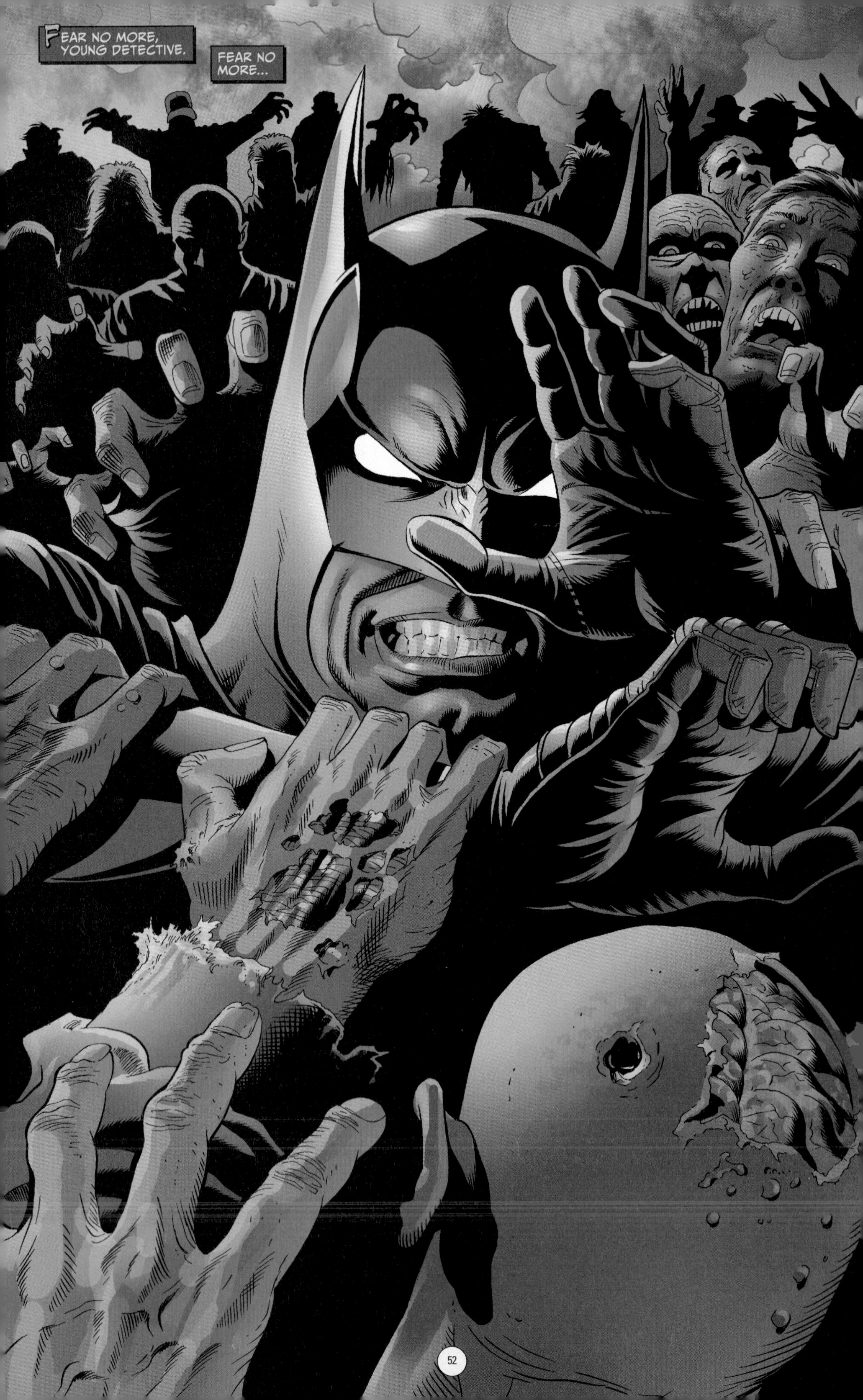
FEAR NO MORE, YOUNG DETECTIVE.
FEAR NO MORE...

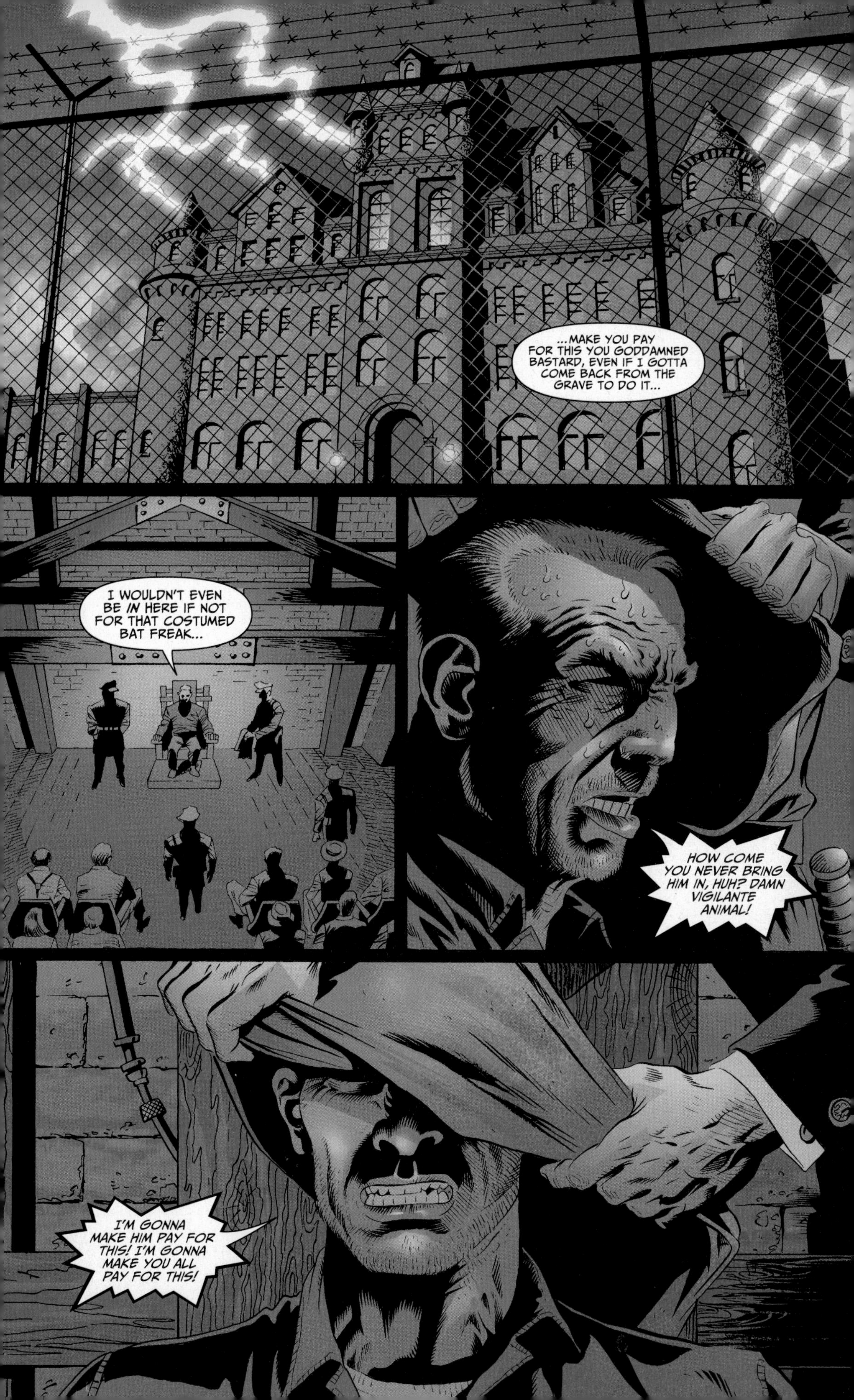
...MAKE YOU PAY FOR THIS YOU GODDAMNED BASTARD, EVEN IF I GOTTA COME BACK FROM THE GRAVE TO DO IT...
I WOULDN'T EVEN BE IN HERE IF NOT FOR THAT COSTUMED BAT FREAK...
HOW COME YOU NEVER BRING HIM IN, HUH? DAMN VIGILANTE ANIMAL!
I'M GONNA MAKE HIM PAY FOR THIS! I'M GONNA MAKE YOU ALL PAY FOR THIS!

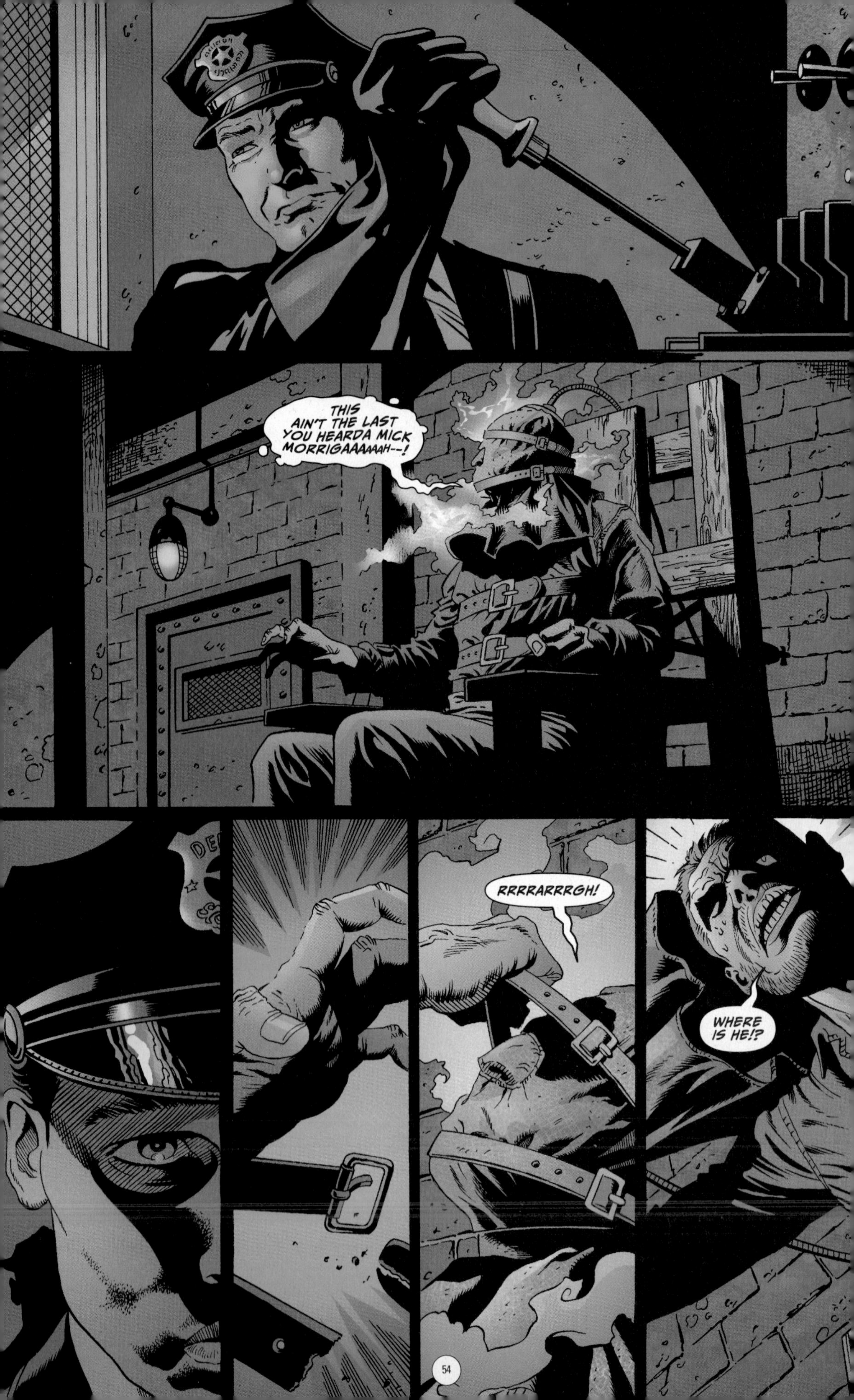
THIS AIN'T THE LAST YOU HEARDA MICK MORRIGAAAAAAH--!
RRRRARRRGH!
WHERE IS HE!?

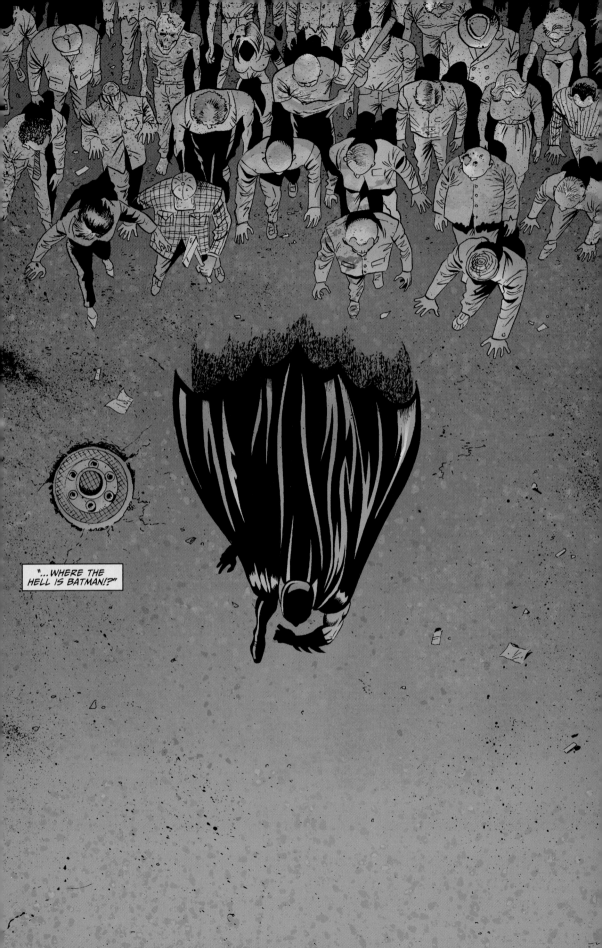

"...WHERE THE HELL IS BATMAN!?"

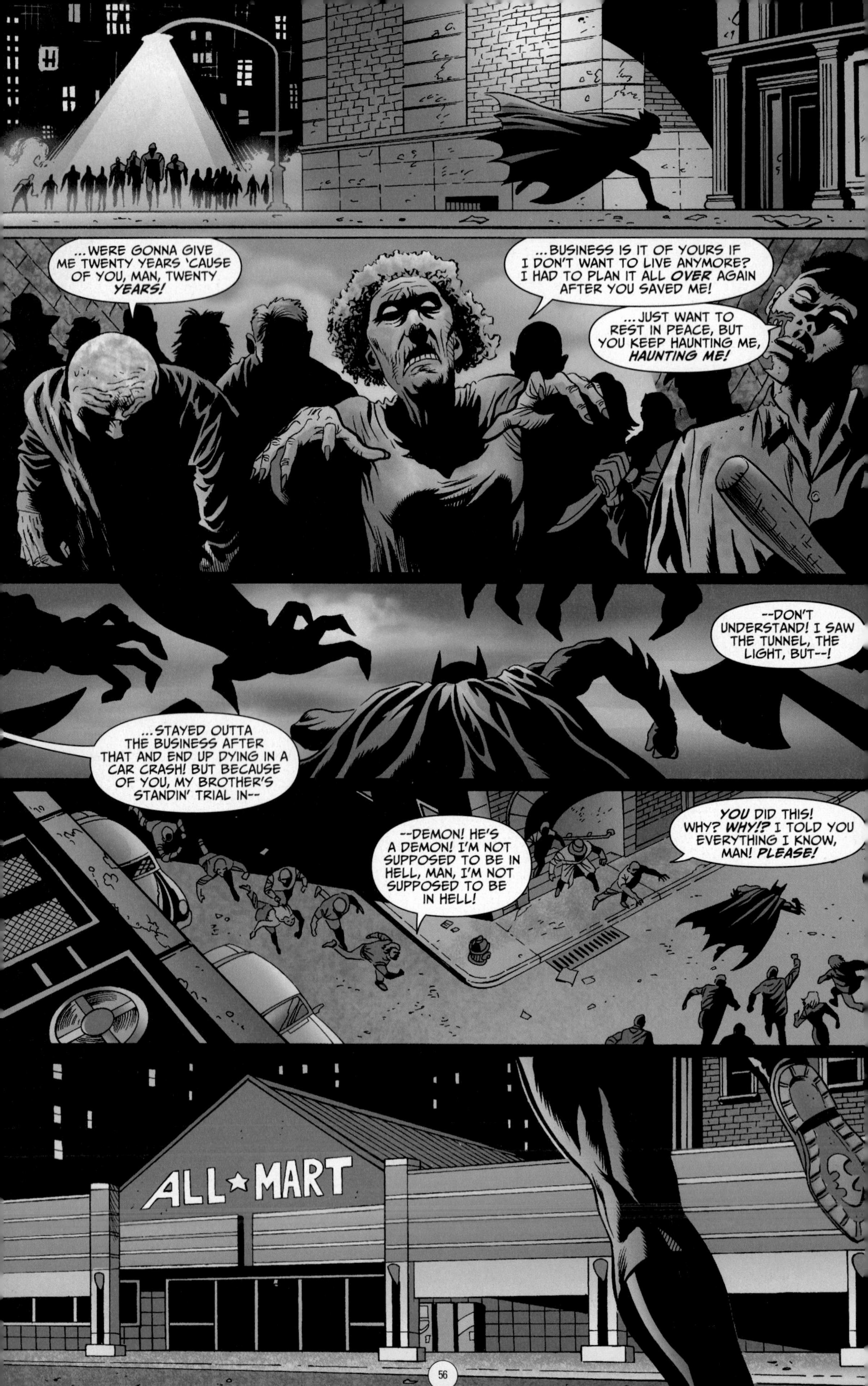
...WERE GONNA GIVE ME TWENTY YEARS 'CAUSE OF YOU, MAN, TWENTY YEARS!
...BUSINESS IS IT OF YOURS IF I DON'T WANT TO LIVE ANYMORE? I HAD TO PLAN IT ALL OVER AGAIN AFTER YOU SAVED ME!
...JUST WANT TO REST IN PEACE, BUT YOU KEEP HAUNTING ME, HAUNTING ME!
--DON'T UNDERSTAND! I SAW THE TUNNEL, THE LIGHT, BUT--!
...STAYED OUTTA THE BUSINESS AFTER THAT AND END UP DYING IN A CAR CRASH! BUT BECAUSE OF YOU, MY BROTHER'S STANDIN' TRIAL IN--
--DEMON! HE'S A DEMON! I'M NOT SUPPOSED TO BE IN HELL, MAN, I'M NOT SUPPOSED TO BE IN HELL!
YOU DID THIS! WHY? WHY!? I TOLD YOU EVERYTHING I KNOW, MAN! PLEASE!
ALL★MART

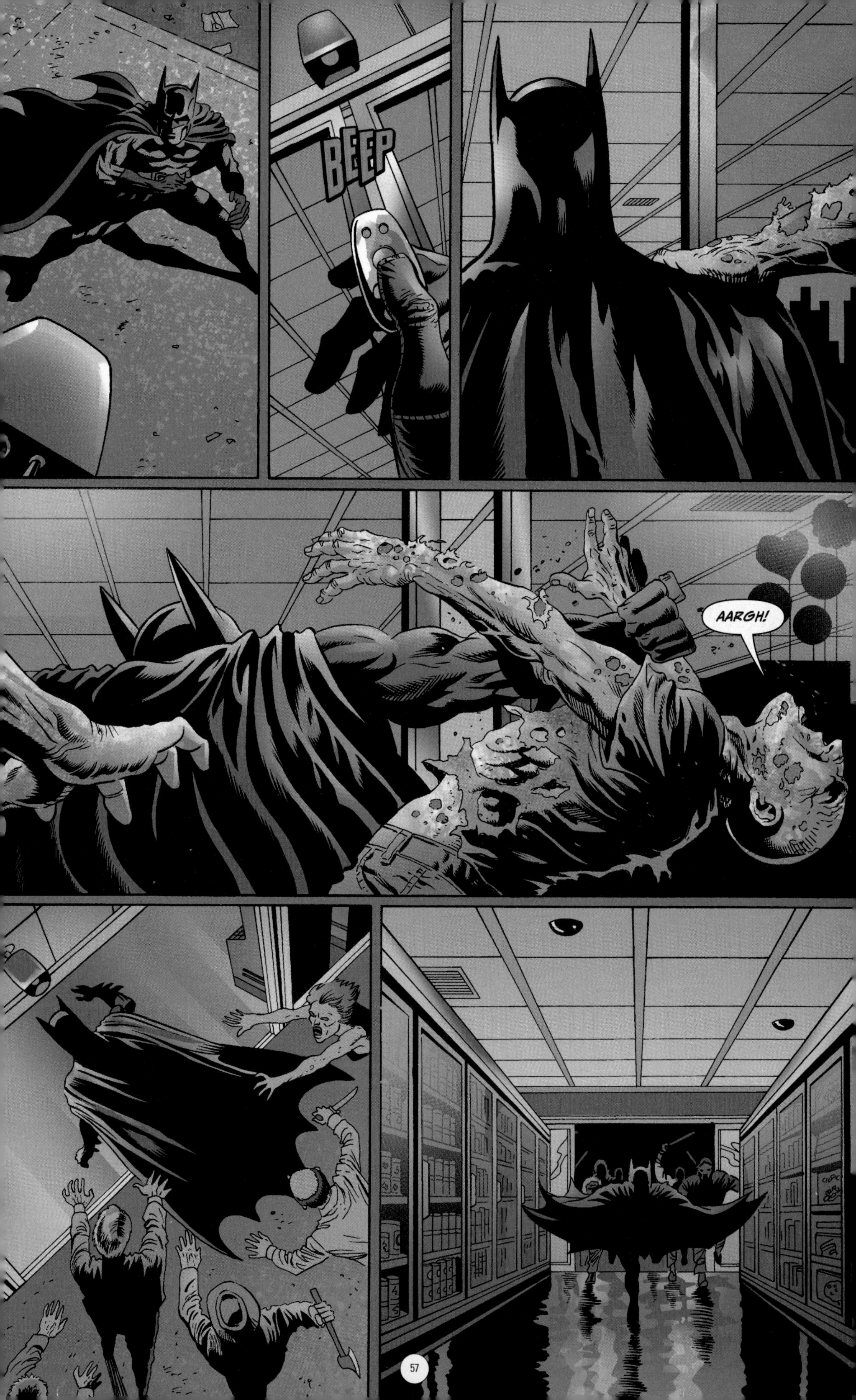

BEEP
AARGH!

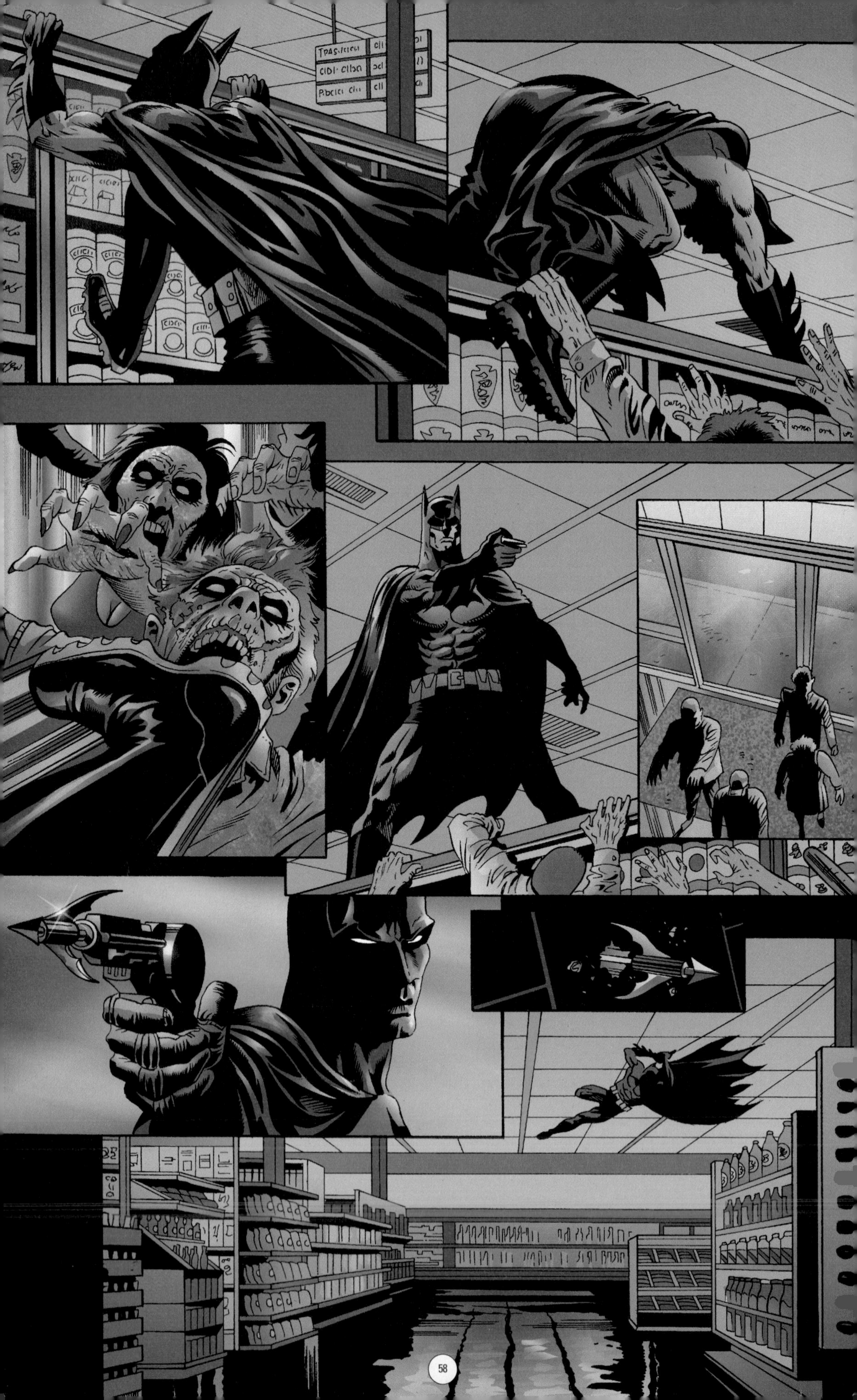

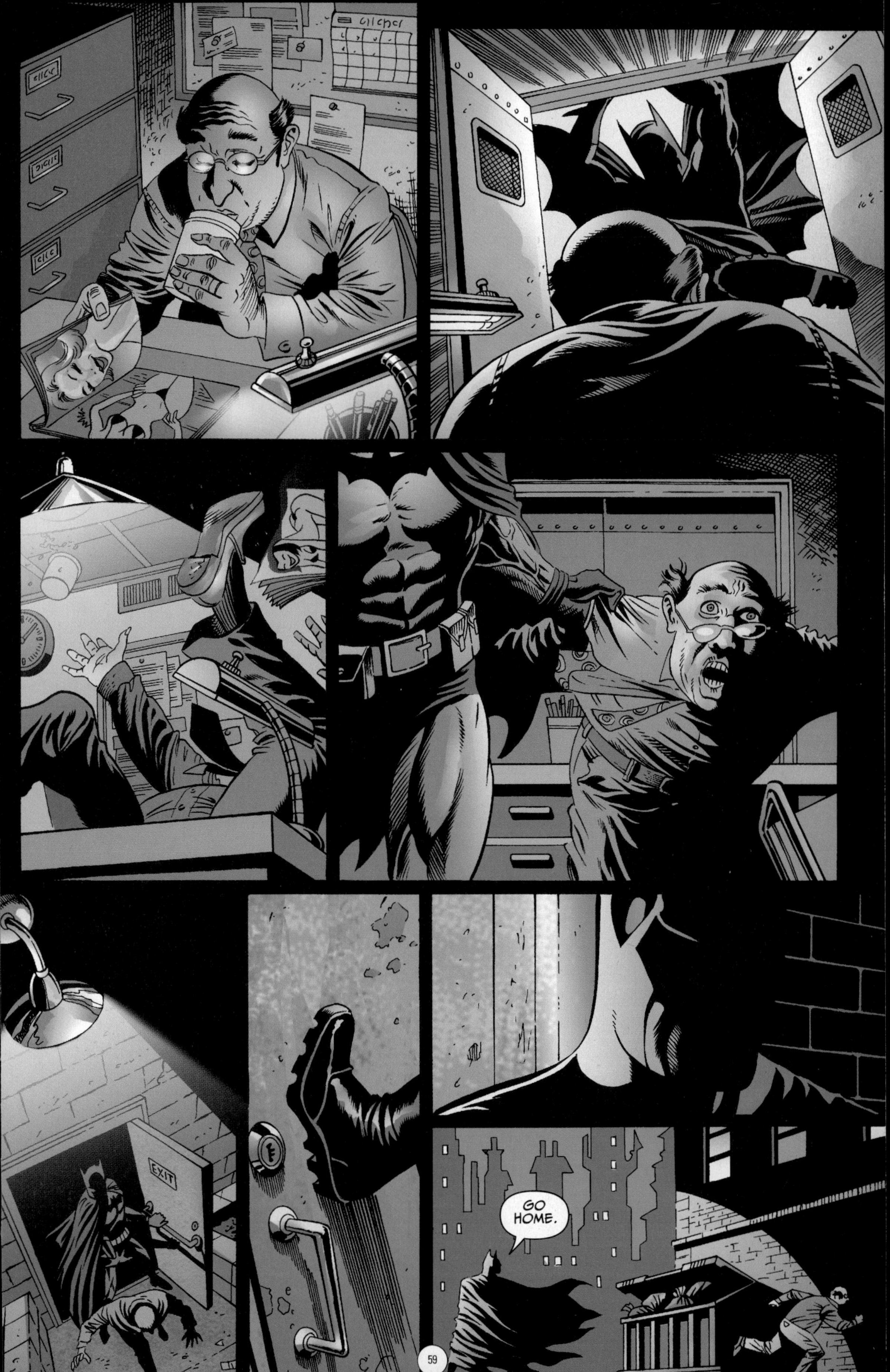
GO HOME.
EXIT

ALFRED—

My DEAR DETECTIVE—

19 JULY 2001, CAIRO

THOUGH I CANNOT HELP BUT HOPE THAT THE DELIVERY OF THIS LETTER PROVES UNNECESSARY, I WRITE IT NOW WITH THE GREAT COMPASSION AND RESPECT I HAVE ALWAYS FELT TOWARDS YOU.

IT IS STILL MY INTENTION TO WIN YOU TO MY CAUSE—NO MAN WITH YOUR INTELLIGENCE COULD FAIL TO ABSOLUTE...

INTERDEPENDENCY OF ALL LIFE ON THIS PLANET AND THE FINAL NECESSITY OF ...ECTING THE LARGER ...ISM OF WHICH WE ARE ...ALL A PART—

...BUT I WOULD BE ...NOT TO PLAN FOR ...BILITY ...YOUR ...IR ...Y B... ...A...

—GOT ANYTHING?

INDEED, SIR. YOUR HUNCH WAS CORRECT.

THERE IS A SECOND LETTER ENCODED WITHIN RA'S' FIRST, THIS ONE IN ARABIC.

I'M WORKING ON THE TRANSLATION NOW.

GOOD.

WE'LL NEED EVERY CLUE WE CAN GET.

SEND ME WHAT YOU'VE GOT.

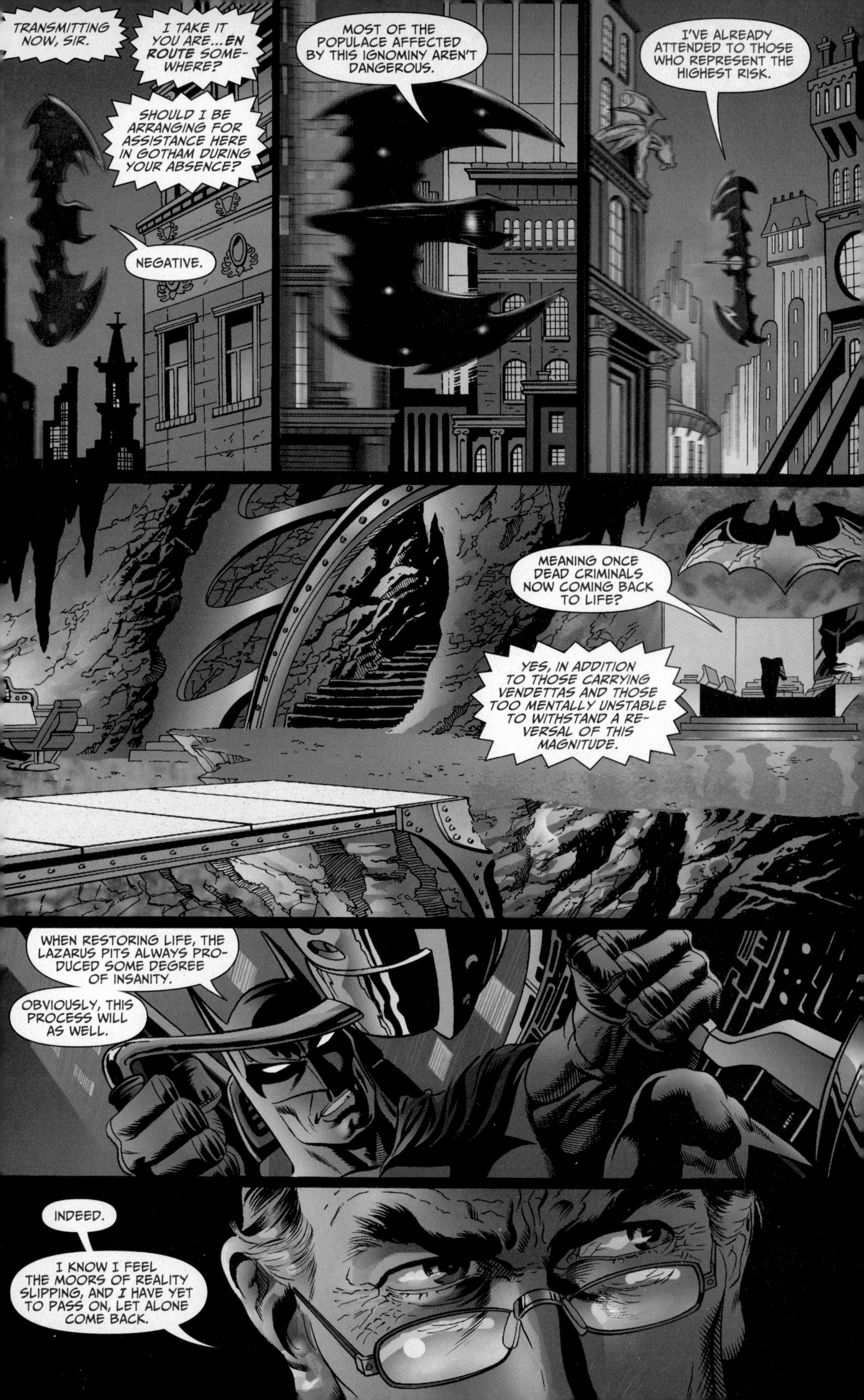
TRANSMITTING NOW, SIR.
I TAKE IT YOU ARE... EN ROUTE SOME-WHERE?
SHOULD I BE ARRANGING FOR ASSISTANCE HERE IN GOTHAM DURING YOUR ABSENCE?
NEGATIVE.
MOST OF THE POPULACE AFFECTED BY THIS IGNOMINY AREN'T DANGEROUS.
I'VE ALREADY ATTENDED TO THOSE WHO REPRESENT THE HIGHEST RISK.
MEANING ONCE DEAD CRIMINALS NOW COMING BACK TO LIFE?
YES, IN ADDITION TO THOSE CARRYING VENDETTAS AND THOSE TOO MENTALLY UNSTABLE TO WITHSTAND A RE-VERSAL OF THIS MAGNITUDE.
WHEN RESTORING LIFE, THE LAZARUS PITS ALWAYS PRO-DUCED SOME DEGREE OF INSANITY.
OBVIOUSLY, THIS PROCESS WILL AS WELL.
INDEED.
I KNOW I FEEL THE MOORS OF REALITY SLIPPING, AND I HAVE YET TO PASS ON, LET ALONE COME BACK.

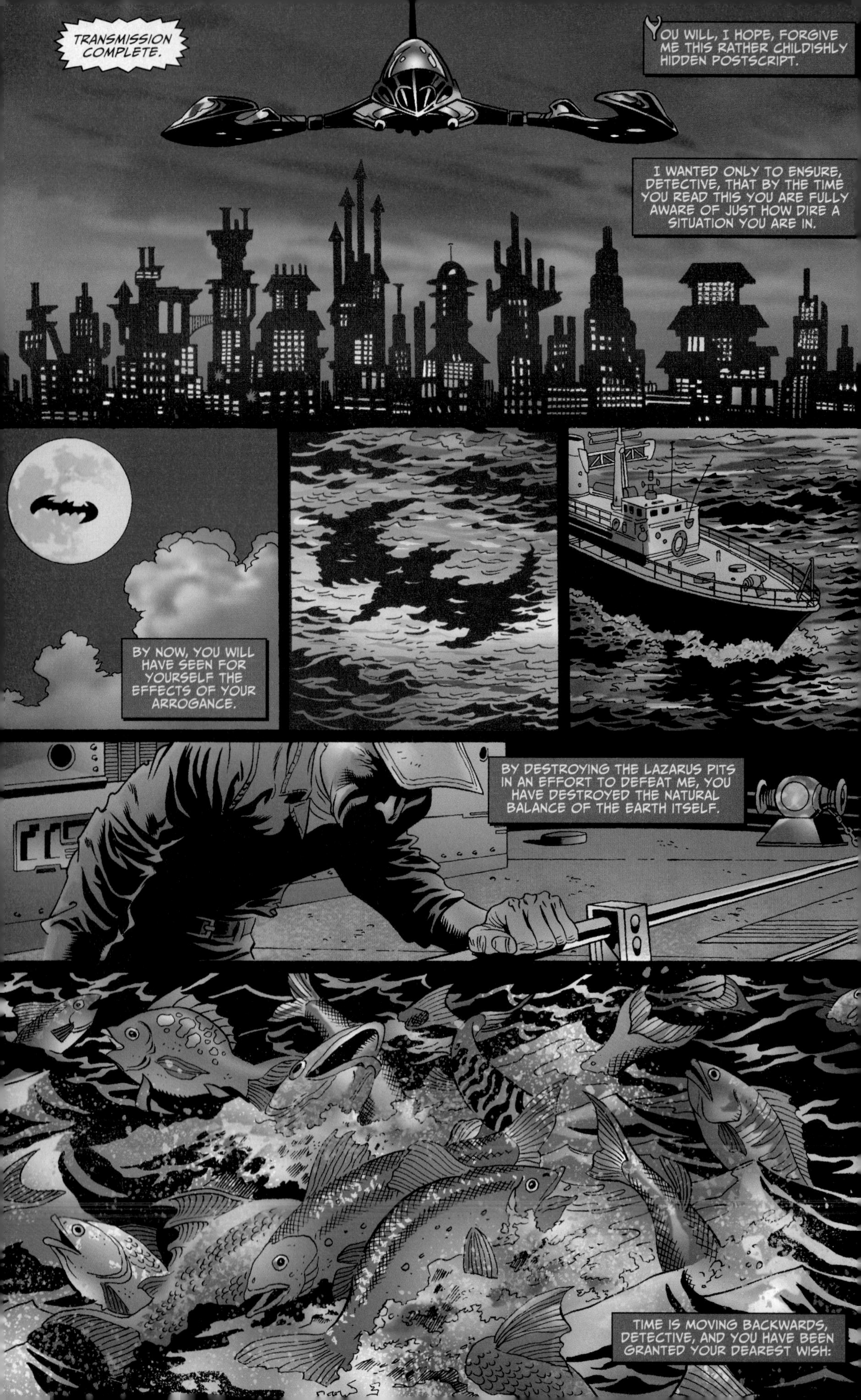
TRANSMISSION COMPLETE.
YOU WILL, I HOPE, FORGIVE ME THIS RATHER CHILDISHLY HIDDEN POSTSCRIPT.
I WANTED ONLY TO ENSURE, DETECTIVE, THAT BY THE TIME YOU READ THIS YOU ARE FULLY AWARE OF JUST HOW DIRE A SITUATION YOU ARE IN.
BY NOW, YOU WILL HAVE SEEN FOR YOURSELF THE EFFECTS OF YOUR ARROGANCE.
BY DESTROYING THE LAZARUS PITS IN AN EFFORT TO DEFEAT ME, YOU HAVE DESTROYED THE NATURAL BALANCE OF THE EARTH ITSELF.
TIME IS MOVING BACKWARDS, DETECTIVE, AND YOU HAVE BEEN GRANTED YOUR DEAREST WISH:

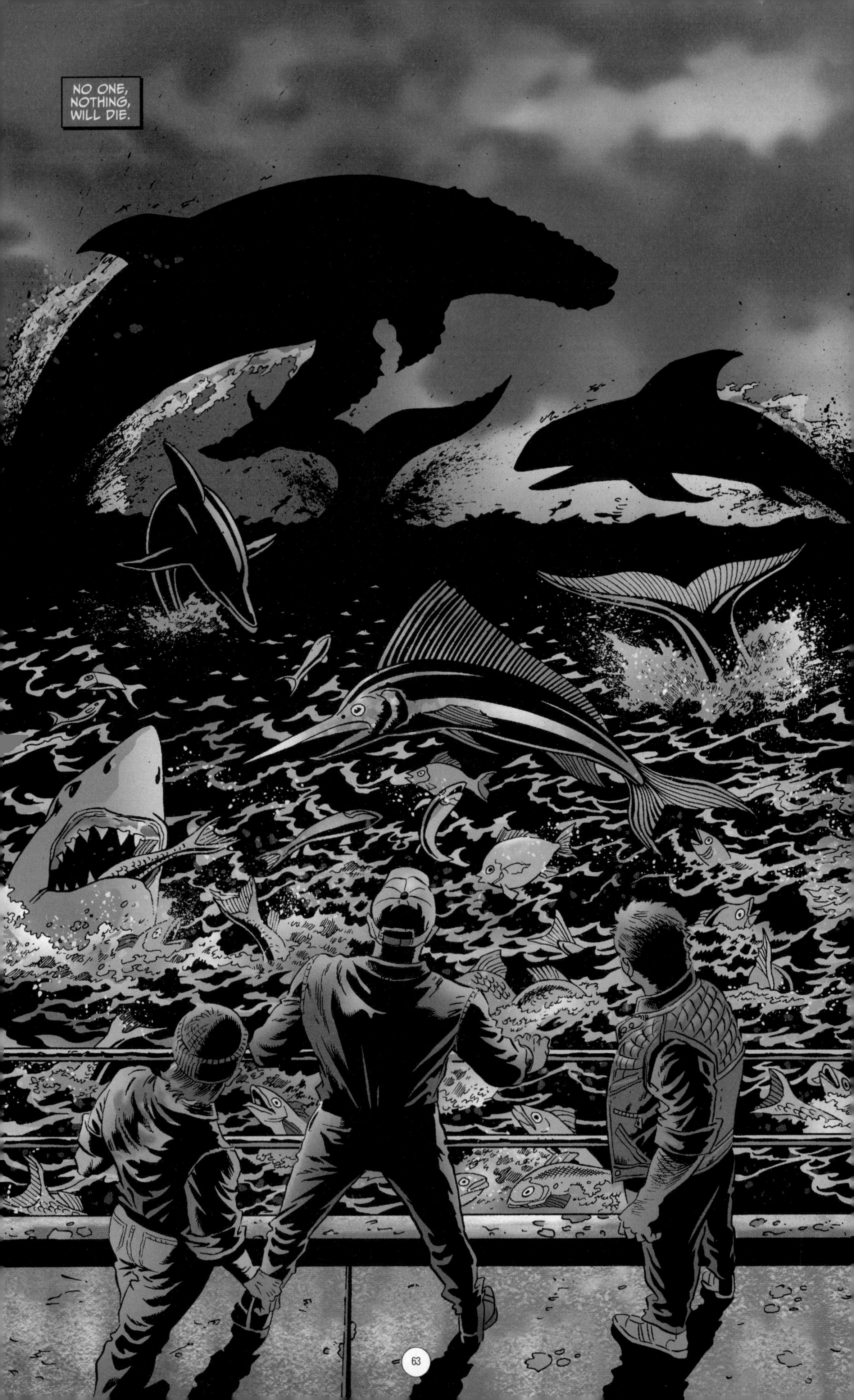
NO ONE,
NOTHING,
WILL DIE.

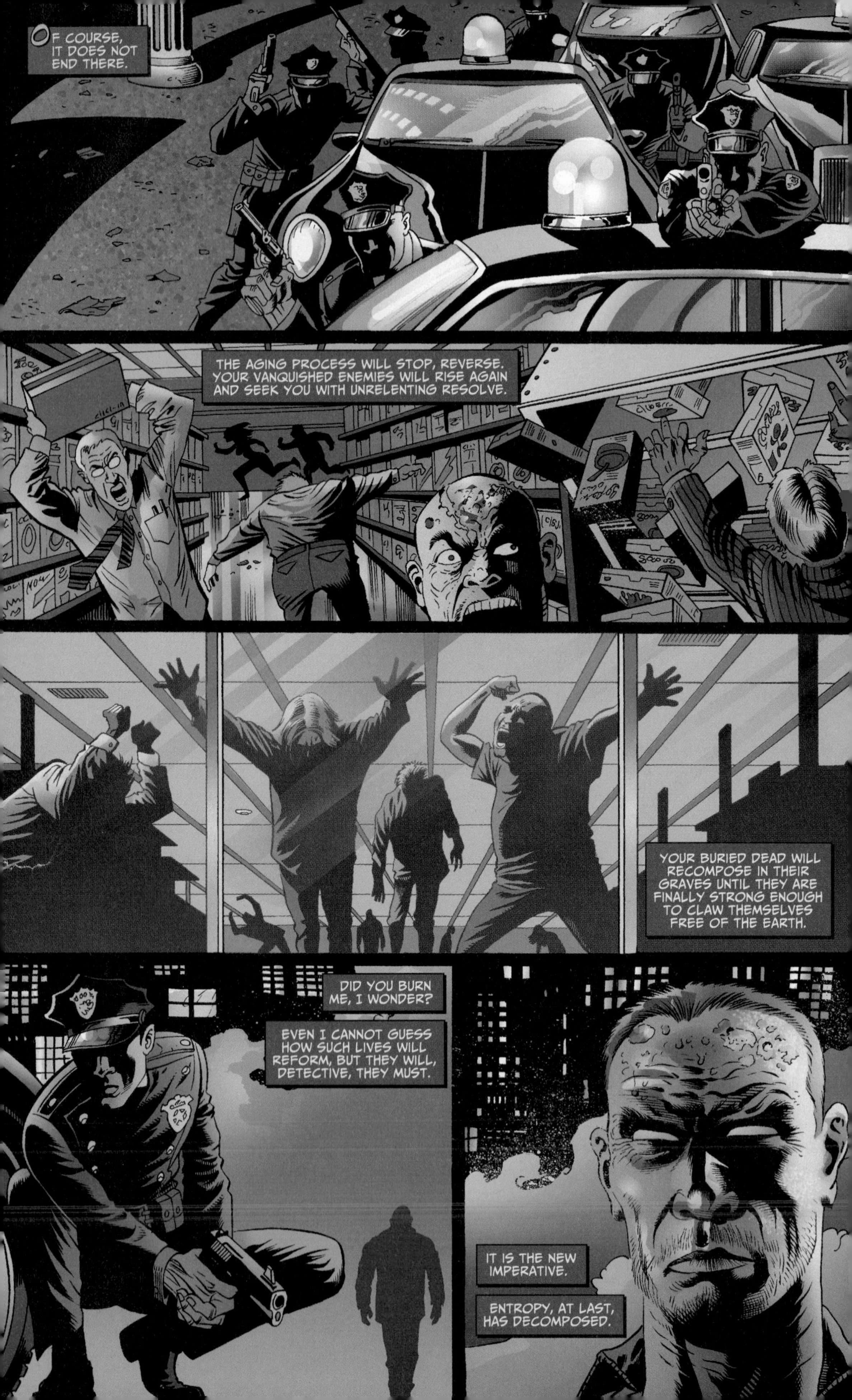
OF COURSE, IT DOES NOT END THERE.
THE AGING PROCESS WILL STOP, REVERSE. YOUR VANQUISHED ENEMIES WILL RISE AGAIN AND SEEK YOU WITH UNRELENTING RESOLVE.
YOUR BURIED DEAD WILL RECOMPOSE IN THEIR GRAVES UNTIL THEY ARE FINALLY STRONG ENOUGH TO CLAW THEMSELVES FREE OF THE EARTH.
DID YOU BURN ME, I WONDER?
EVEN I CANNOT GUESS HOW SUCH LIVES WILL REFORM, BUT THEY WILL, DETECTIVE, THEY MUST.
IT IS THE NEW IMPERATIVE.
ENTROPY, AT LAST, HAS DECOMPOSED.

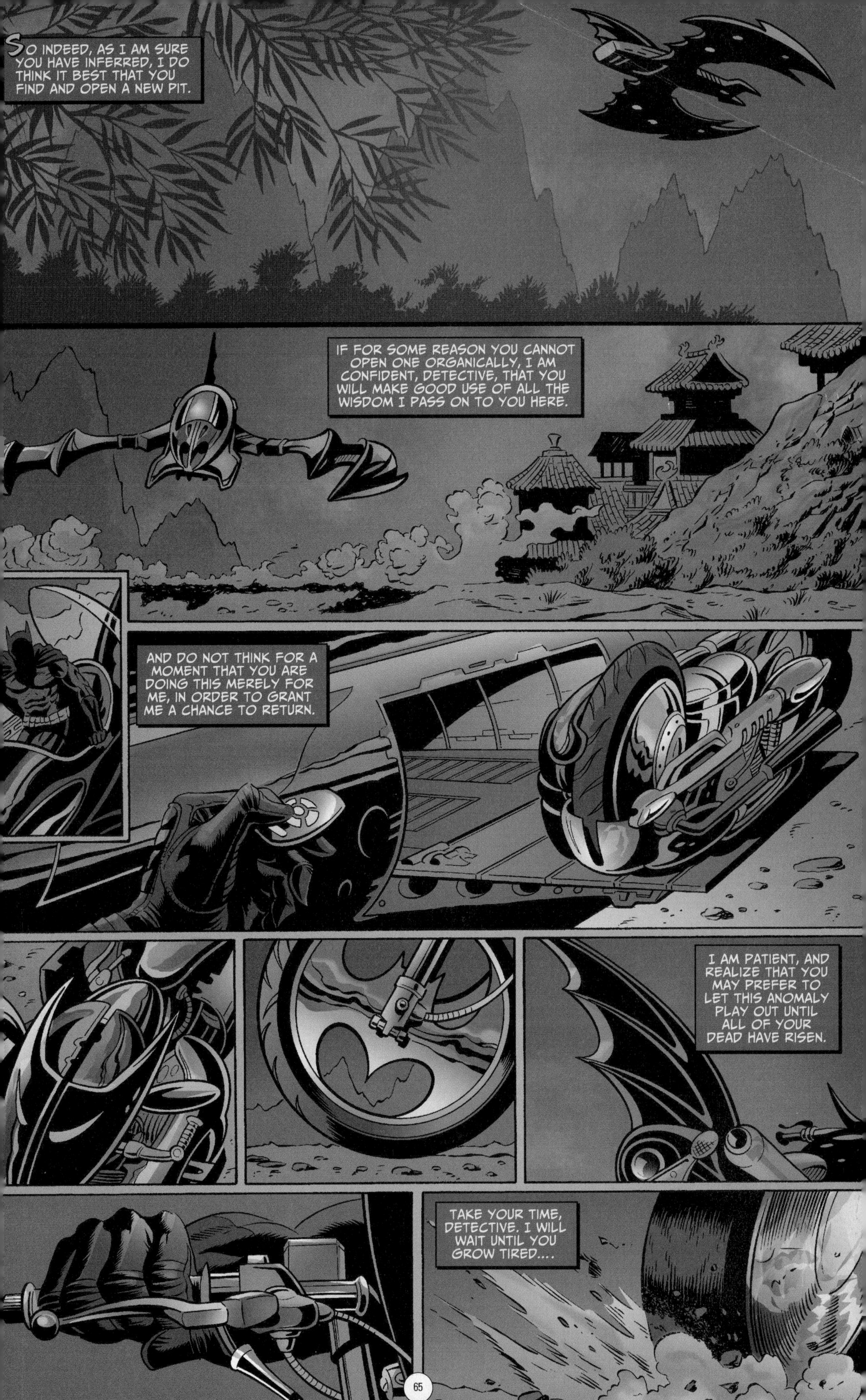
SO INDEED, AS I AM SURE YOU HAVE INFERRED, I DO THINK IT BEST THAT YOU FIND AND OPEN A NEW PIT.
IF FOR SOME REASON YOU CANNOT OPEN ONE ORGANICALLY, I AM CONFIDENT, DETECTIVE, THAT YOU WILL MAKE GOOD USE OF ALL THE WISDOM I PASS ON TO YOU HERE.
AND DO NOT THINK FOR A MOMENT THAT YOU ARE DOING THIS MERELY FOR ME, IN ORDER TO GRANT ME A CHANCE TO RETURN.
I AM PATIENT, AND REALIZE THAT YOU MAY PREFER TO LET THIS ANOMALY PLAY OUT UNTIL ALL OF YOUR DEAD HAVE RISEN.
TAKE YOUR TIME, DETECTIVE. I WILL WAIT UNTIL YOU GROW TIRED....

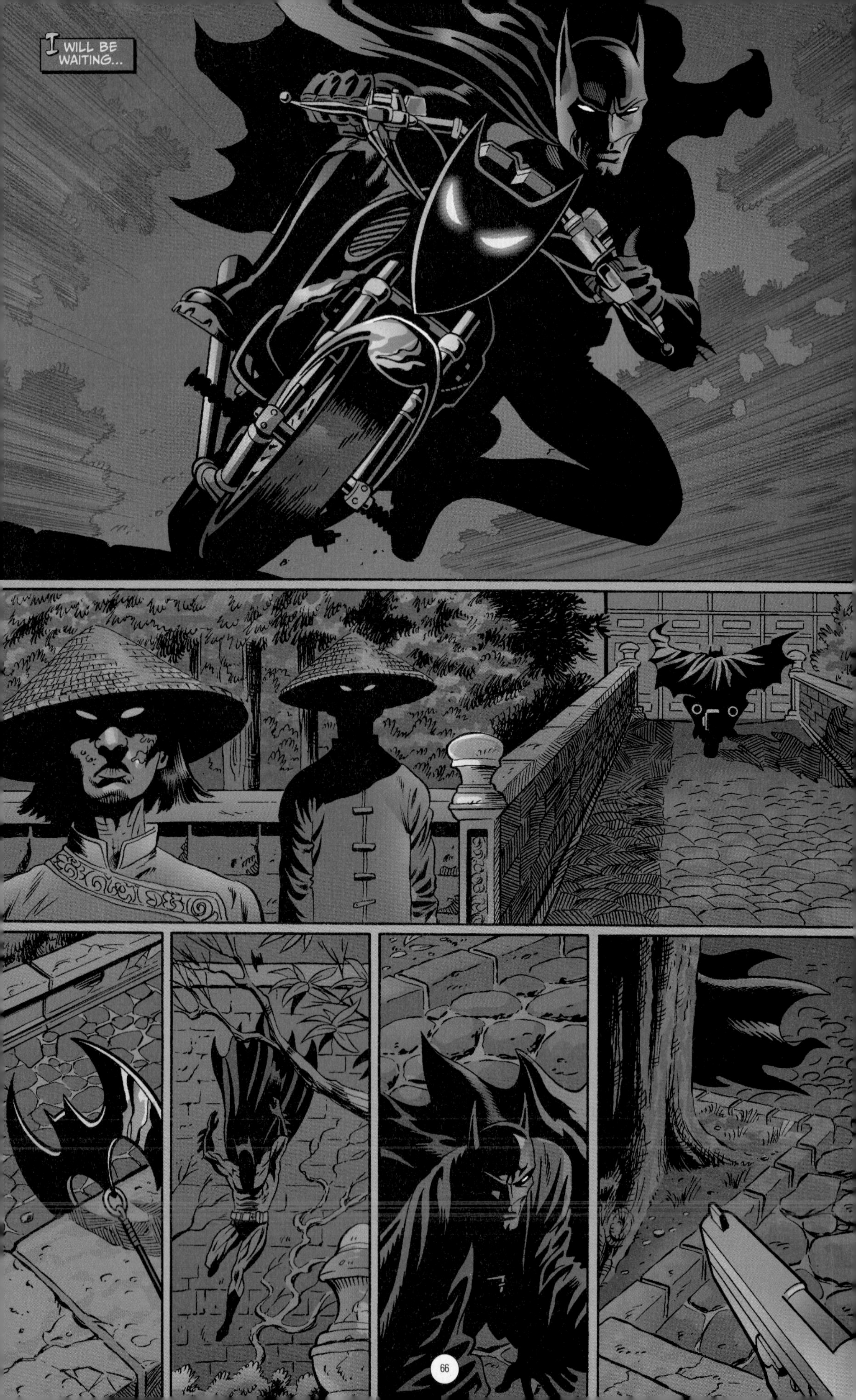
I WILL BE WAITING...

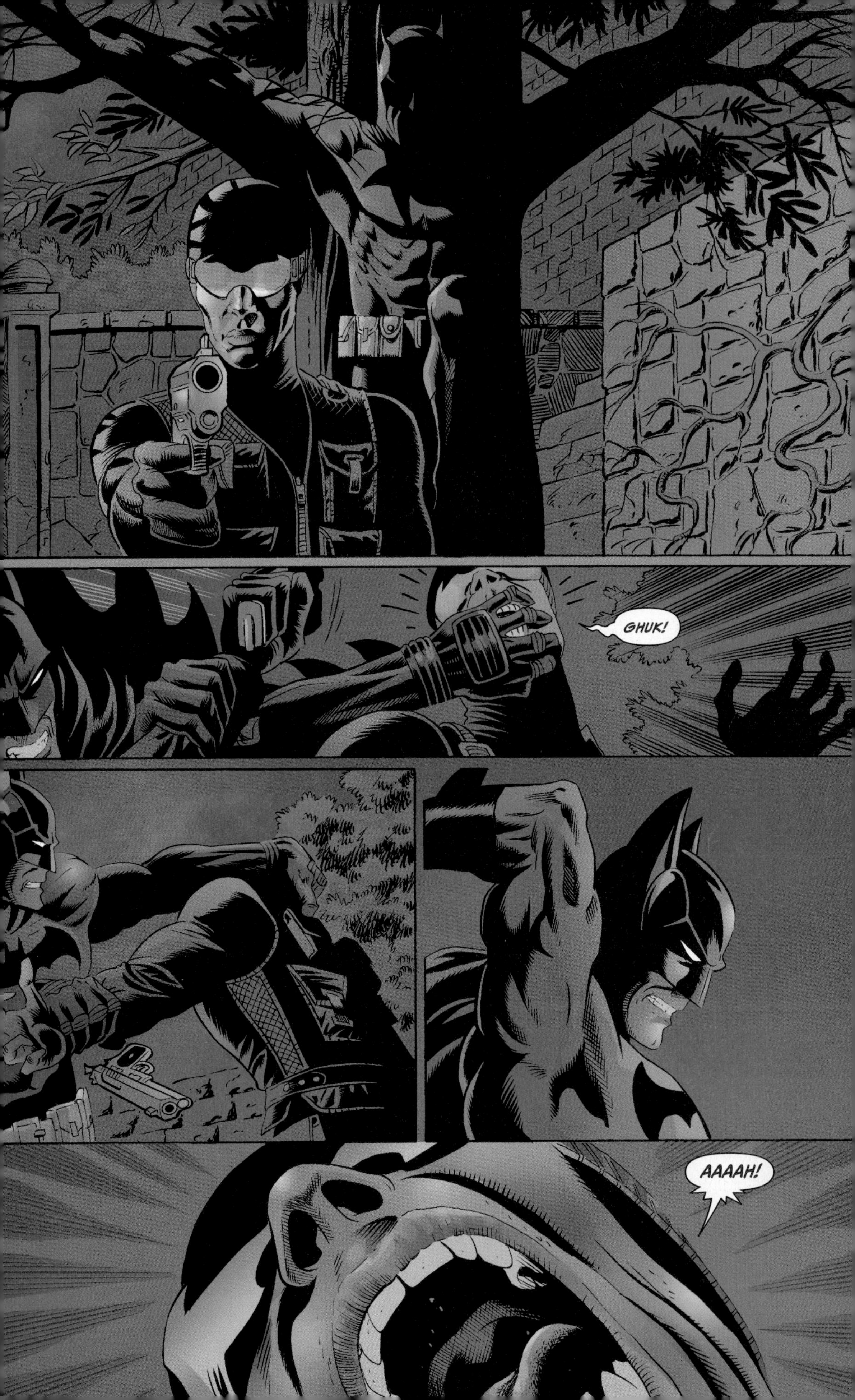
GHUK!
AAAAH!

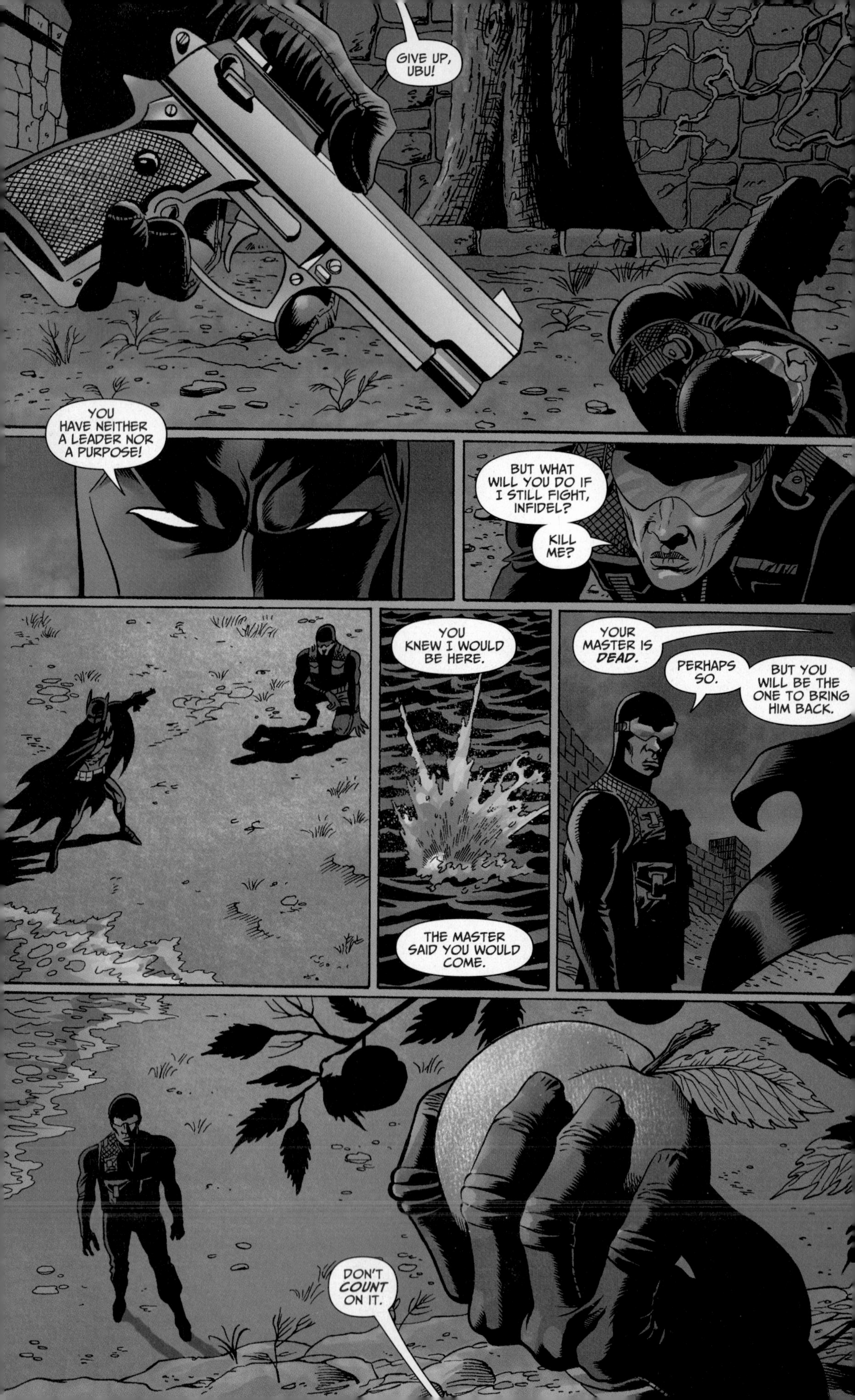
GIVE UP, UBU!
YOU HAVE NEITHER A LEADER NOR A PURPOSE!
BUT WHAT WILL YOU DO IF I STILL FIGHT, INFIDEL?
KILL ME?
YOU KNEW I WOULD BE HERE.
THE MASTER SAID YOU WOULD COME.
YOUR MASTER IS DEAD.
PERHAPS SO.
BUT YOU WILL BE THE ONE TO BRING HIM BACK.
DON'T COUNT ON IT.

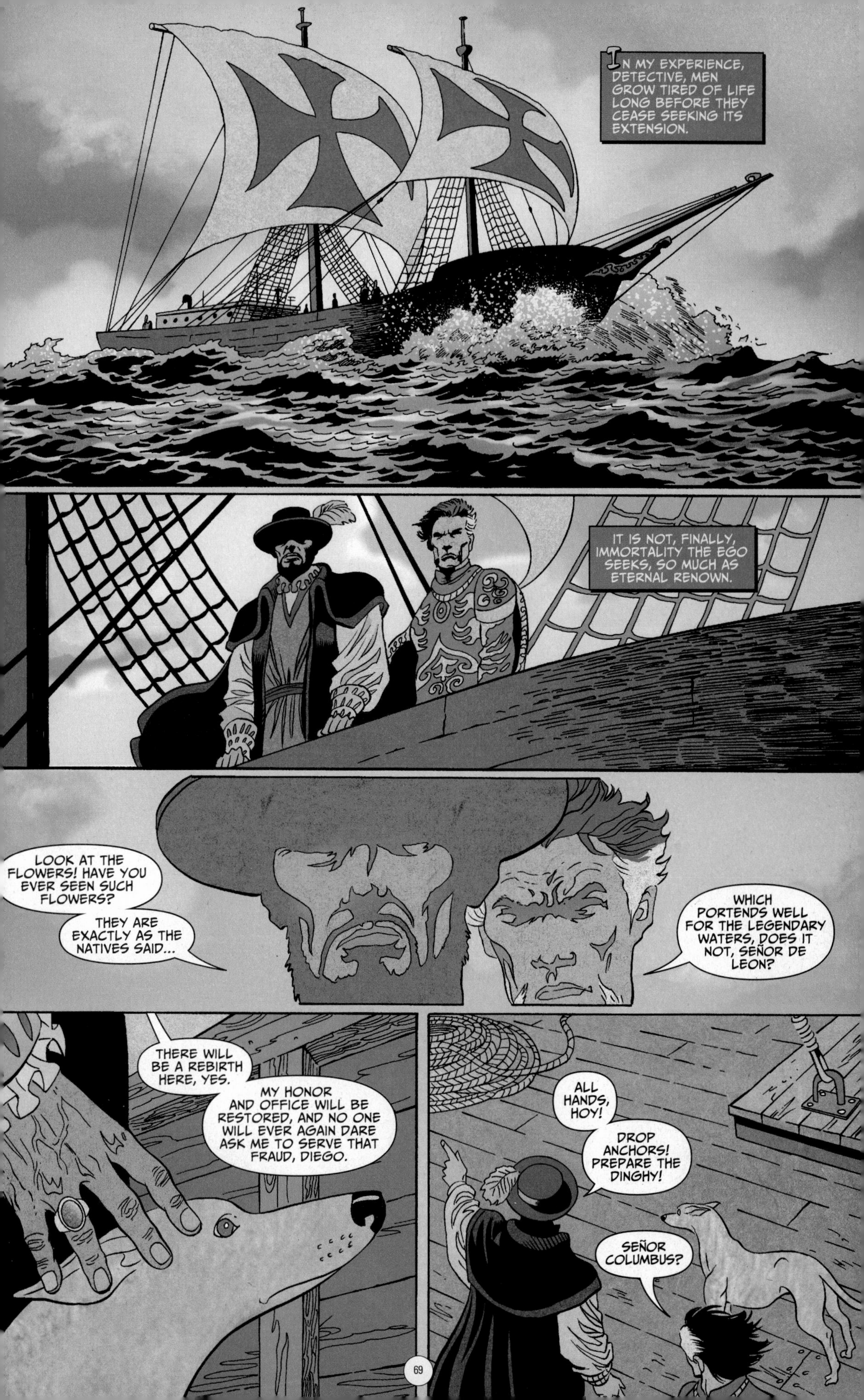
IN MY EXPERIENCE, DETECTIVE, MEN GROW TIRED OF LIFE LONG BEFORE THEY CEASE SEEKING ITS EXTENSION.
IT IS NOT, FINALLY, IMMORTALITY THE EGO SEEKS, SO MUCH AS ETERNAL RENOWN.
LOOK AT THE FLOWERS! HAVE YOU EVER SEEN SUCH FLOWERS?
THEY ARE EXACTLY AS THE NATIVES SAID...
WHICH PORTENDS WELL FOR THE LEGENDARY WATERS, DOES IT NOT, SEÑOR DE LEON?
THERE WILL BE A REBIRTH HERE, YES.
MY HONOR AND OFFICE WILL BE RESTORED, AND NO ONE WILL EVER AGAIN DARE ASK ME TO SERVE THAT FRAUD, DIEGO.
ALL HANDS, HOY!
DROP ANCHORS! PREPARE THE DINGHY!
SEÑOR COLUMBUS?

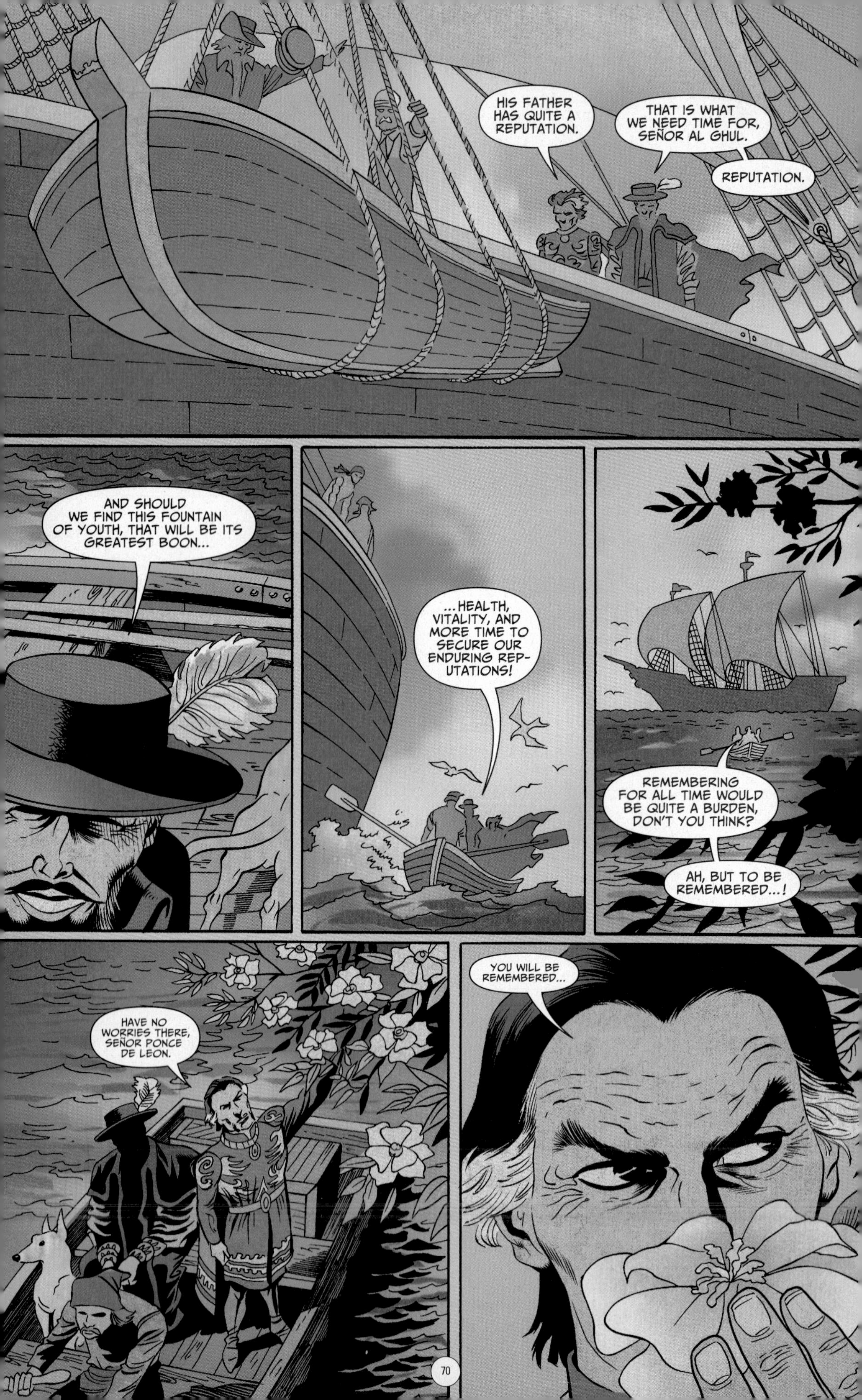
HIS FATHER HAS QUITE A REPUTATION.
THAT IS WHAT WE NEED TIME FOR, SEÑOR AL GHUL.
REPUTATION.
AND SHOULD WE FIND THIS FOUNTAIN OF YOUTH, THAT WILL BE ITS GREATEST BOON...
...HEALTH, VITALITY, AND MORE TIME TO SECURE OUR ENDURING REP-UTATIONS!
REMEMBERING FOR ALL TIME WOULD BE QUITE A BURDEN, DON'T YOU THINK?
AH, BUT TO BE REMEMBERED...!
HAVE NO WORRIES THERE, SEÑOR PONCE DE LEON.
YOU WILL BE REMEMBERED...

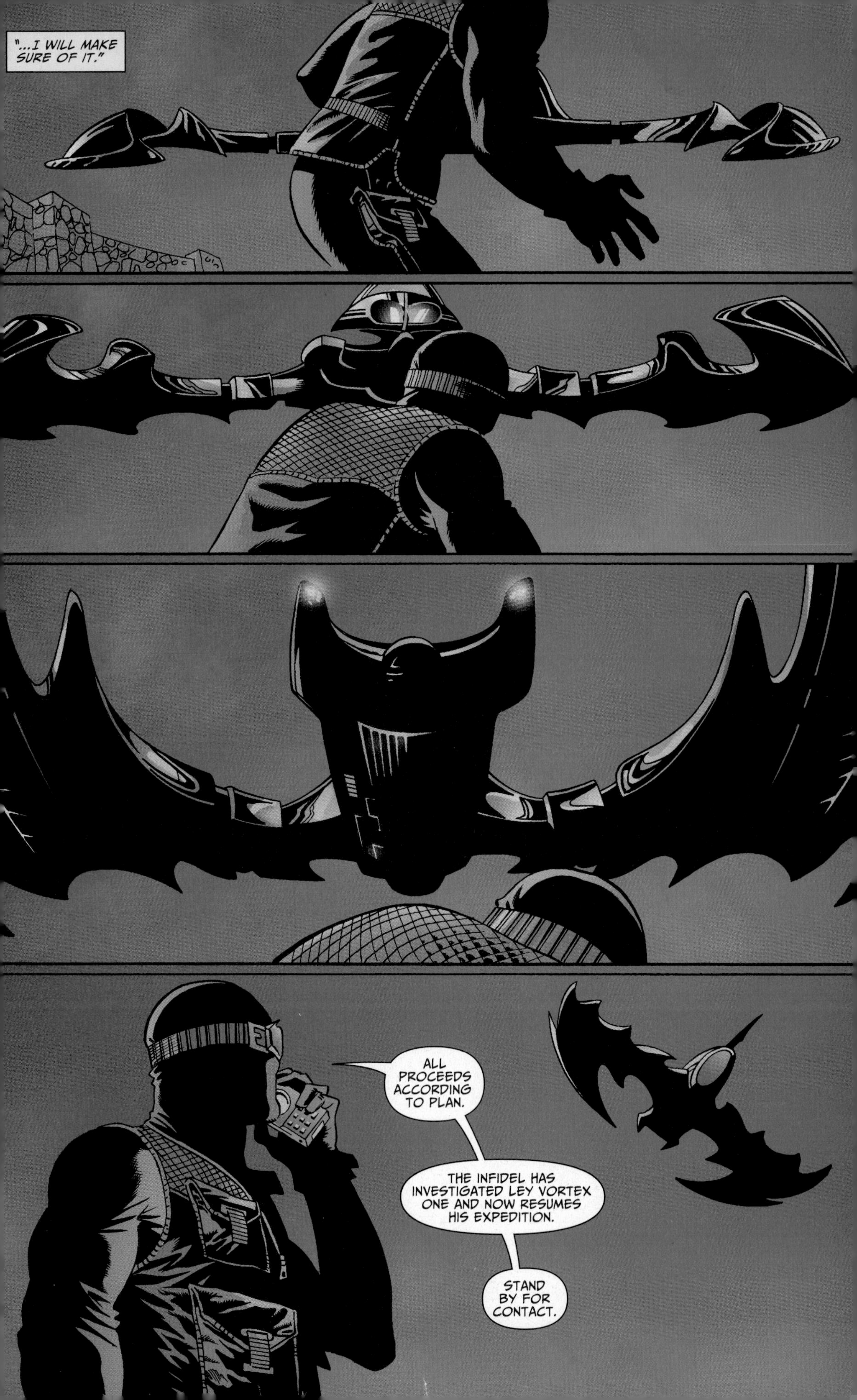
"...I WILL MAKE SURE OF IT."
ALL PROCEEDS ACCORDING TO PLAN.
THE INFIDEL HAS INVESTIGATED LEY VORTEX ONE AND NOW RESUMES HIS EXPEDITION.
STAND BY FOR CONTACT.

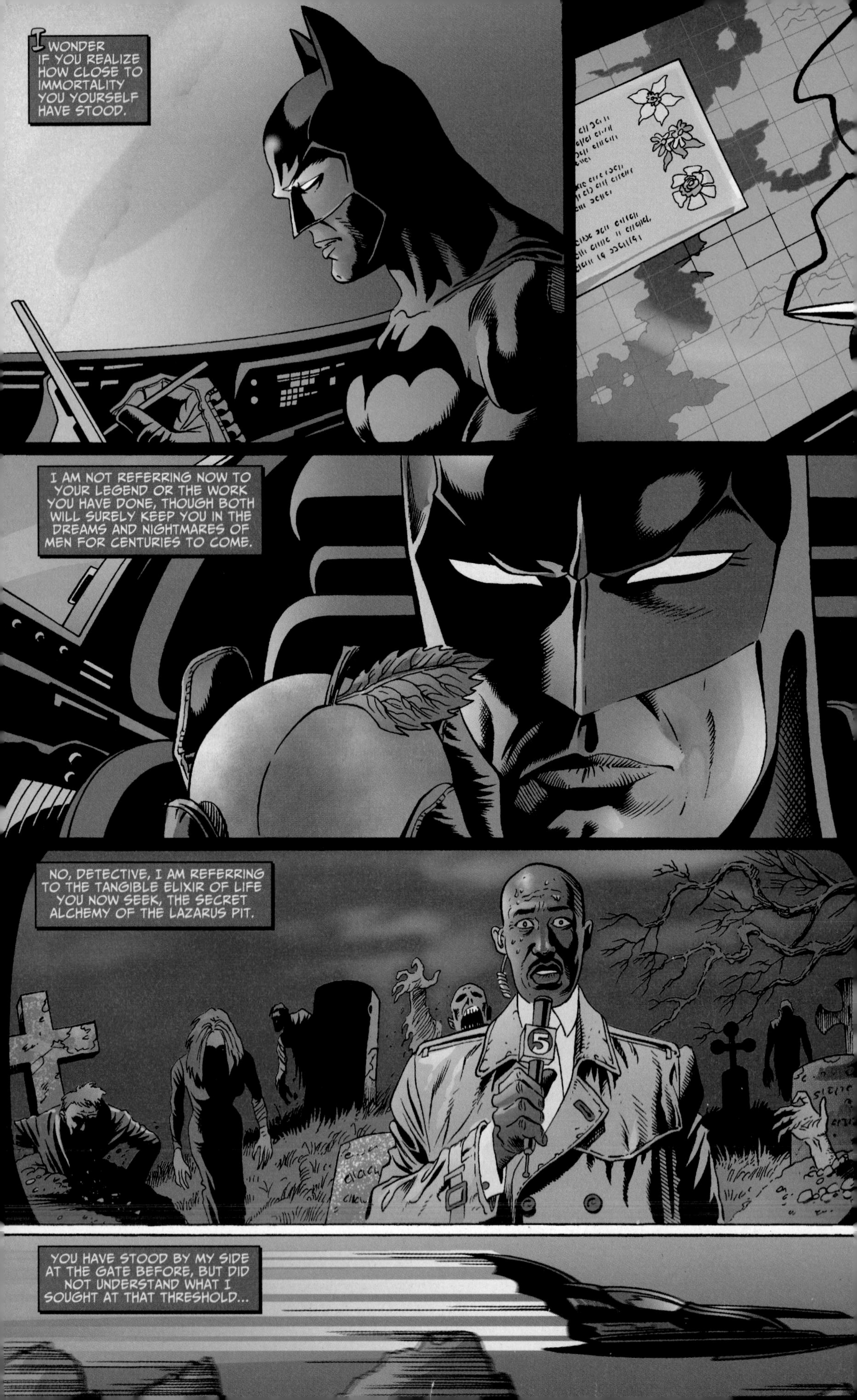
I WONDER IF YOU REALIZE HOW CLOSE TO IMMORTALITY YOU YOURSELF HAVE STOOD.
I AM NOT REFERRING NOW TO YOUR LEGEND OR THE WORK YOU HAVE DONE, THOUGH BOTH WILL SURELY KEEP YOU IN THE DREAMS AND NIGHTMARES OF MEN FOR CENTURIES TO COME.
NO, DETECTIVE, I AM REFERRING TO THE TANGIBLE ELIXIR OF LIFE YOU NOW SEEK, THE SECRET ALCHEMY OF THE LAZARUS PIT.
YOU HAVE STOOD BY MY SIDE AT THE GATE BEFORE, BUT DID NOT UNDERSTAND WHAT I SOUGHT AT THAT THRESHOLD...

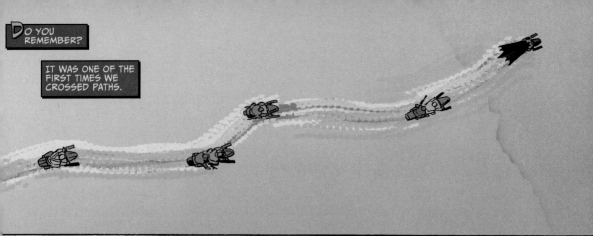

DO YOU REMEMBER?

IT WAS ONE OF THE FIRST TIMES WE CROSSED PATHS.

BUDDA BUDDA BUDDA BUDDA

SPOING SPANG SPANG SPOING

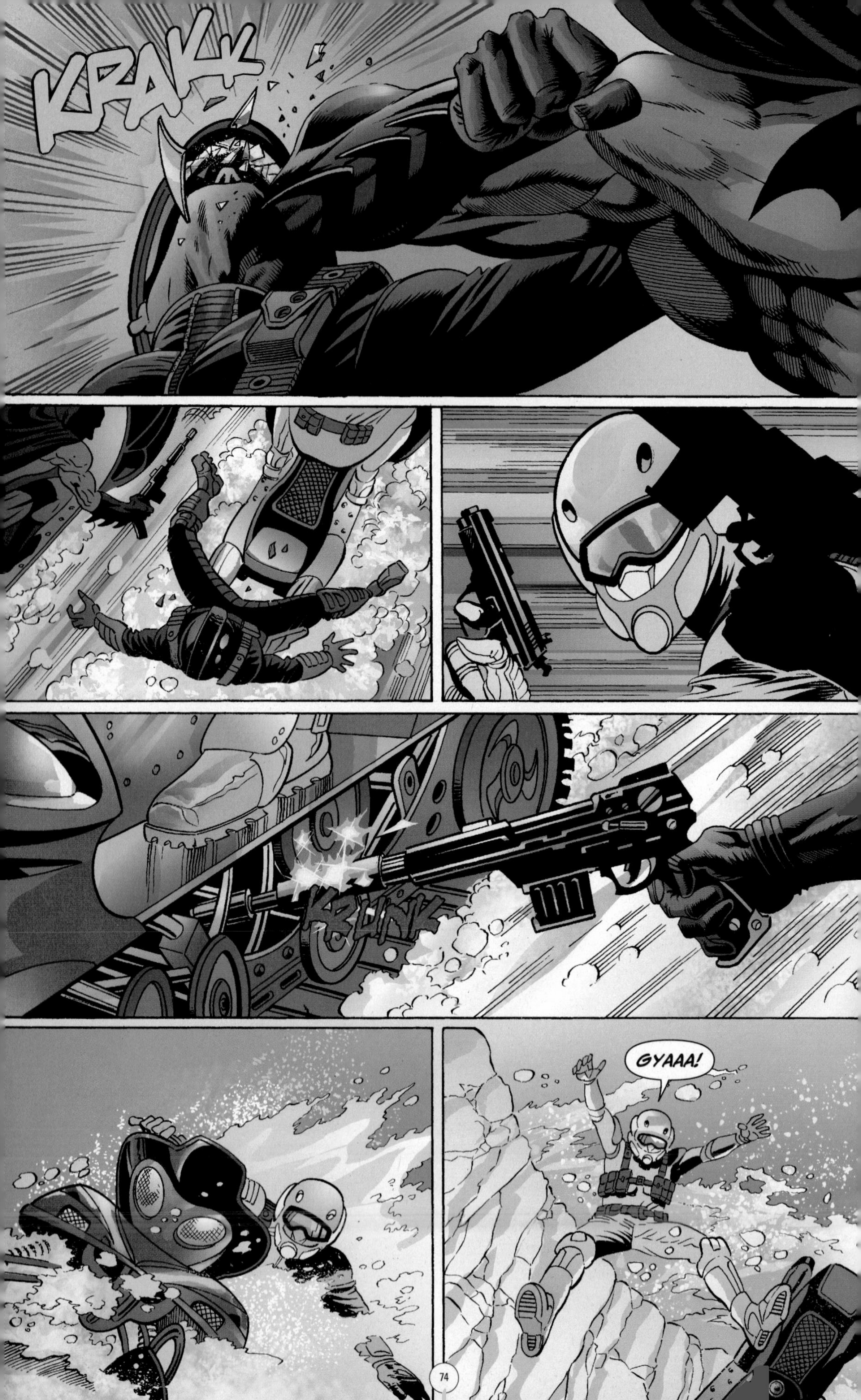
KRAKK
KBLINK
GYAAA!

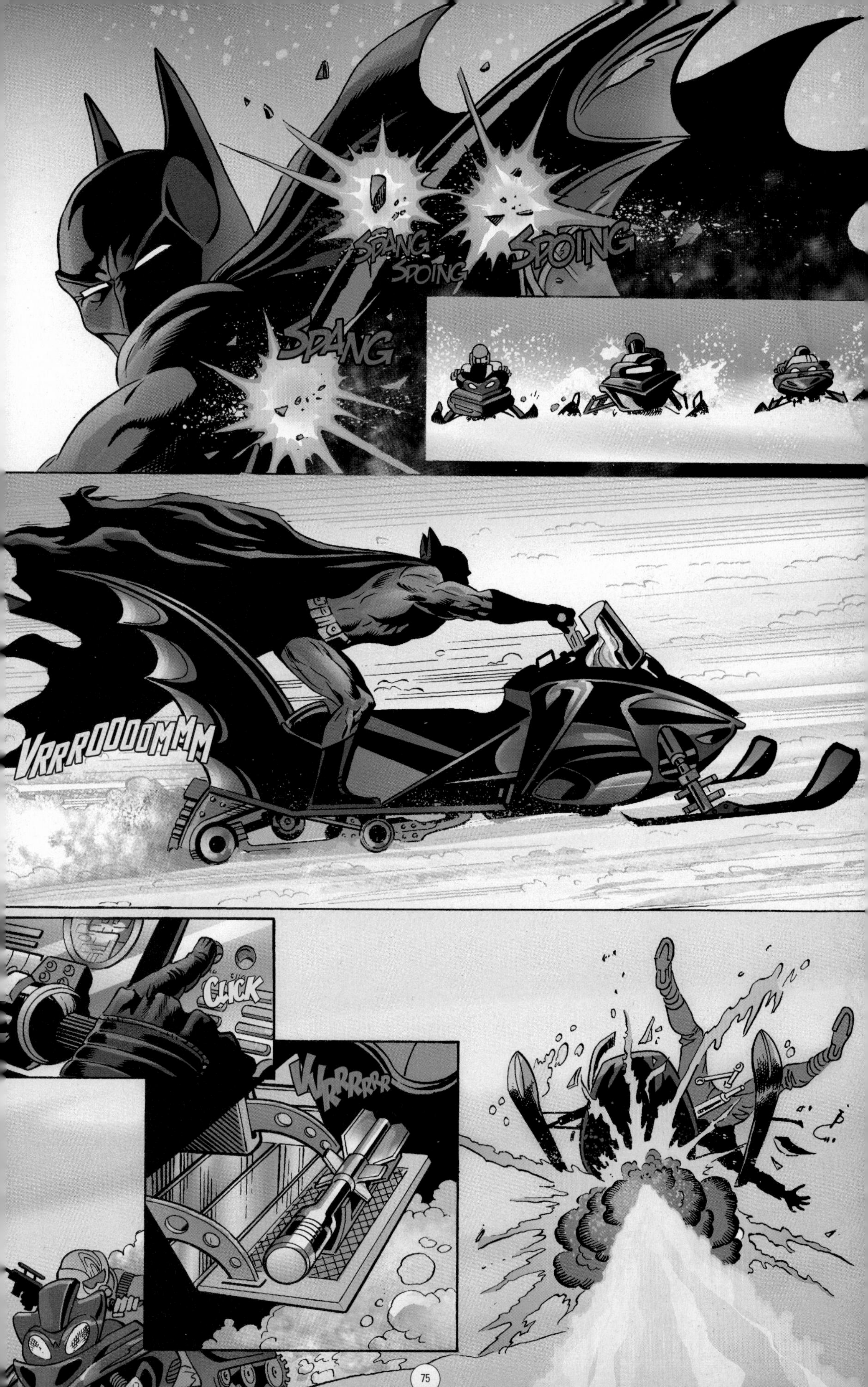
SPANG
SPOING
SPOING
SPANG
VRRROOOOMMM
CLICK
WRRRRRR

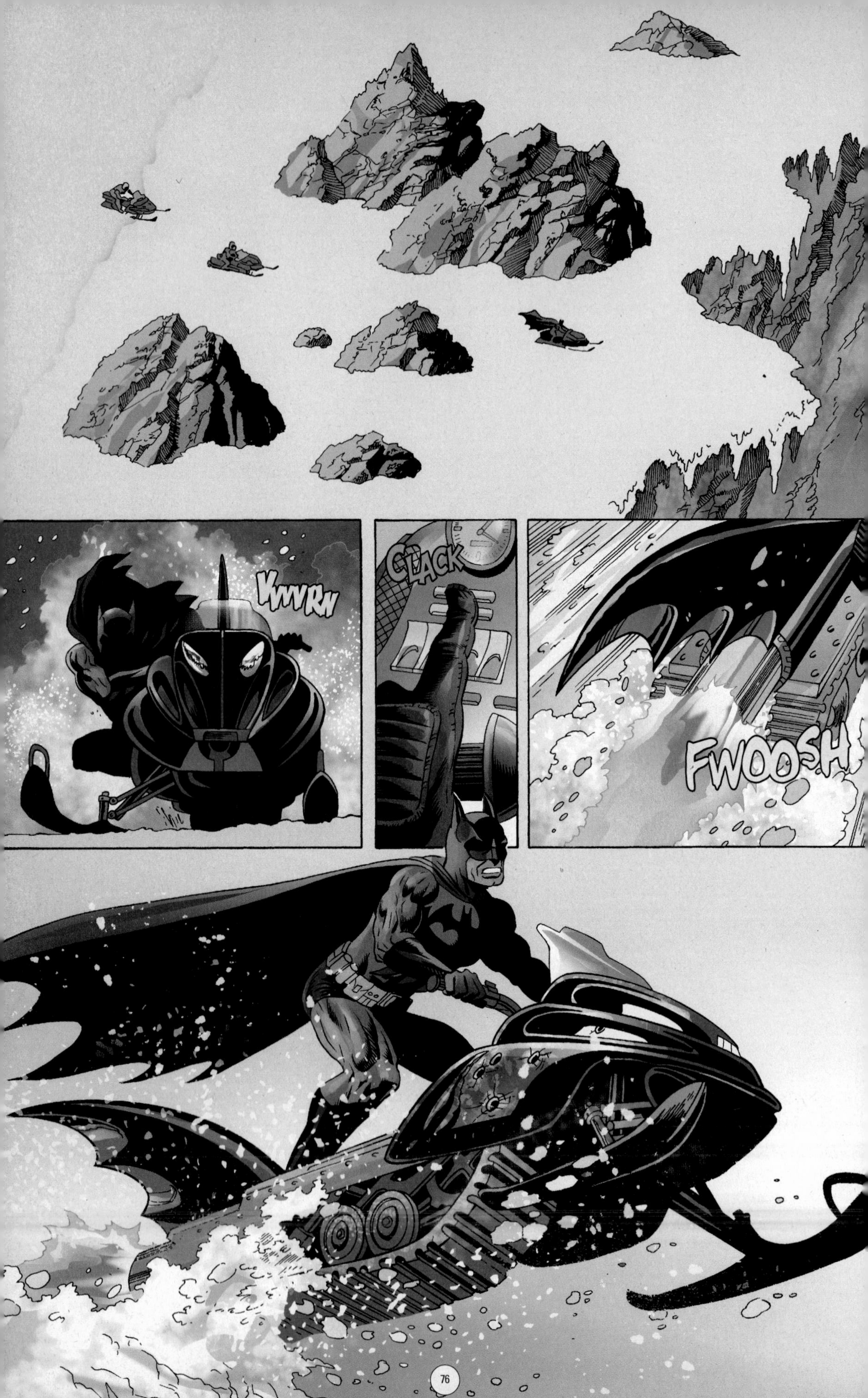
VVVVRN
CLACK
FWOOSH

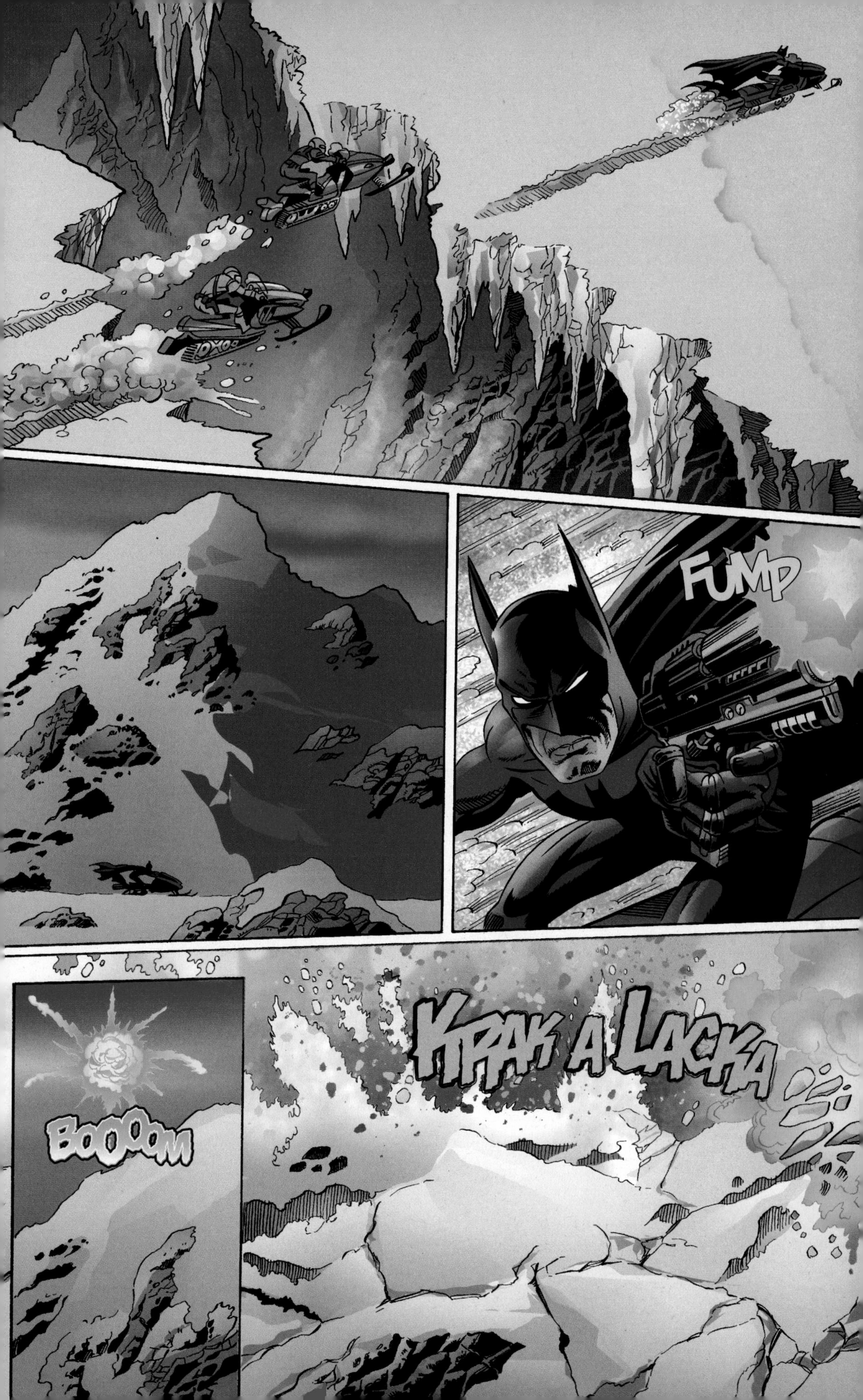
FUMP
BOOOOM
KRAK A LACKA

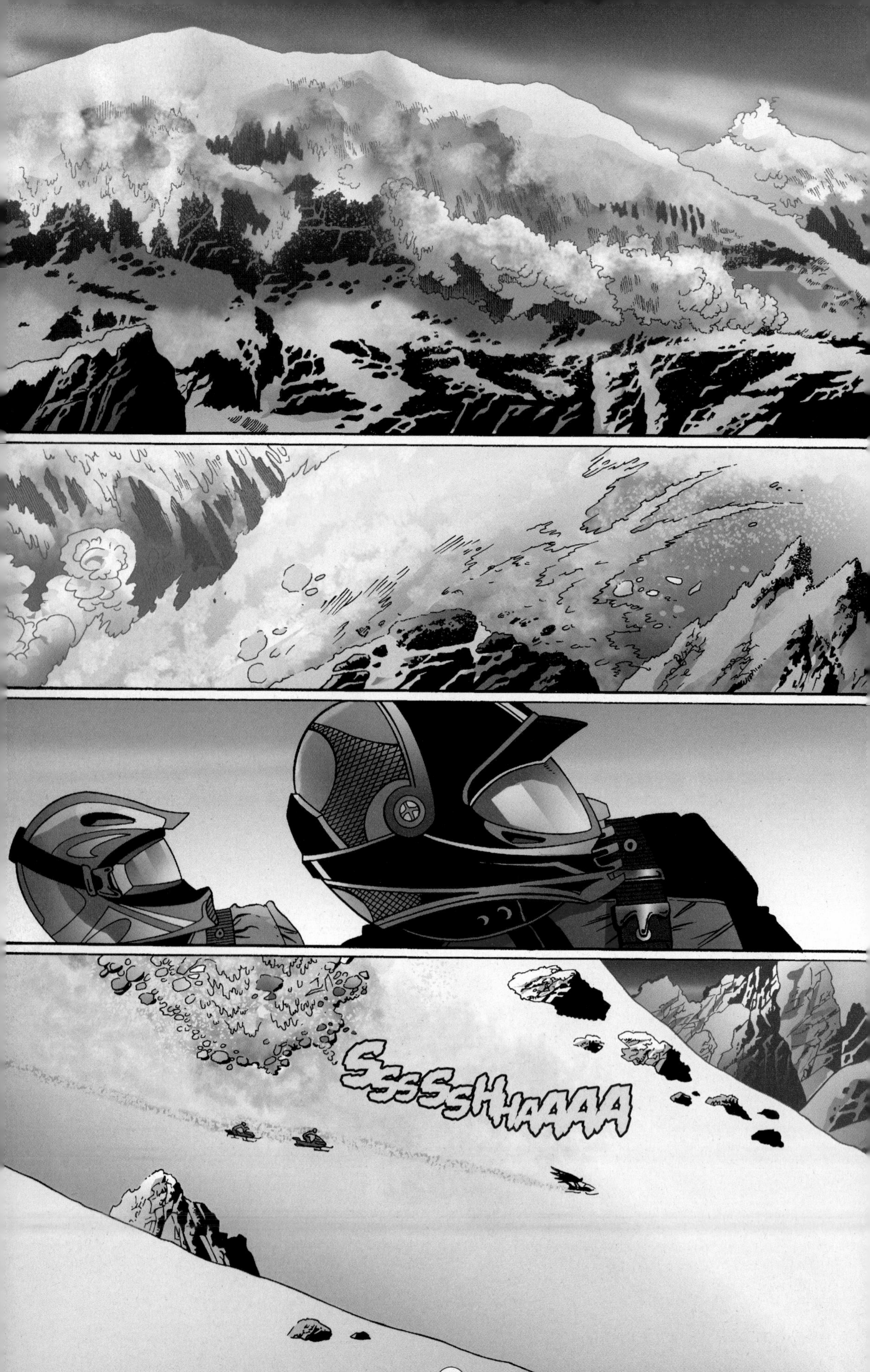
SsssSsHAAAAA

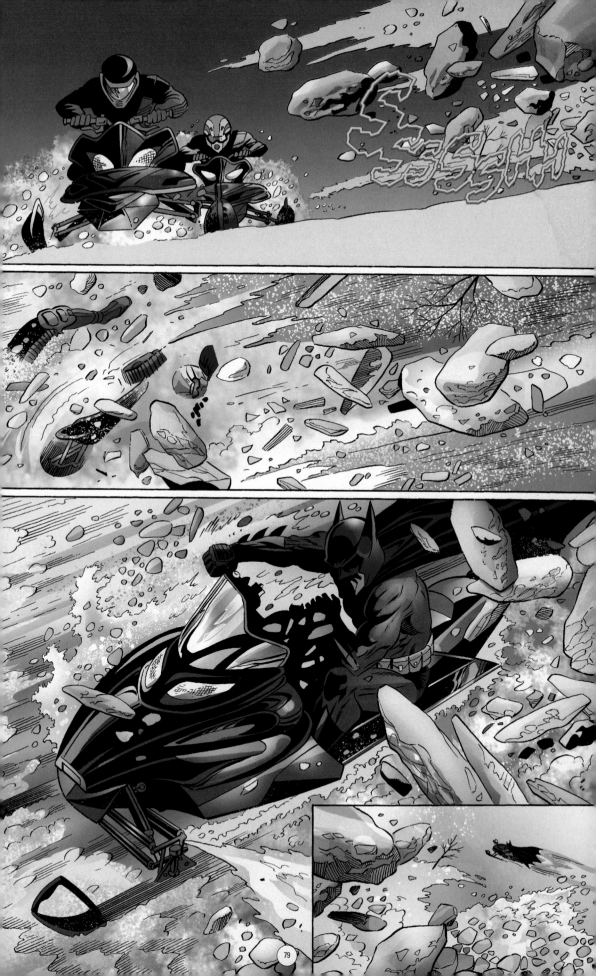

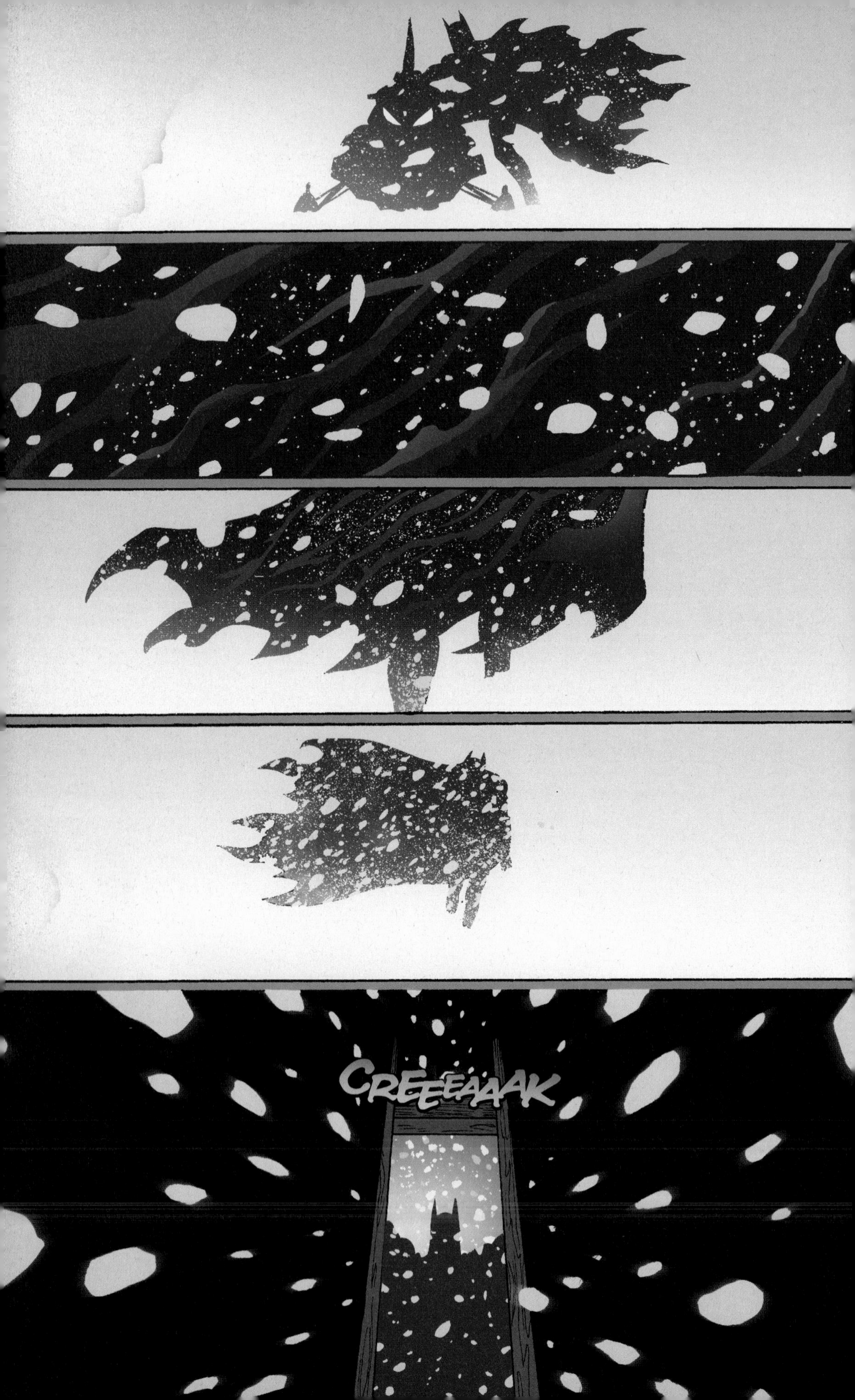
CREEEAAAK

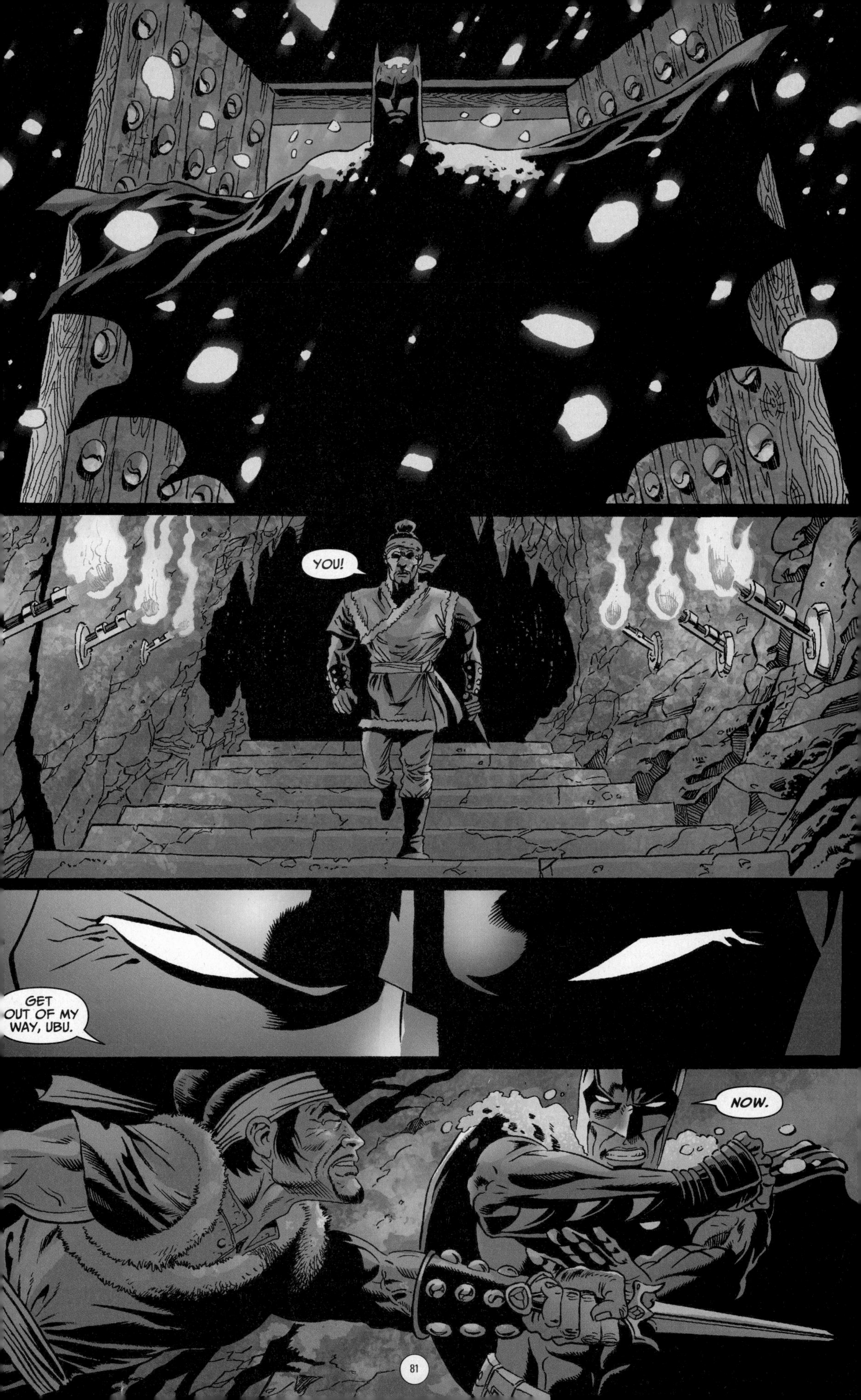
YOU!
GET OUT OF MY WAY, UBU.
NOW.

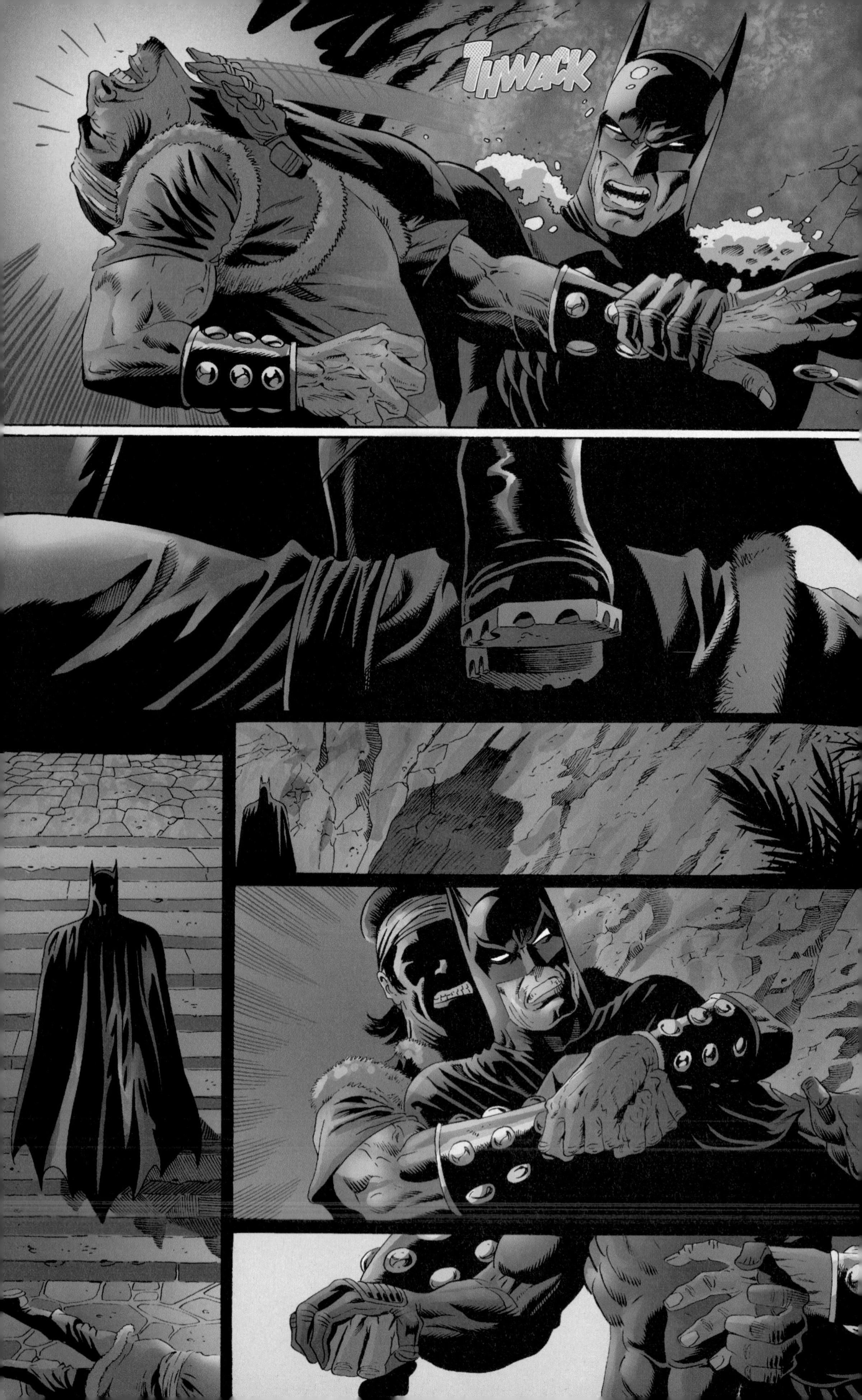
THWACK

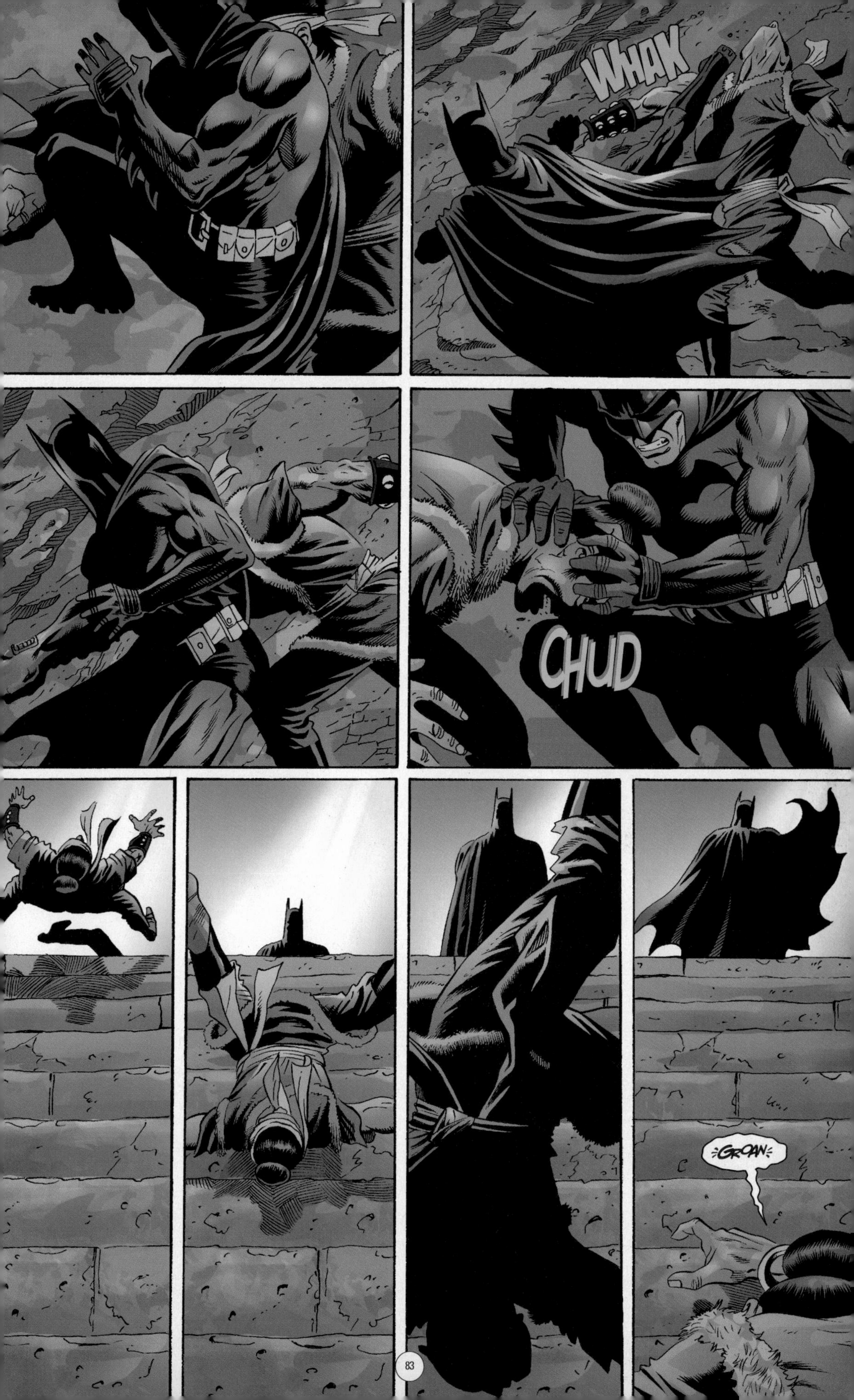
WHAK
CHUD
GROAN

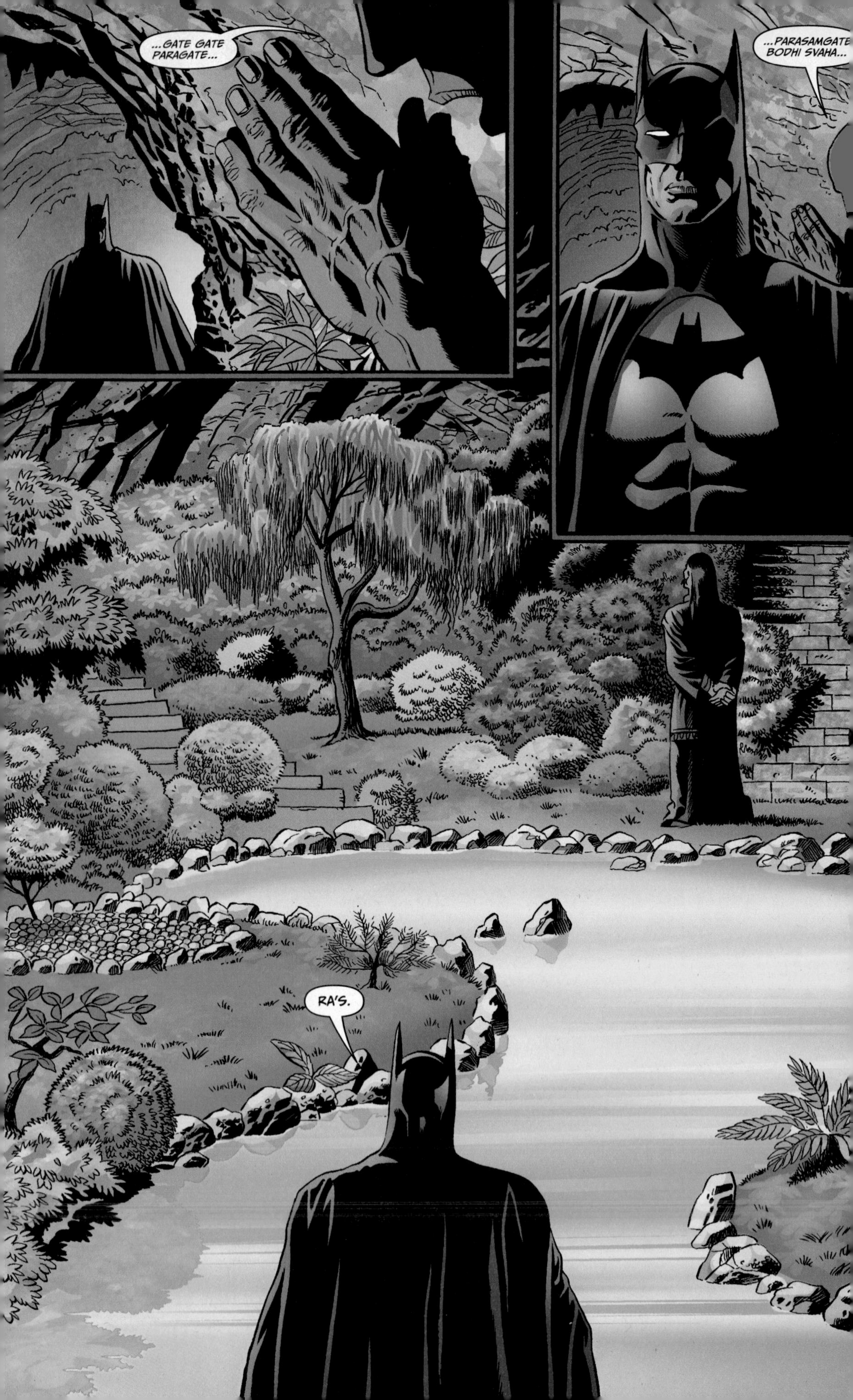
...GATE GATE PARAGATE...
...PARASAMGATE BODHI SVAHA...
RA'S.

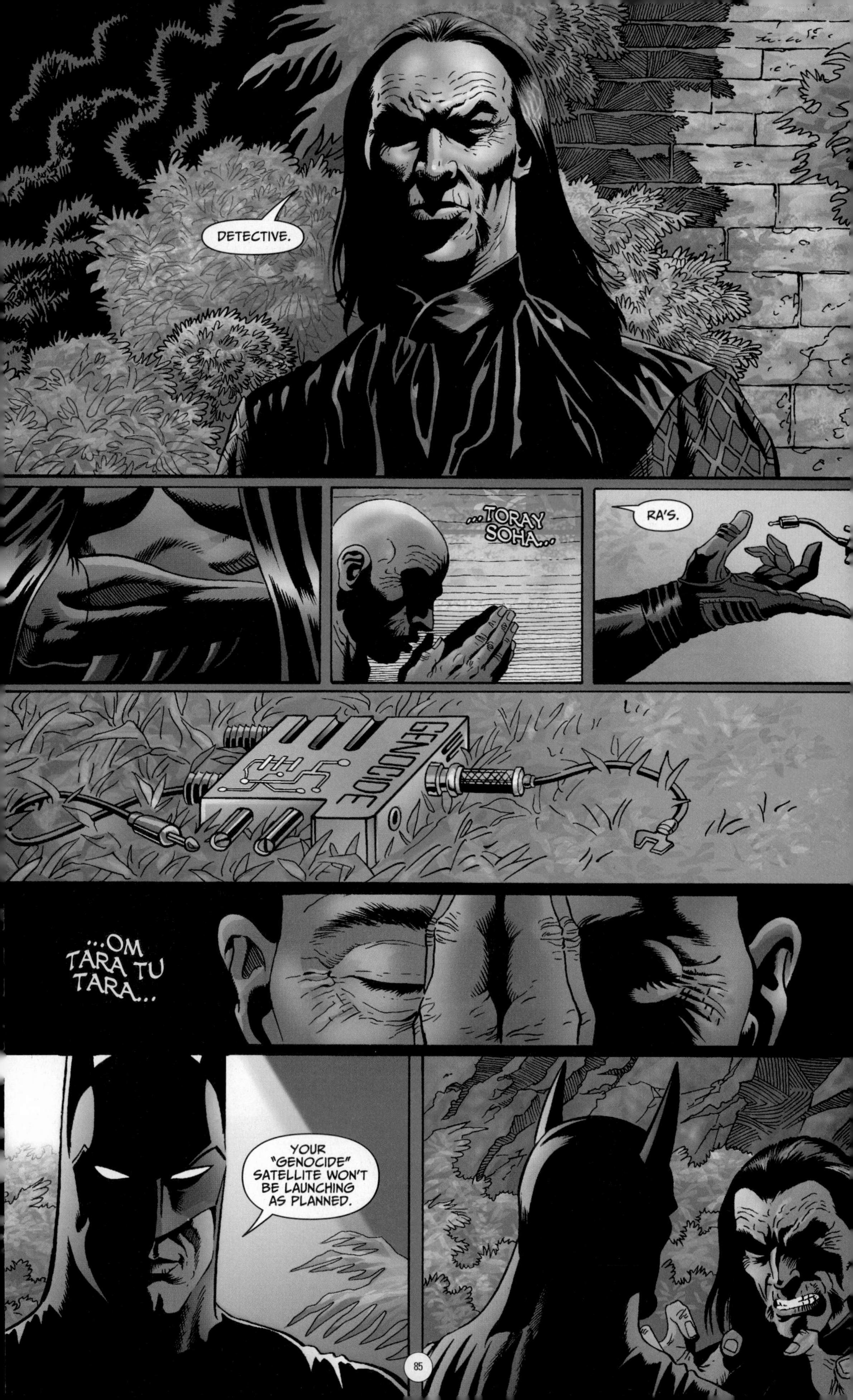
DETECTIVE.
...TORAY SOHA...
RA'S.
GENOCIDE
...OM TARA TU TARA...
YOUR "GENOCIDE" SATELLITE WON'T BE LAUNCHING AS PLANNED.

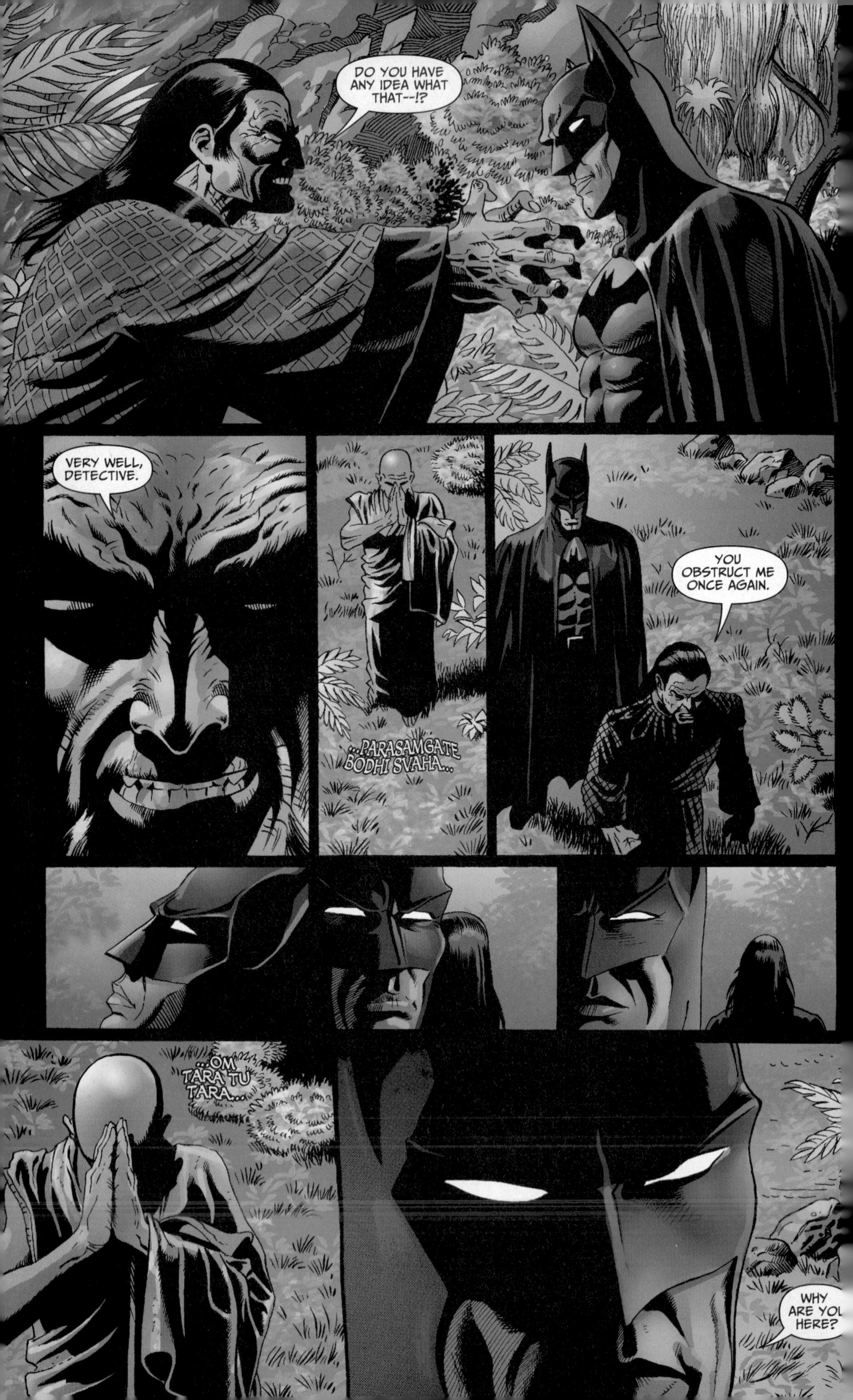
DO YOU HAVE ANY IDEA WHAT THAT--!?
VERY WELL, DETECTIVE.
...PARASAMGATE BODHI SVAHA...
YOU OBSTRUCT ME ONCE AGAIN.
...OM TARA TU TARA...
WHY ARE YOU HERE?

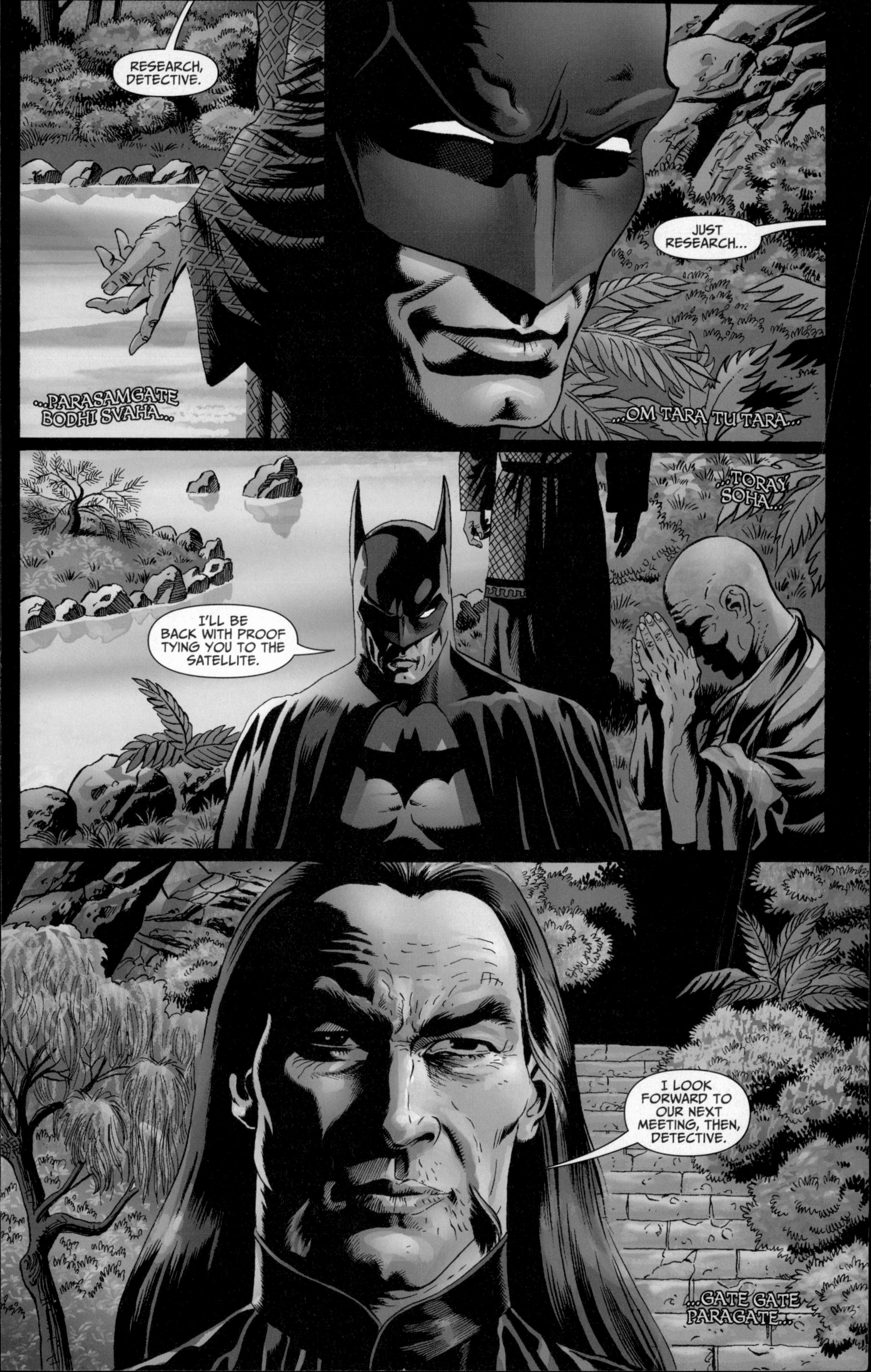
RESEARCH, DETECTIVE.
JUST RESEARCH...
...PARASAMGATE BODHI SVAHA...
...OM TARA TU TARA...
...TORAY SOHA...
I'LL BE BACK WITH PROOF TYING YOU TO THE SATELLITE.
I LOOK FORWARD TO OUR NEXT MEETING, THEN, DETECTIVE.
...GATE GATE PARAGATE...

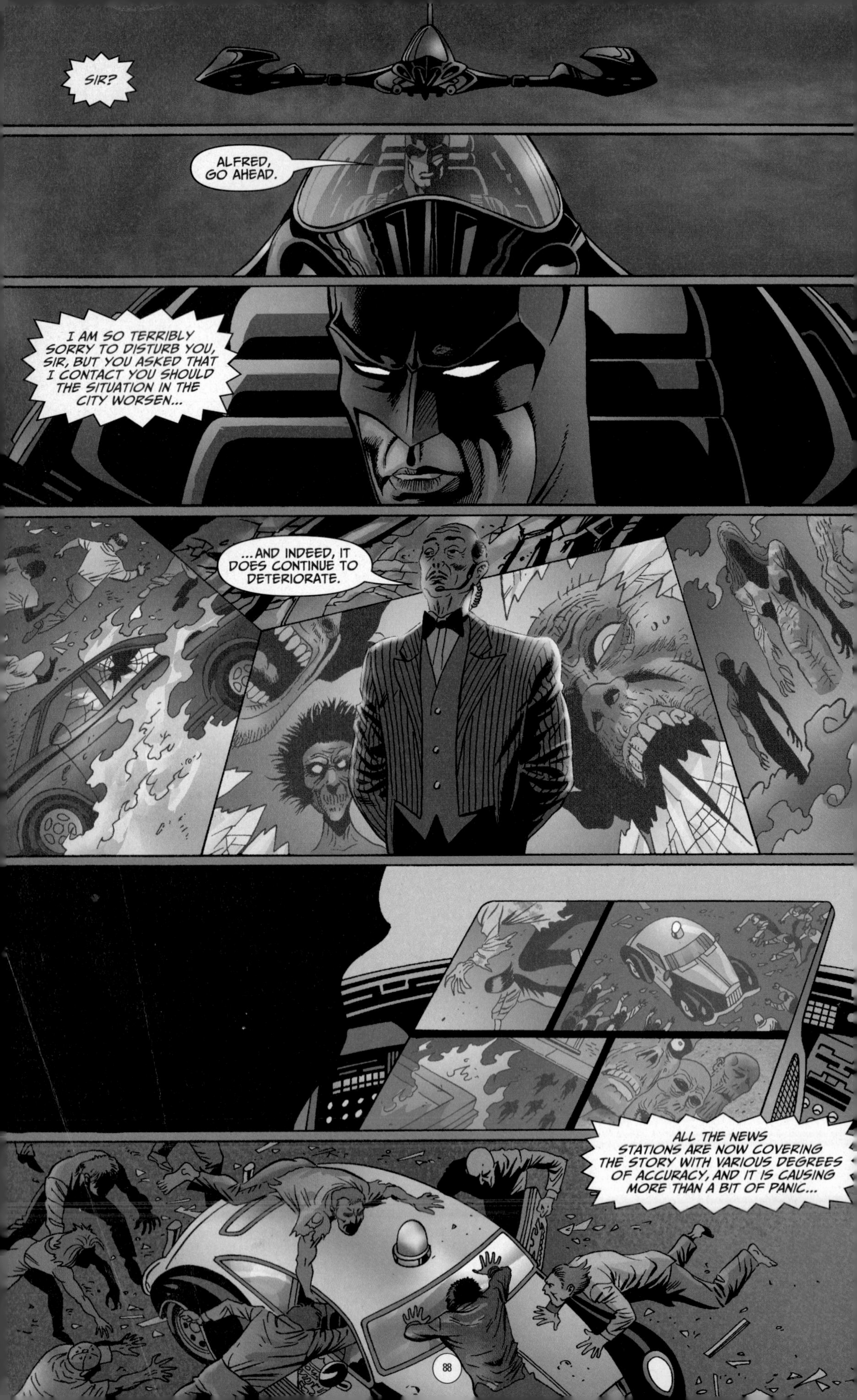
SIR?
ALFRED, GO AHEAD.
I AM SO TERRIBLY SORRY TO DISTURB YOU, SIR, BUT YOU ASKED THAT I CONTACT YOU SHOULD THE SITUATION IN THE CITY WORSEN...
...AND INDEED, IT DOES CONTINUE TO DETERIORATE.
ALL THE NEWS STATIONS ARE NOW COVERING THE STORY WITH VARIOUS DEGREES OF ACCURACY, AND IT IS CAUSING MORE THAN A BIT OF PANIC...

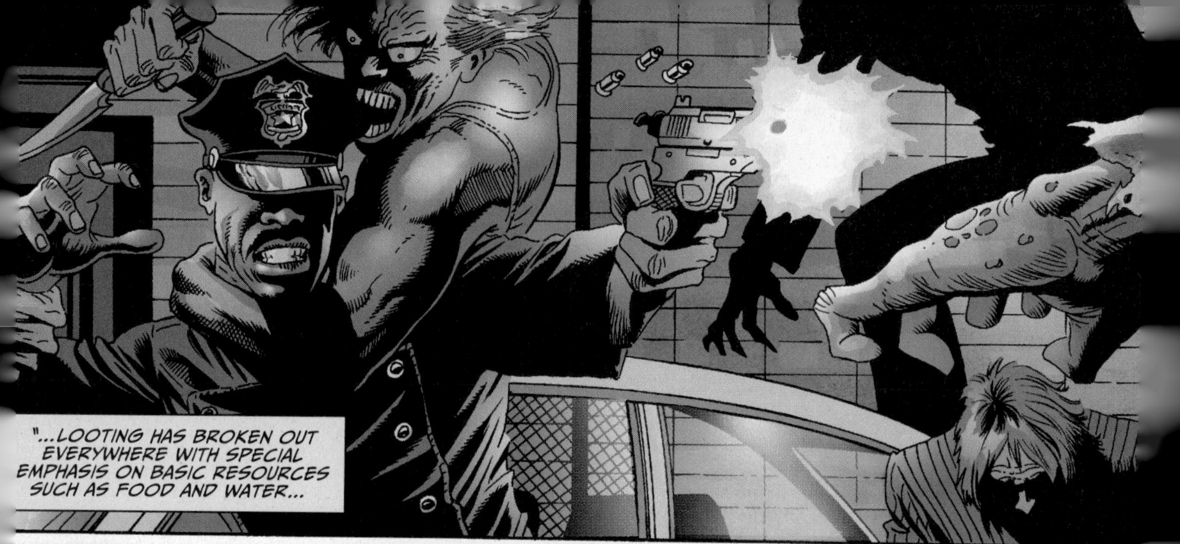
"...LOOTING HAS BROKEN OUT EVERYWHERE WITH SPECIAL EMPHASIS ON BASIC RESOURCES SUCH AS FOOD AND WATER...

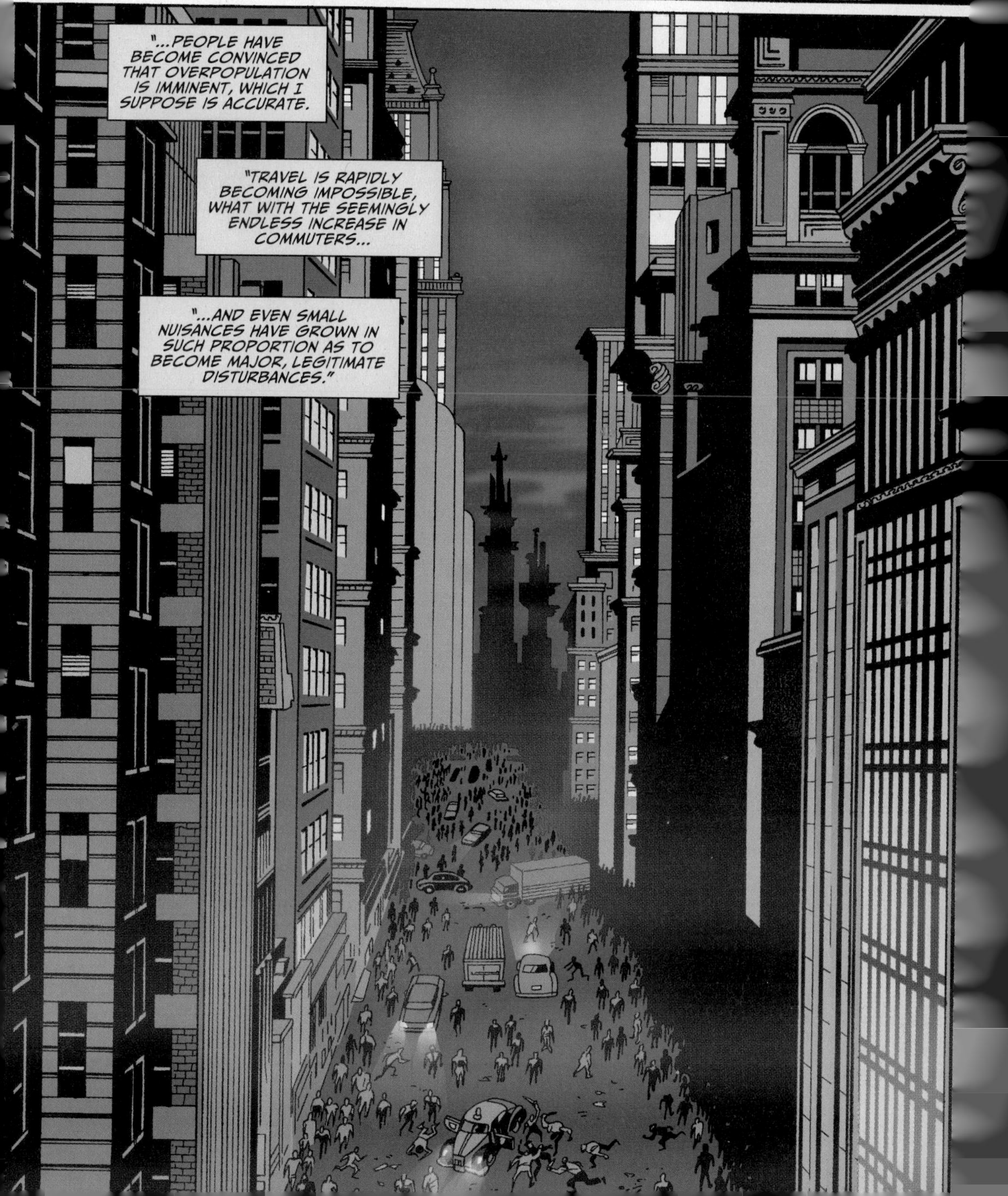
"...PEOPLE HAVE BECOME CONVINCED THAT OVERPOPULATION IS IMMINENT, WHICH I SUPPOSE IS ACCURATE.
"TRAVEL IS RAPIDLY BECOMING IMPOSSIBLE, WHAT WITH THE SEEMINGLY ENDLESS INCREASE IN COMMUTERS...
"...AND EVEN SMALL NUISANCES HAVE GROWN IN SUCH PROPORTION AS TO BECOME MAJOR, LEGITIMATE DISTURBANCES."

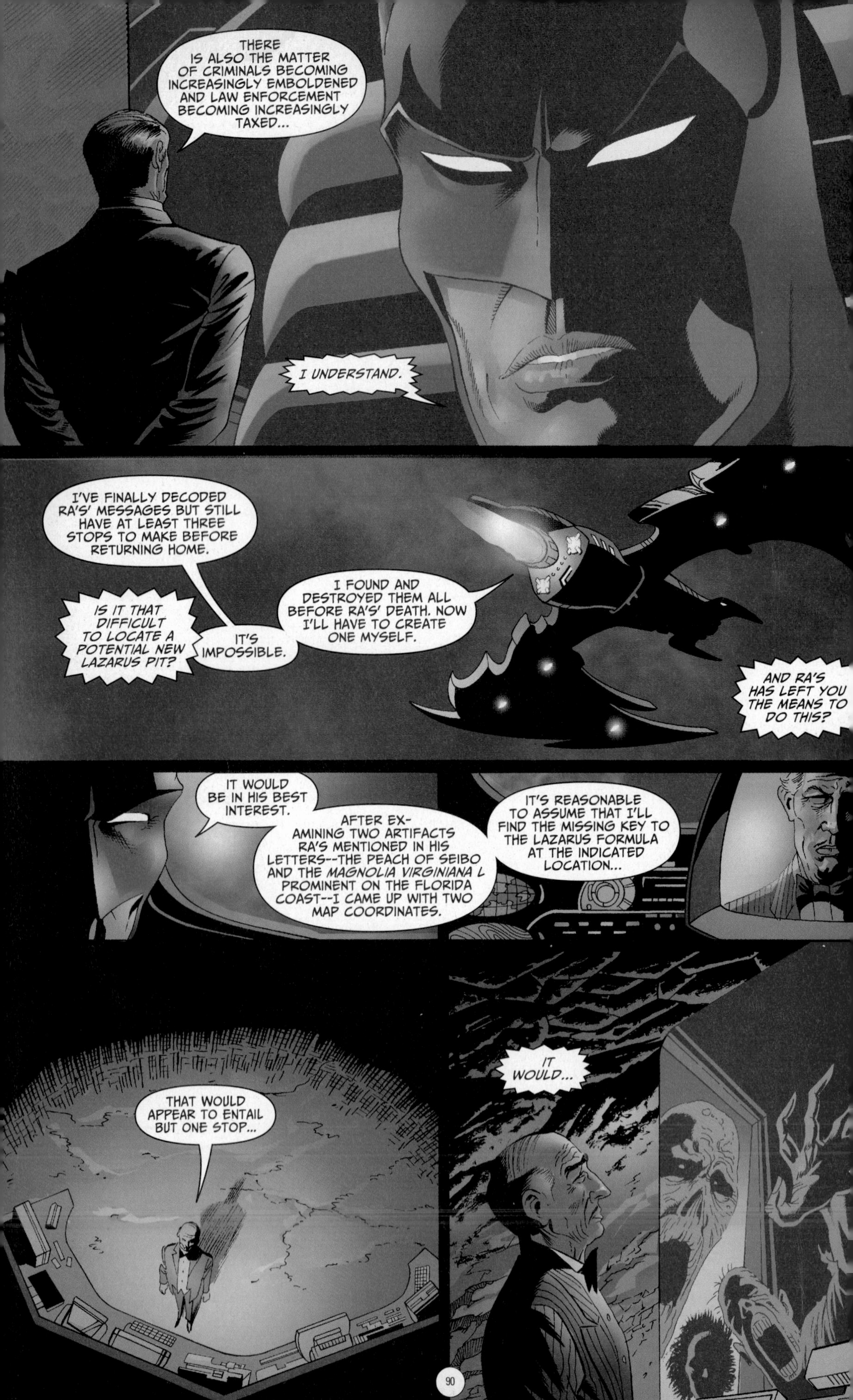
THERE IS ALSO THE MATTER OF CRIMINALS BECOMING INCREASINGLY EMBOLDENED AND LAW ENFORCEMENT BECOMING INCREASINGLY TAXED...
I UNDERSTAND.
I'VE FINALLY DECODED RA'S' MESSAGES BUT STILL HAVE AT LEAST THREE STOPS TO MAKE BEFORE RETURNING HOME.
IS IT THAT DIFFICULT TO LOCATE A POTENTIAL NEW LAZARUS PIT?
IT'S IMPOSSIBLE.
I FOUND AND DESTROYED THEM ALL BEFORE RA'S' DEATH. NOW I'LL HAVE TO CREATE ONE MYSELF.
AND RA'S HAS LEFT YOU THE MEANS TO DO THIS?
IT WOULD BE IN HIS BEST INTEREST.
AFTER EX-AMINING TWO ARTIFACTS RA'S MENTIONED IN HIS LETTERS--THE PEACH OF SEIBO AND THE MAGNOLIA VIRGINIANA L PROMINENT ON THE FLORIDA COAST--I CAME UP WITH TWO MAP COORDINATES.
IT'S REASONABLE TO ASSUME THAT I'LL FIND THE MISSING KEY TO THE LAZARUS FORMULA AT THE INDICATED LOCATION...
THAT WOULD APPEAR TO ENTAIL BUT ONE STOP...
IT WOULD...

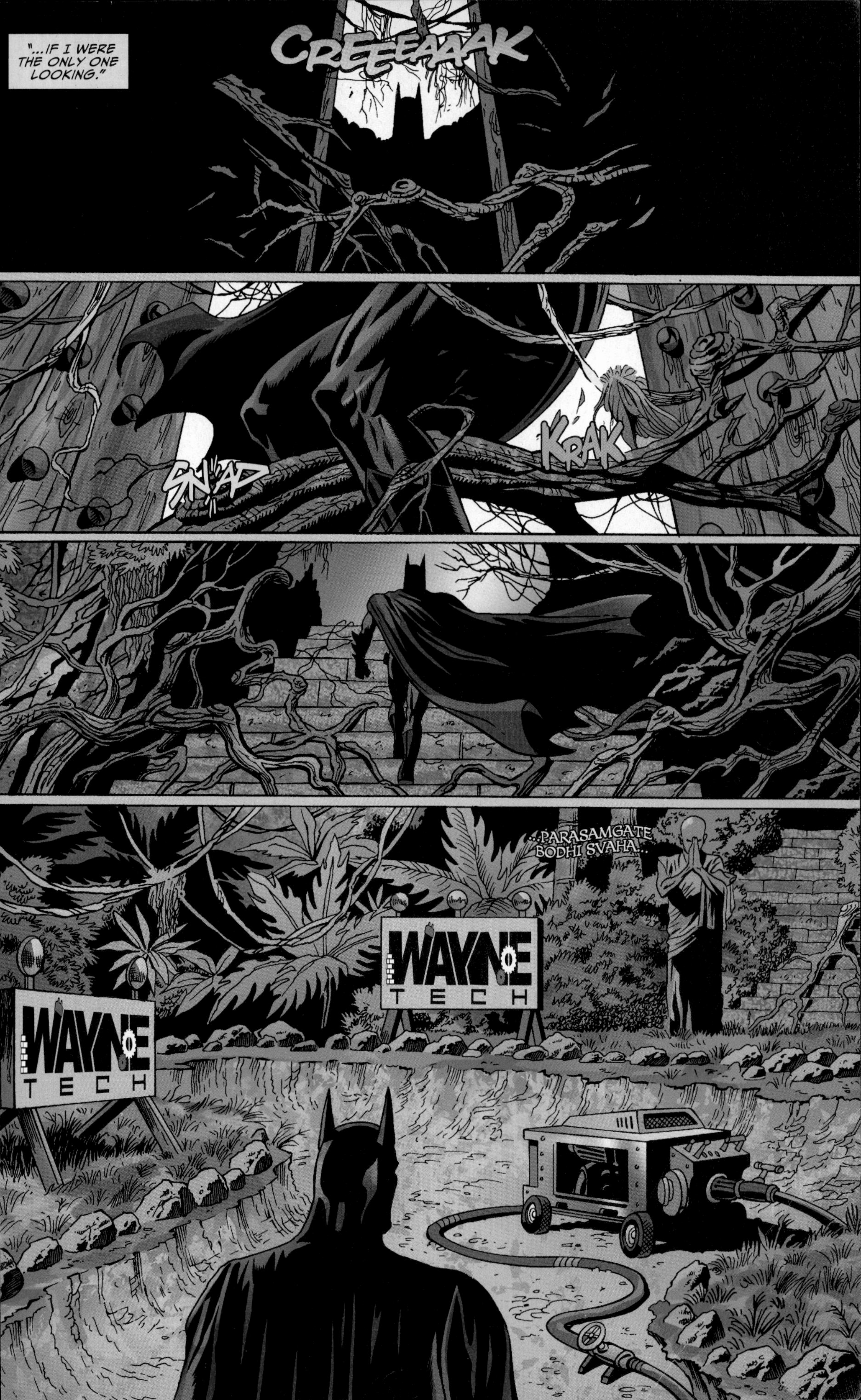

"...IF I WERE THE ONLY ONE LOOKING."
CREEEAAAK
SNAP
KRAK
...PARASAMGATE BODHI SVAHA...
WAYNE TECH
WAYNE TECH

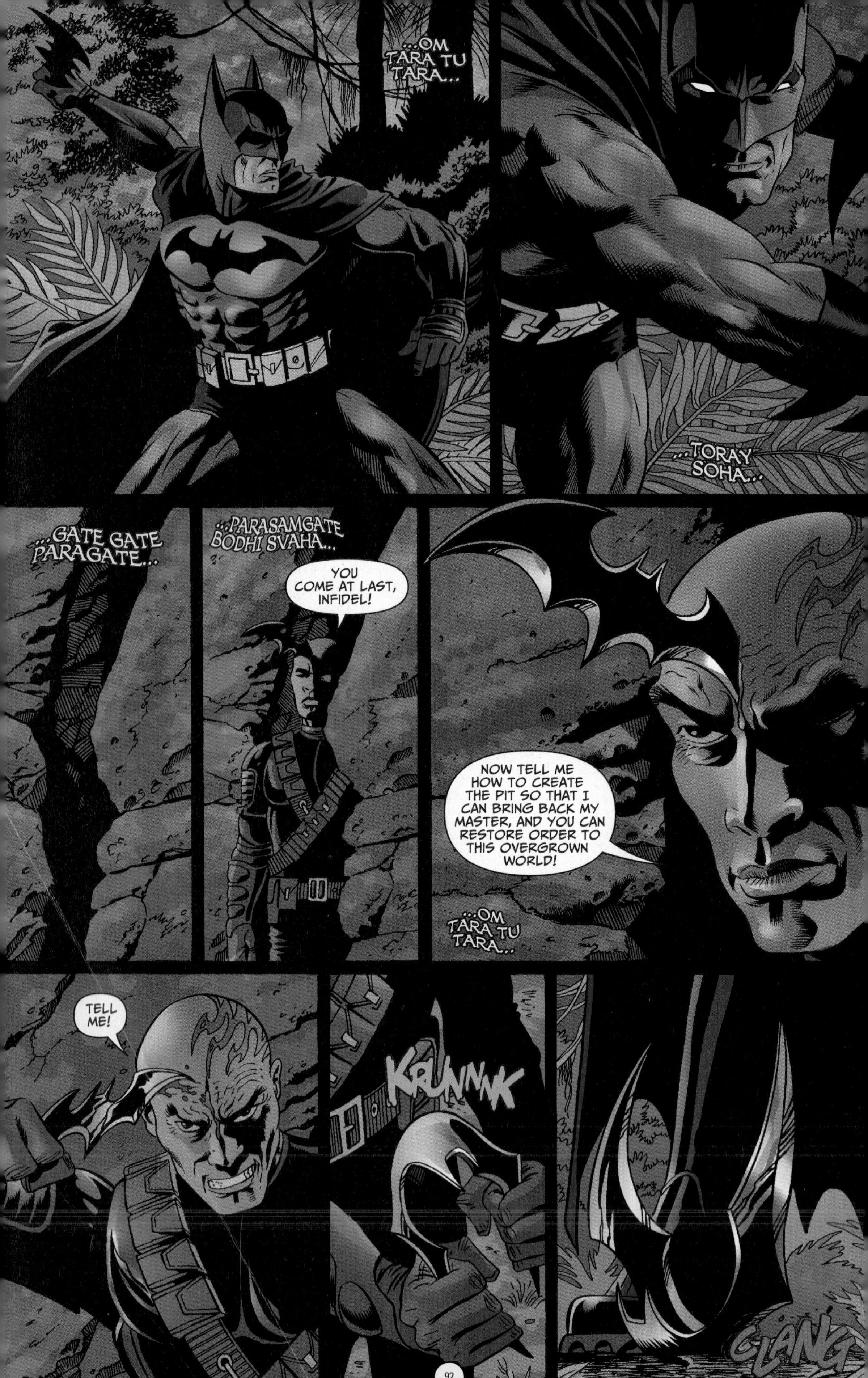
...OM TARA TU TARA...
...TORAY SOHA...
...GATE GATE PARAGATE...
...PARASAMGATE BODHI SVAHA...
YOU COME AT LAST, INFIDEL!
NOW TELL ME HOW TO CREATE THE PIT SO THAT I CAN BRING BACK MY MASTER, AND YOU CAN RESTORE ORDER TO THIS OVERGROWN WORLD!
...OM TARA TU TARA...
TELL ME!
KRUNNNK
CLANG

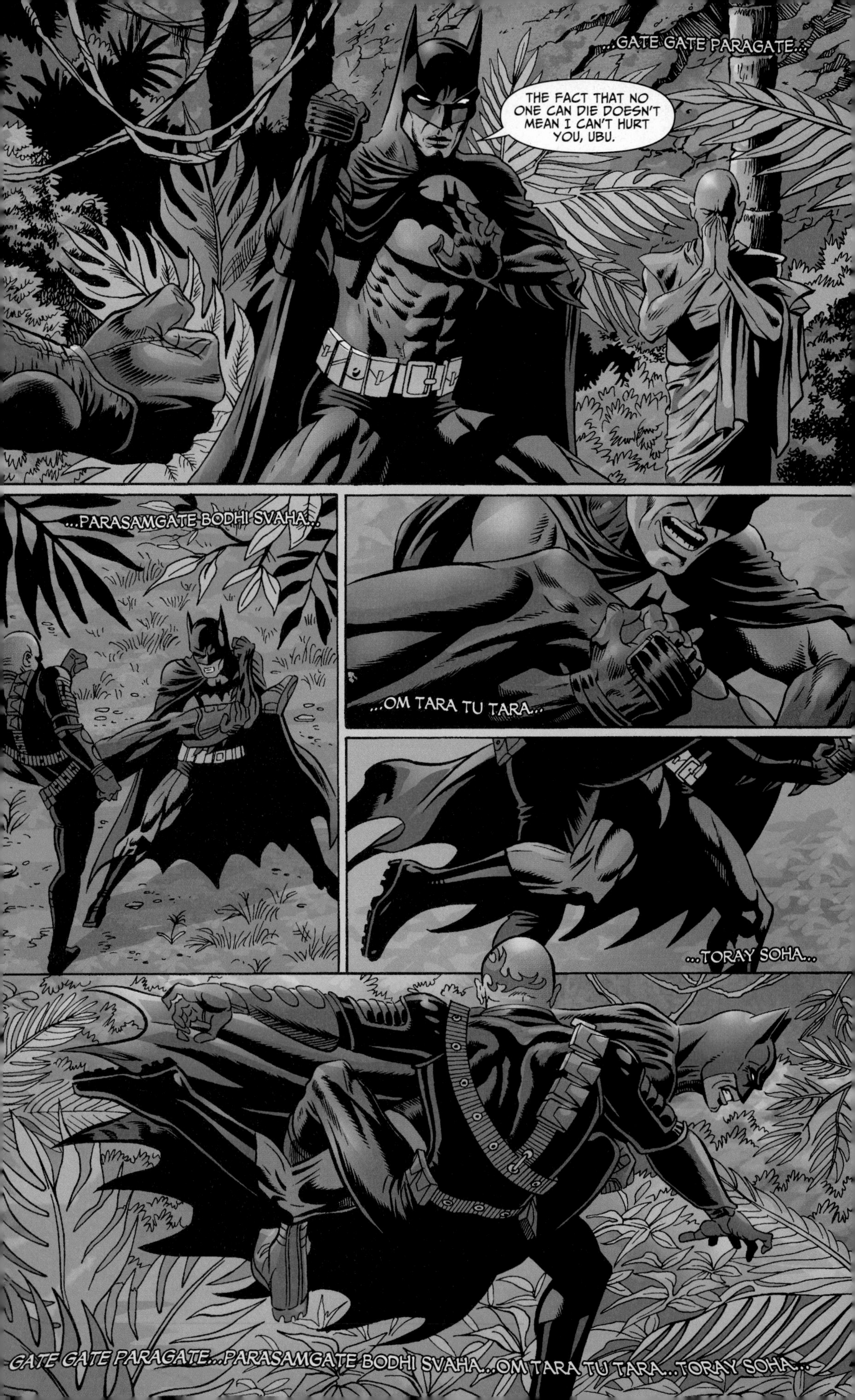
...GATE GATE PARAGATE...
THE FACT THAT NO ONE CAN DIE DOESN'T MEAN I CAN'T HURT YOU, UBU.
...PARASAMGATE BODHI SVAHA...
...OM TARA TU TARA...
...TORAY SOHA...
GATE GATE PARAGATE...PARASAMGATE BODHI SVAHA...OM TARA TU TARA...TORAY SOHA...

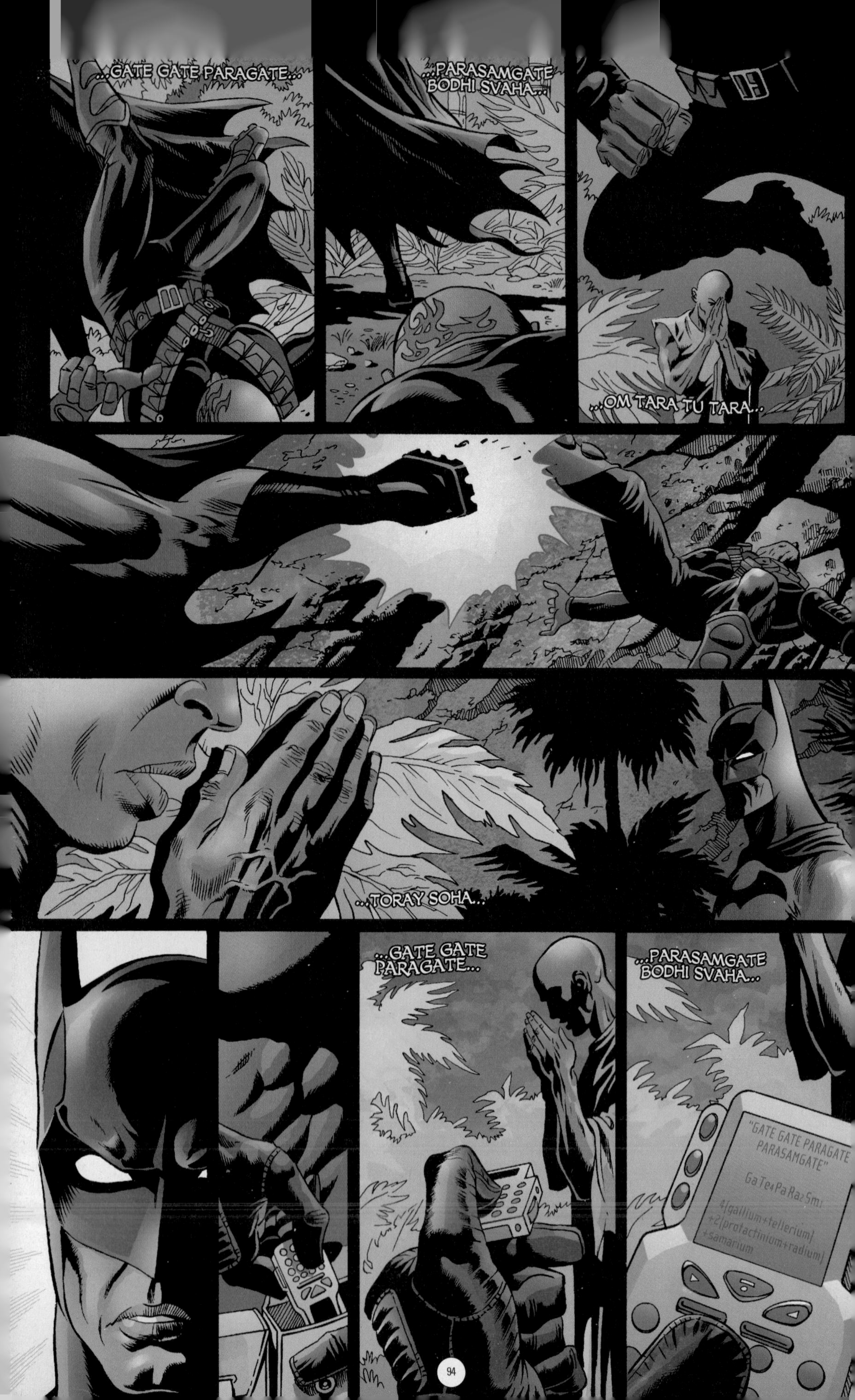

...GATE GATE PARAGATE...
...PARASAMGATE BODHI SVAHA...
...OM TARA TU TARA...
...TORAY SOHA...
...GATE GATE PARAGATE...
...PARASAMGATE BODHI SVAHA...
"GATE GATE PARAGATE PARASAMGATE"
Ga Te4 Pa Ra2 Sm:
4(gallium+tellerium)
+2(protactinium+radium)
+samarium

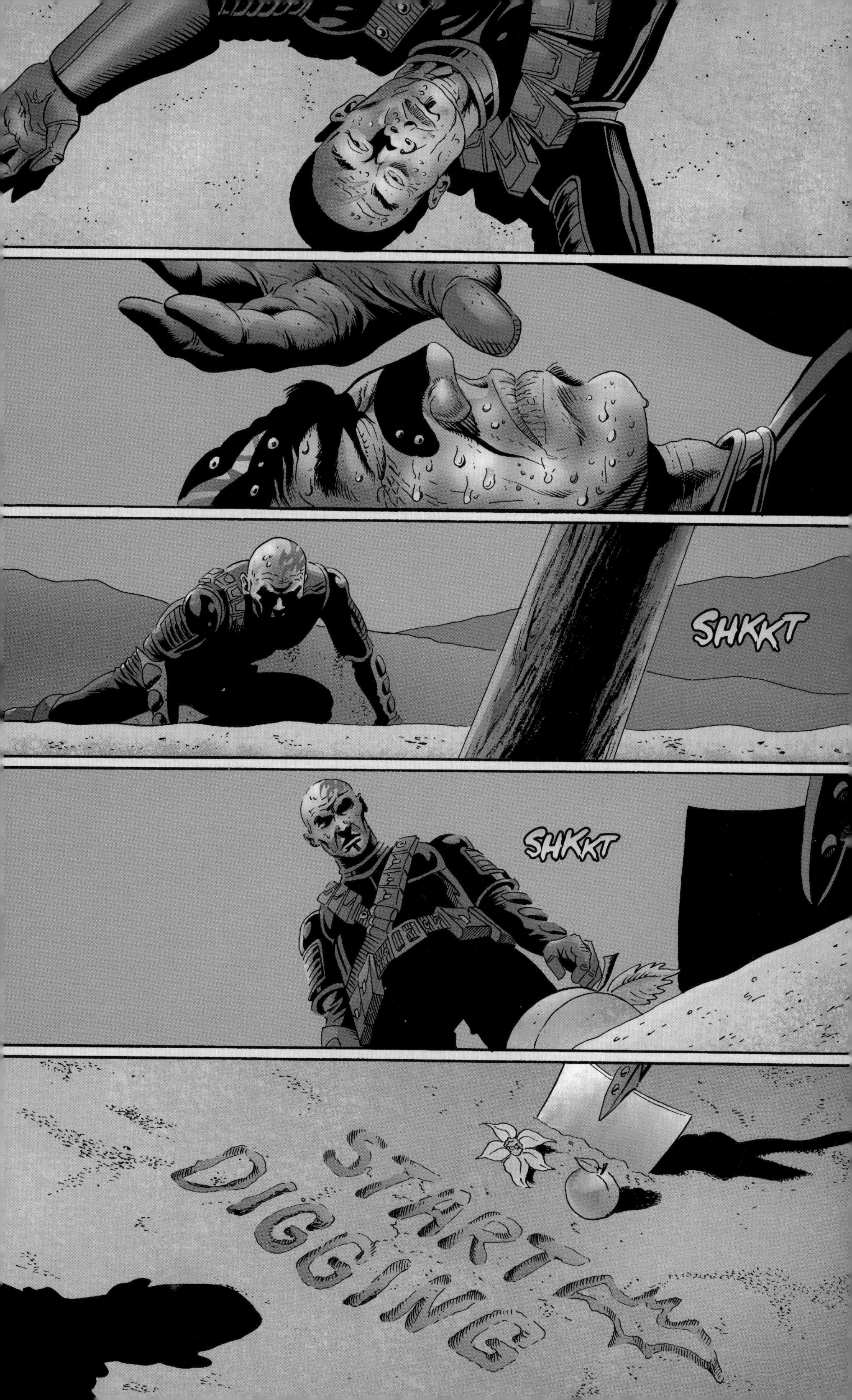
SHKKT
SHKKT
START DIGGING

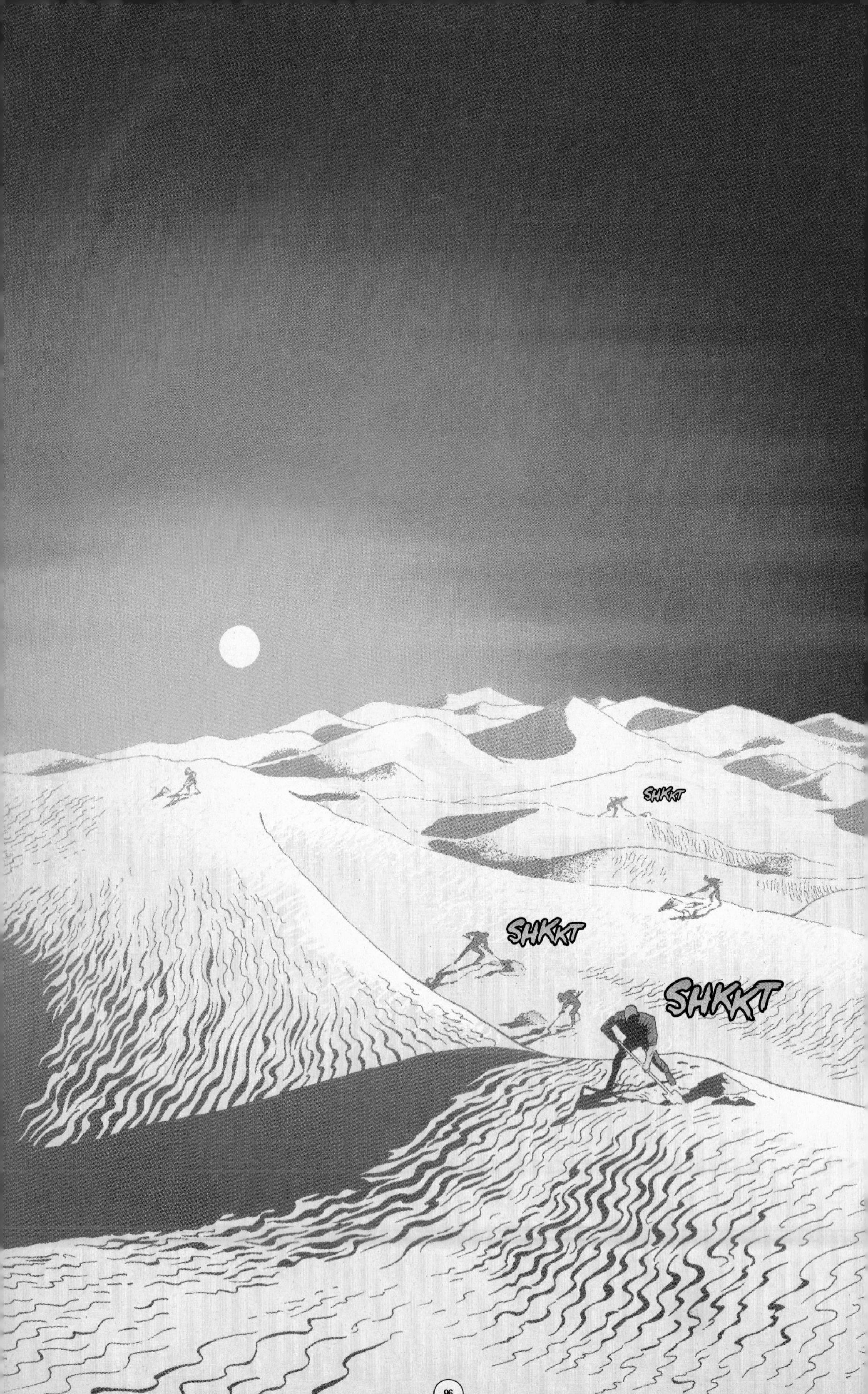
SHKKT
SHKKT
SHKKT

Gotham Gazette

★★★ ★★★

R.I.P. GOTHAM
CITY'S CORPSES FIND PEACE ONCE AGAIN

by Maureen Michaels

An inexplicable medical crisis came to an end early today with the re-interment of hundreds of recently buried Gotham citizens and a dramatic increase in reported hospital mortality rates. "It really was like death took a holiday," says Dr. William Prince, head of the Gotham General Intensive Care Unit. "Our job here is to save lives whenever possible, but something happened that really threw off the entire balance of existence. I'm sorry for the families who are now losing loved ones after frankly miraculous recoveries, but I'm relieved to see more recognizable fatality patterns reestablishing themselves in the I.C.U."

"We were just over-whelmed," agrees Dr. Femi Opara, medical administrator for the privately-run Saint Mary's medical center in Coventry. "You always want the best for your patients, but we reached a point here where we simply ran out of resources and explanations for what was happening. Even those who were benefiting from it were concerned. What was happening was unnatural." Indeed, speculation concerning possible causes for the sixty-four-hour ban on death and accompanying

temporary reversal of the aging process range from fantastical to conspiratorial, with little in the way of provable hypotheses. "I think Superman must have reversed the planet's spin on its axis," insists Burnley resident Al Evans. "He probably did it to save one particular person, without being aware of the potential side effects."

....continued A6

MICK MORRIGAN, DEAD AGAIN
SURVIVING ELECTRIC CHAIR VICTIM FOUND DEAD IN GROCERY PARKING LOT

By William Baumgarner

Witnesses and officials at Blackgate Prison were stunned last Tuesday when convicted murdered Mick Morrigan not only survived electrocution, but also subsequently broke free of the electric chair and the prison vowing revenge on Gotham City's mysterious Batman, whom Morrigan seemed to blame for his incarceration.

"We've had people survive the initial electrocution once or twice before," admits Blackgate warden Tom Lansky. "But it's usually just a glitch in the machinery that we can fix up pretty fast. With Morrigan, everything was working and we all thought he was dead,

....continued B11

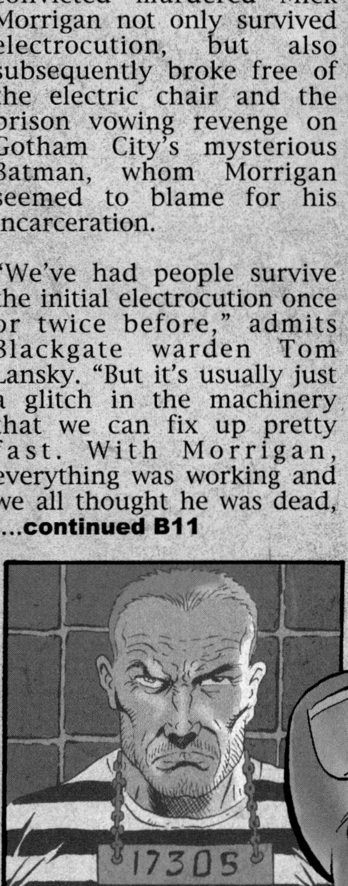

17305

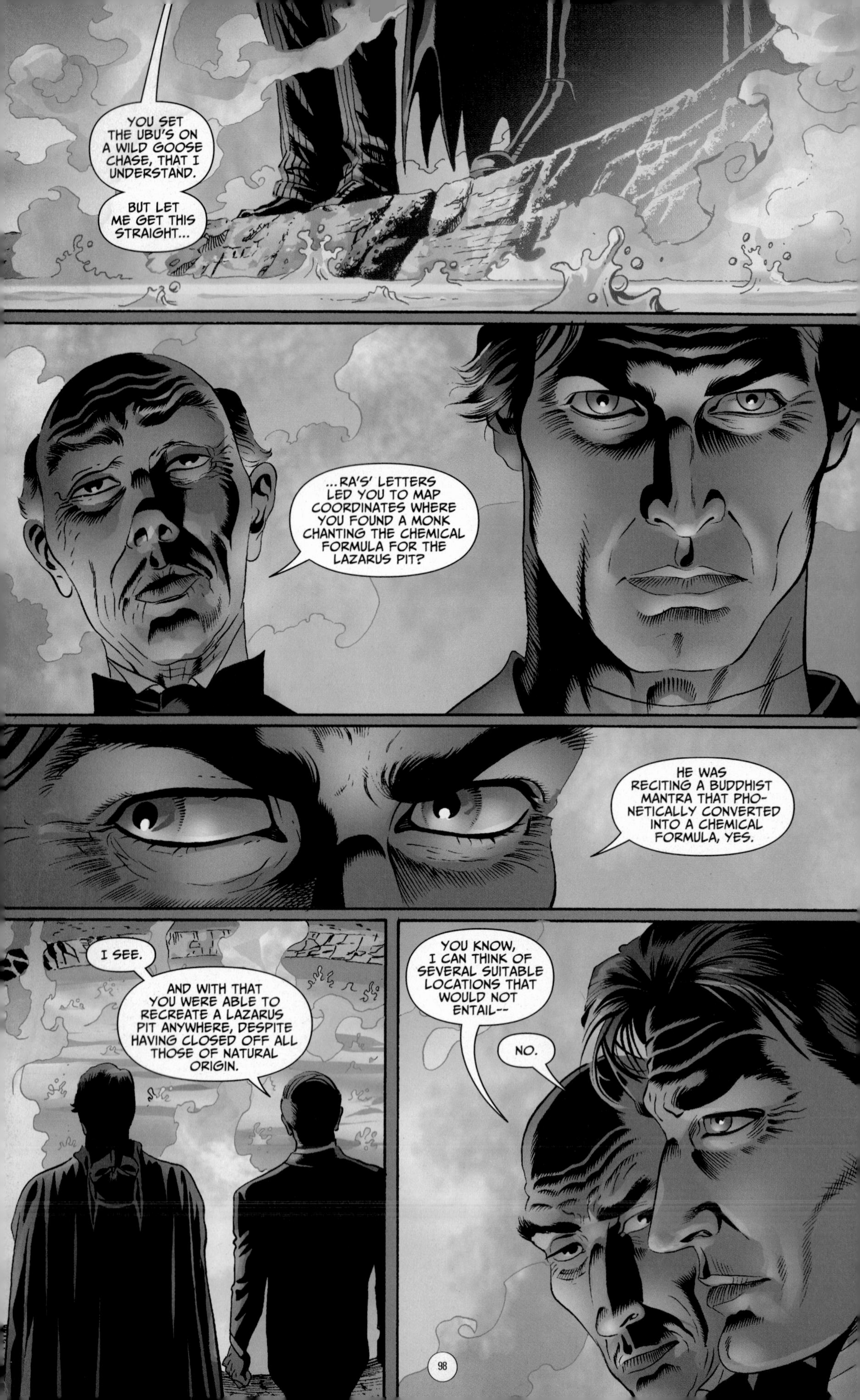

YOU SET THE UBU'S ON A WILD GOOSE CHASE, THAT I UNDERSTAND.
BUT LET ME GET THIS STRAIGHT...
...RA'S' LETTERS LED YOU TO MAP COORDINATES WHERE YOU FOUND A MONK CHANTING THE CHEMICAL FORMULA FOR THE LAZARUS PIT?
HE WAS RECITING A BUDDHIST MANTRA THAT PHO-NETICALLY CONVERTED INTO A CHEMICAL FORMULA, YES.
I SEE.
AND WITH THAT YOU WERE ABLE TO RECREATE A LAZARUS PIT ANYWHERE, DESPITE HAVING CLOSED OFF ALL THOSE OF NATURAL ORIGIN.
YOU KNOW, I CAN THINK OF SEVERAL SUITABLE LOCATIONS THAT WOULD NOT ENTAIL--
NO.

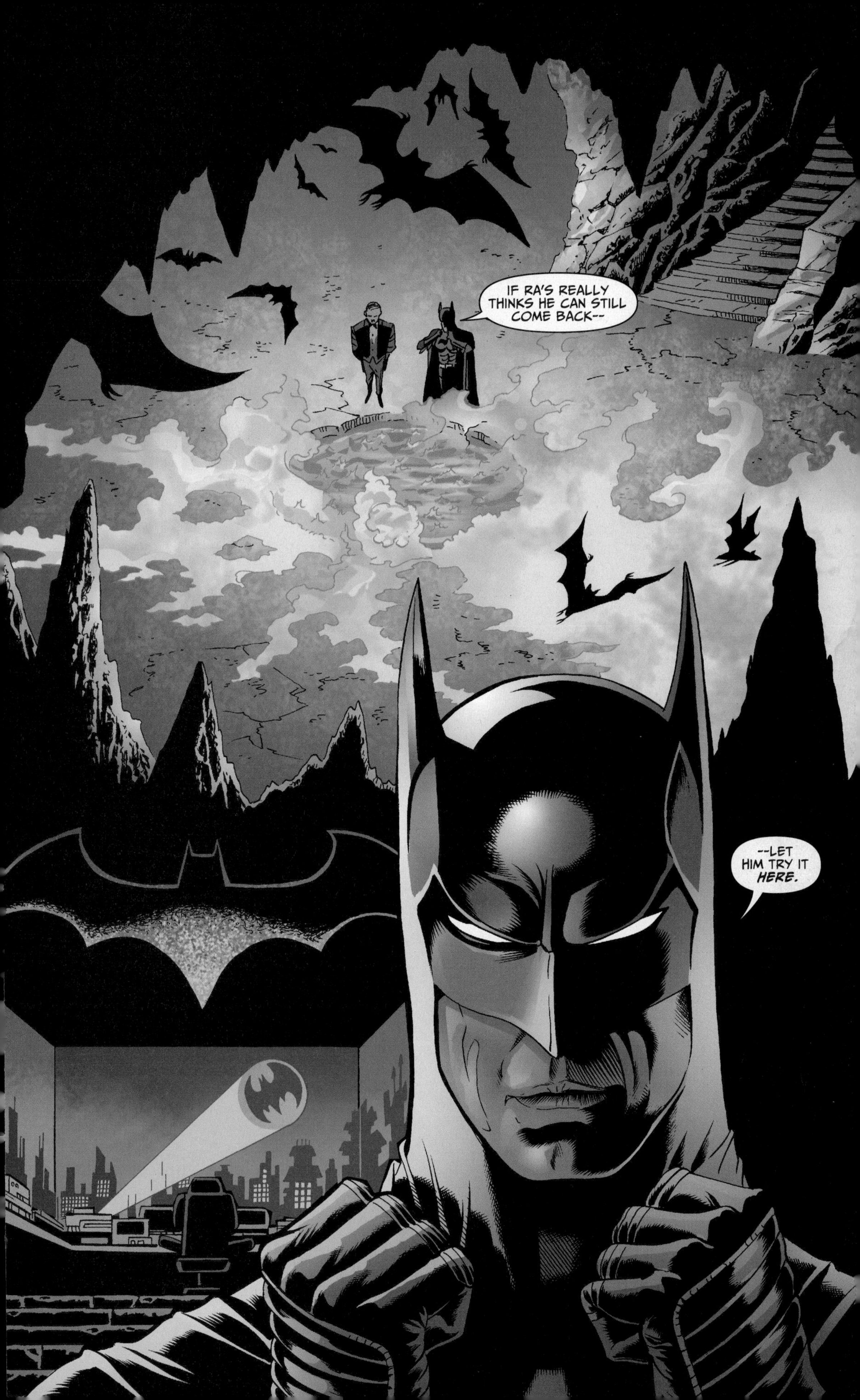
IF RA'S REALLY THINKS HE CAN STILL COME BACK--
--LET HIM TRY IT *HERE*.

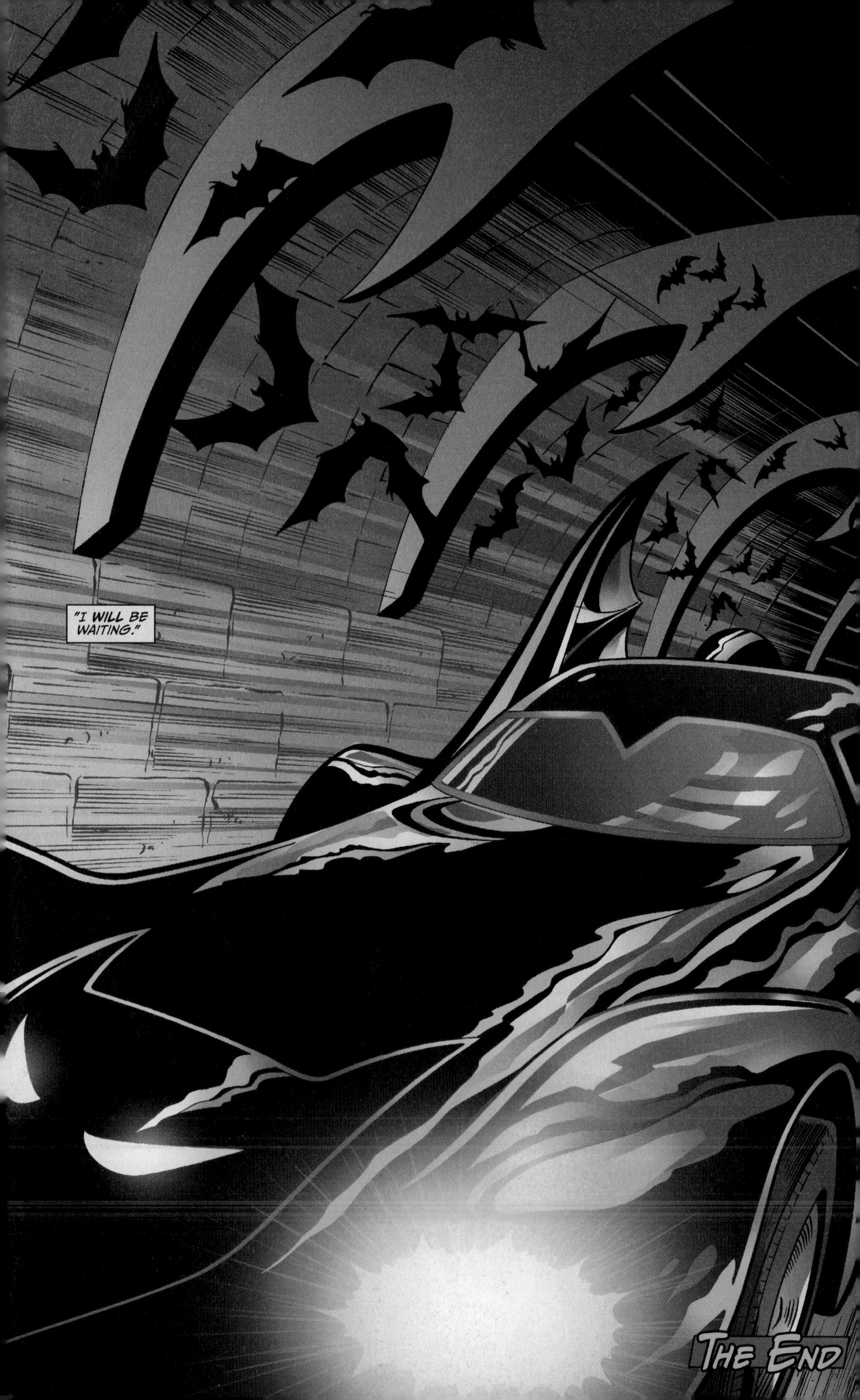
"I WILL BE WAITING."
THE END

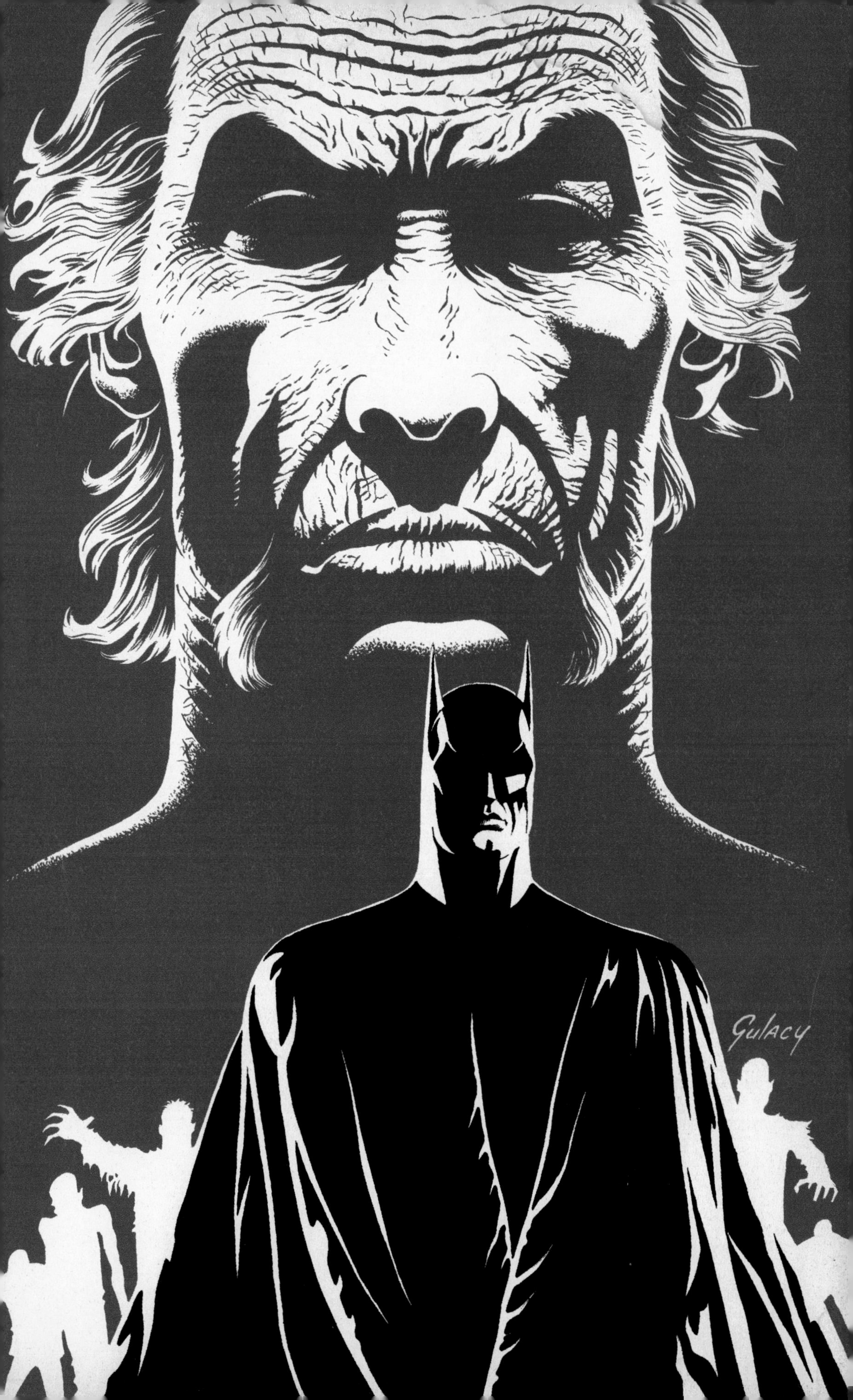
GULACY

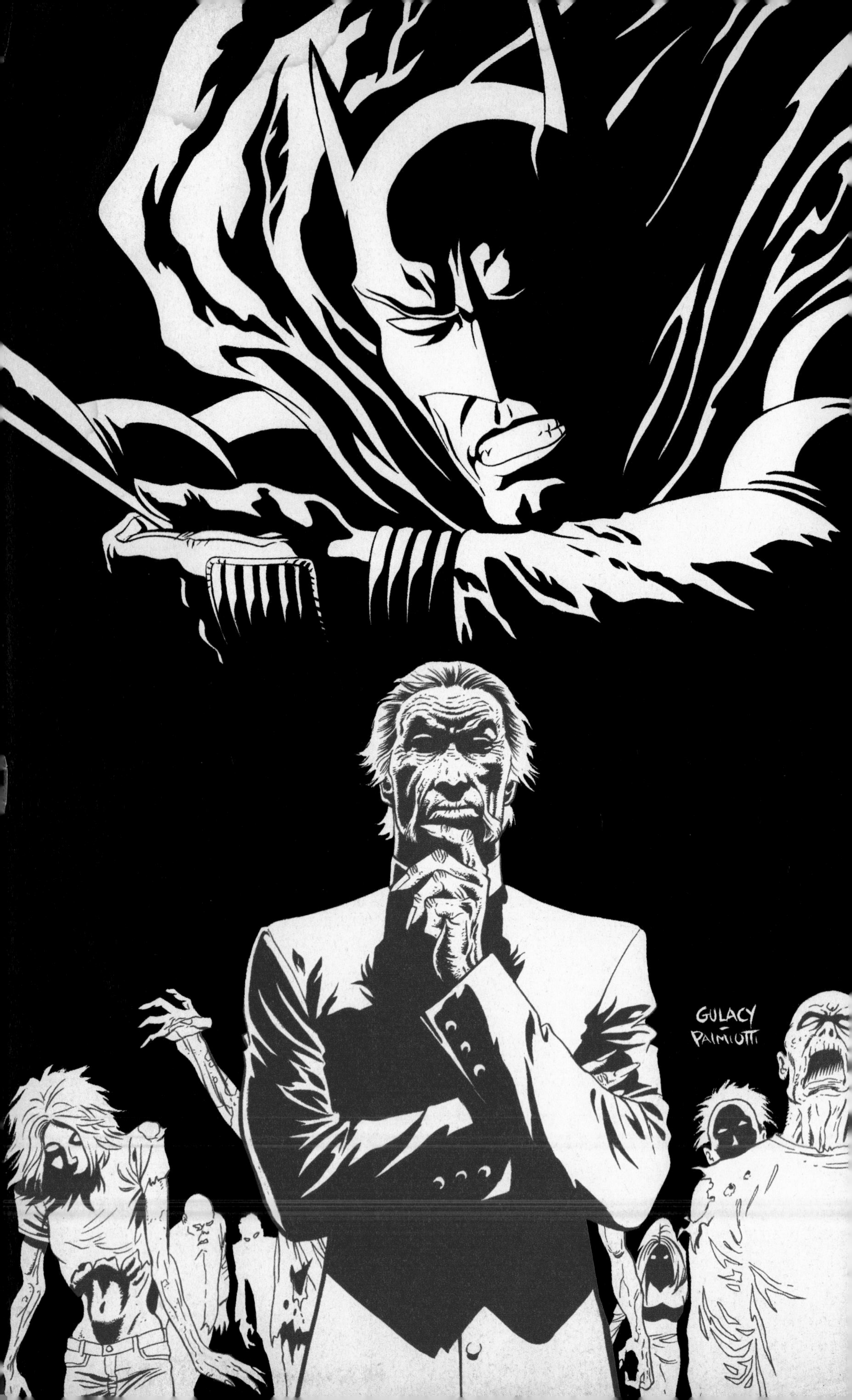
GULACY
PALMIOTTI

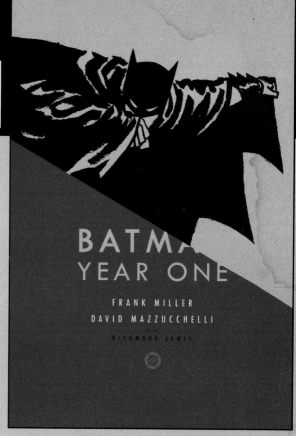

AND DON'T MISS THESE OTHER GREAT TITLES FEATURING **BATMAN!**

BATMAN: NO MAN'S LAND VOLUME 1

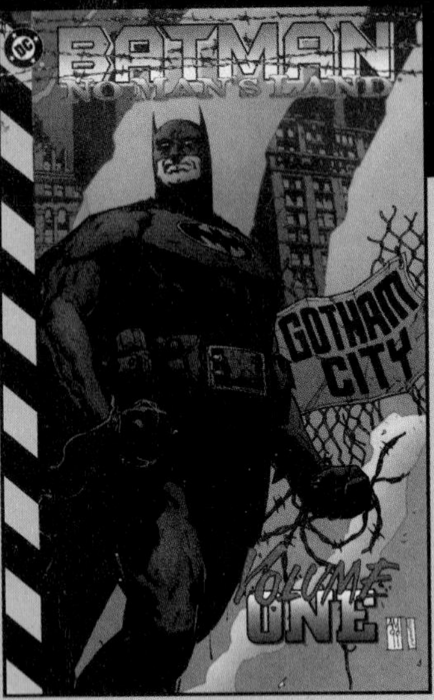
BATMAN
NO MAN'S LAND
GOTHAM CITY
VOLUME ONE

VARIOUS

THE BATMAN CHRONICLES VOLUME 1

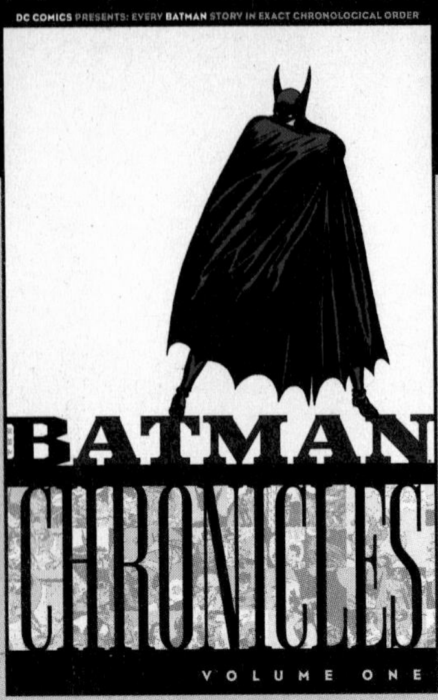
DC COMICS PRESENTS: EVERY BATMAN STORY IN EXACT CHRONOLOGICAL ORDER
BATMAN
CHRONICLES
VOLUME ONE

BOB KANE
VARIOUS

BATMAN: BRUCE WAYNE: MURDERER?

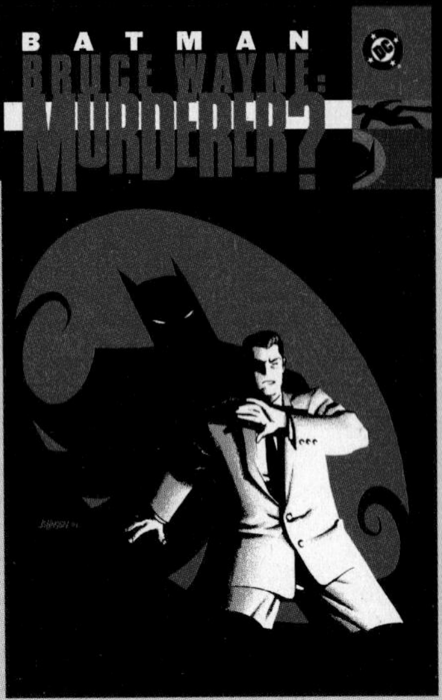
BATMAN
BRUCE WAYNE:
MURDERER?

VARIOUS

BATMAN: HUSH VOLUME 1

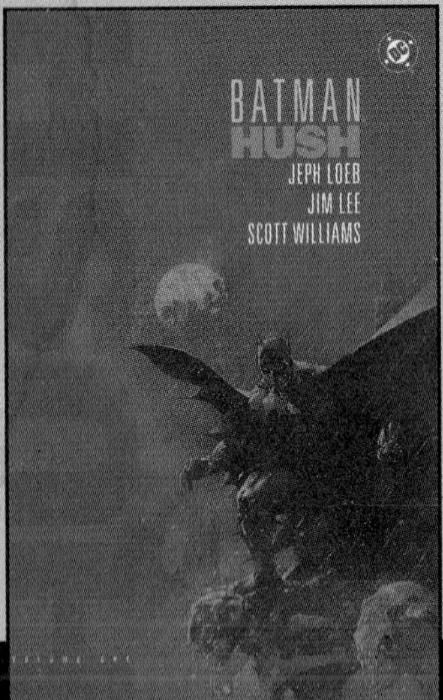
BATMAN
HUSH
JEPH LOEB
JIM LEE
SCOTT WILLIAMS

JEPH LOEB
JIM LEE
SCOTT WILLIAMS

BATMAN: HUSH VOLUME 2

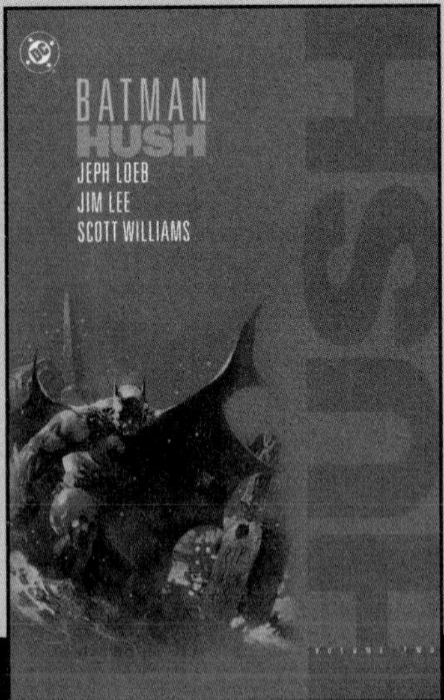
BATMAN
HUSH
JEPH LOEB
JIM LEE
SCOTT WILLIAMS

JEPH LOEB
JIM LEE
SCOTT WILLIAMS

BATMAN: KNIGHTFALL VOLUME 1

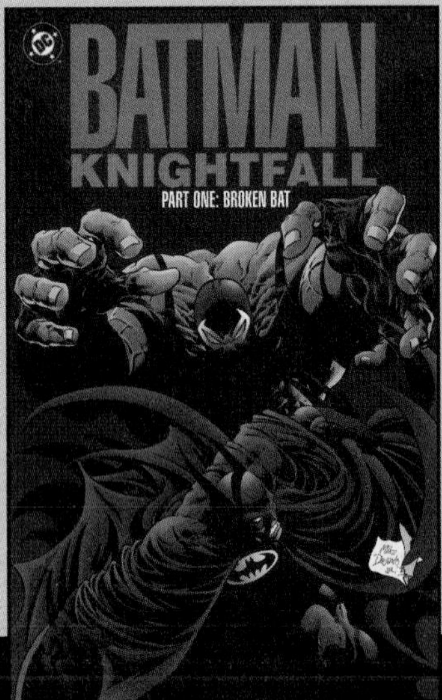
BATMAN
KNIGHTFALL
PART ONE: BROKEN BAT

VARIOUS